Top Decisions

*Strategic Decision-Making
in Organizations*

David J. Hickson
Richard J. Butler
David Cray
Geoffrey R. Mallory
David C. Wilson

Top Decisions

Strategic Decision-Making in Organizations

Jossey-Bass Publishers
San Francisco • London • 1986

91649

TOP DECISIONS
Strategic Decision-Making in Organizations
    by David J. Hickson, Richard J. Butler, David Cray, Geoffrey R. Mallory,
    and David C. Wilson

Library of Congress Cataloging-in-Publication Data
Main entry under title:

Top decisions.

    Based on studies carried out at the Bradford
Management Centre in Britain, 1970–1984.
    Bibliography: p. 273
    Includes index.
    1. Decision-making. I. Hickson, David John.
II. University of Bradford. Management Centre.
HD30.23.T67   1985b   658.4'012   85-10071
ISBN 0-87589-653-7

Manufactured in the United States of America

The paper in this book meets the guidelines for
permanence and durability of the Committee on
Production Guidelines for Book Longevity of the
Council on Library Resources.

JACKET DESIGN BY WILLI BAUM

FIRST EDITION

Code 8604

The Jossey-Bass Management Series

Consulting Editors
Organizations and Management

Warren Bennis
University of Southern California

Richard O. Mason
Southern Methodist University

Ian I. Mitroff
University of Southern California

Foreword

The Bradford studies of decision-making had their origin as long ago as 1970, when I arrived at Bradford Management Centre with the express purpose of setting up an organizational analysis research unit. I had from the start an interest in power, and this was widened by the work of Stewart Clegg, one of the first doctoral candidates in the new unit. After Richard Butler, who shared this interest, joined Bradford in 1973 to be jointly responsible for the unit, and over the years to shoulder a full share of the strains of research, preparatory thinking and fieldwork got underway on interorganizational power.

More substantial research began when the team grew with the coming of Runo Axelsson (from Umea, Sweden) and of David Wilson. We realized that both interorganizational and intraorganizational power are felt throughout processes of strategic decision-making, and that these processes had received insufficient empirical study. There were very few comparable cases, no really large-scale comparative research, and no attempt to assess the relative contributions of possible ingredients of explanation. So the emphasis was shifted onto decision-making processes.

The studies continued until 1984, and indeed continue beyond that in further data analyses and publications. They were made possible by the British Social Science Research Council (SSRC), which awarded a series of one- to two-year grants, though this disjointed and shortsighted funding resulted in an uphill struggle to carry through large-scale, long-term research on small-scale, short-term grants. The burden of continual crises which was laid upon the precariously funded team began when Graham Astley (from the University of Washington, Seattle), who had for two years replaced Runo Axelsson, left because the money ran out. It did so at a difficult stage when success was in the balance and morale faltering.

David Wilson nevertheless held on, living insecurely month by month from grant to grant, and so did Geoffrey Mallory, who joined the team to begin an equally hazardous life (finally becoming temporary lecturer to cover my teaching while this book was drafted). Both kept going from commitment to the research and loyalty to the team, enduring periods without pay between funding and continuing as active as ever as "honorary research fellows." At the worst moments they were sustained by vital bridging sums made available by the Management Centre's director, Chris Higgins, whose support for the team was constant throughout, even though years passed before any results were evident. When David Cray (from Wisconsin) succeeded Graham Astley, he brought a fresh vitality and comradeship that led the team through and out of its lowest months, even though he too had to return across the Atlantic, not to the United States but to Canada, when once more the money ran out. But he somehow found ways to continue an essential contribution from afar.

It was these three, David Wilson, Geoffrey Mallory, and David Cray, who together with Richard Butler and myself, maintained their commitment through thick and thin, through exhausting days closeted in discussion, through wet and windy moorland walks searching for inspiration, through English fish and chips, Chinese takeaways, and Pakistani eating houses—and Yorkshire beer, of course—to make this book possible.

Many others helped along the way. Graham Kenny, visiting fellow for six months on leave from the New South Wales Institute of Technology in Sydney, pitched in to analyze data that was lying unexploited, and then he too continued to contribute from Canada. Paul Jackson, of the Medical Research Council's Social and Applied Psychology Unit at the University of Sheffield, gave advice on data analysis at difficult junctures. Suzana Rodrigues, doctoral candidate from Belo Horizonte, Brazil, completed a thesis closely associated with the main studies which provided another source of ideas.

Judith Hyde's flying fingers typed so much on the way toward this book that her work and friendship are inherent in it. She had to leave us when she moved from her native North of England to South Wales, so, sadly, she was never able to type its actual words.

Gill Sharpley lived through every crisis to see the whole thing from beginning to end, an experienced friend in need for all who came and went, in good times and bad. She made typed coherence from a multitude of scrambled manuscripts and research proposals, and many times gamely endured retyping drafts which she had previously been assured were absolutely final and would not need doing again. With Susan Woodruffe cheerfully and efficiently taking over some of the typing when its sheer volume became overwhelming, and Jenny Braithwaite drawing the figures, Gill produced the bulk of the book and kept her head amid the churning piles of paper. She must surely owe the world her own book on her inside view of research groups!

The culminating ingredient was NIAS, the Netherlands Institute for Advanced Study in Humanities and Social Sciences, at Wassenaar near The Hague. NIAS provided a fellowship and a year of peace and quiet, broken only by the cooing of its flock of doves, for me to write much of the first draft of the book. Without NIAS there could not have been a book. NIAS also provided Anne Simpson's expertise with typewriter and sticky tape, and she herself provided much more—enthusiasm for the work and repeated encouragement. The British SSRC then came forward when completion still looked beyond reach and ensured it with a Personal Research Grant for five months' concentration back home in the Yorkshire moors. The University of Bradford and colleagues in Organizational Analysis readily granted leave of absence twice over.

Even so, as editor-in-chief of *Organization Studies,* I would not have been able to stay away from Bradford for the necessary concentrated effort were it not for imperturbable Pam Waterhouse, editorial secretary. She kept the OS office going faultlessly despite an absentee editor. During my absence, Gill Sharpley's experienced understanding was also invaluable, for she coped smoothly and independently with professorial and departmental affairs so that I was protected from them.

Of course, all of this depended on the willingness of hundreds of executives and administrators to describe for us the making of decisions, and in three instances to permit the decision-making to be followed as it happened. We hope that they gained something from reviewing their own experience and that the book will contribute to the education of their successors, among many others.

This Foreword bears my name alone because it is both on behalf of my co-authors and a tribute to them and their determination in times of adversity, and to everyone else who contributed.

That must certainly include six American and British reviewers of the book manuscript, each of whom blended criticism with heartening support in just the right proportions.

Ultimately, of course, it almost goes without saying that for the five authors it was Marjorie, Ann, Ellen, Ros, and Jo who made it all possible and worthwhile.

November 1985   David J. Hickson

Preface

This book is about how the bigger decisions are made at the top of the bigger organizations. That is, it is about the strategic processes through which those at the top of business firms, commercial companies, state-owned undertakings, health organizations, universities and colleges, public agencies, and indeed all the commonplace public sector and private sector organizations of our times, arrive at their major decisions. It is based on ten years of original research —on a larger and more comprehensive scale than before—known as the Bradford studies of strategic decision-making, carried out in Britain. These studies covered one hundred and fifty case histories that include decisions of every kind, from new product launches to takeover bids, from new services to corporate plans, from large-scale investments to internal reorganizations, and many more. The research was spurred by the fragmentary nature of what was known about decision-making. Previous work had yielded a series of often brilliant insights, but these were disconnected and there was no larger context in which to place them. For a wider understanding, answers had to be found to questions that had been around for years but had no answers.

Are top decisions made in ways so infinitely varied that they defy description? Is each episode unique beyond compare? Or can top decision processes be grouped in a simple way that makes sense of them?

Why is a decision arrived at in one way rather than another? What explains decision-making? Is it a response to the problem being considered, or to the interests implicated, or to both? If both, what mix of problem and interests brings on what kind of decision-making? Who is most influential, those on the inside or those on the outside, such as trade unions and government departments?

Is the process of deciding on a new product quite different from that of deciding on a reorganization or a takeover bid? Are different topics handled in different ways? Or does the organization determine everything? Are decisions taken in private businesses in ways quite different from those in state-owned industries or utilities? Is decision-making in universities and colleges as distinctive as it has been made out to be?

Executives and administrators who have used the findings of research know from experience that it does not give absolute hard and fast answers to questions such as these. It cannot do so. In a provisional world that can be looked at from different points of view, research gives provisional answers. Given always that in this sense what can be achieved is inhibited by the human predicament, this book faces up to these and other questions with the advantage of doubly intensive and extensive information about decision-making in which to look for answers.

It draws on first-hand accounts to open up the board rooms, committee chambers, and corridors of decision-making in a range of different organizations to students, academics, and practitioners. For students it provides a fresh perspective on the essence of management and administration, the making of those strategic decisions that shape economy and society, and by which national economic and social policy is either implemented or frustrated. For academics it provides a broad empirical foundation for teaching, and a perspective into which other research can be fitted and on which further research can be based. For executives and administrators, it is a guide to how things are done elsewhere and a source of ideas on how things might best be done. For all three, students, academics, and practitioners, it offers a straightforward understanding of decision-making as a process that ensues from the problem at hand and from the influence exerted, in an intelligible way.

Part One of the book describes how strategic decisions are made and the problems and interests that enter into their making. Part Two discusses the reasons each is made in the way that it is.

The book begins with the story of a dramatic struggle between two directors and their supporters during the making of a decision in a chemical company. It shows how what happens follows from both the problem that is the subject of decision and the interests that are implicated by it. Chapter Two deals with the first of these, the complexity of the problems in terms of their consequences and of the variety of interests involved, starting with an examination of what constitutes a decision at a strategic level. Chapter Three correspondingly deals with the politicality of the interests in terms of the influence brought to bear, showing which interests most influence which decisions, and the balance of influence between internal top management and external customers, trade unions, agencies of government, corporation head office, and many others. Chapter Four begins with a consideration of how long it takes to make strategic decisions and whether committees slow things down. It goes on to describe the characteristics of how decisions are arrived at and discerns three primary ways of decision-making. This threefold typology of processes is the basis for explanations of why decisions are made in different ways, explanations that are built up in Part Two of the book.

Part Two begins with an analysis, in Chapter Five, of the making of product, personnel, reorganization, boundary, location, input, technology, domain (market), control system, and service decisions, to find how far each tends to be made in a characteristic manner. Chapter Six analyses the features of problems and interests that can lead to each of the three types of process. Contrasting modes of decision-making are found in which each form of process tends to ensue from a different combination of problem complexity and interest politicality. Chapter Seven examines the differences between manufacturing and service organizations, and privately owned and publicly (government) owned organizations, and among professional organizations, including health service units, colleges, and universities, to suggest the extent to which each process of decision-making is typical of the organization concerned rather than of the matter in hand. An overall summary and assessment is given in Chapter Eight, together with some implications for management and administration. Details of research method and data additional to the description given in Chapter One appear in the appendixes.

University of Bradford
   Management Centre
November 1985

Richard J. Butler
David Cray
David J. Hickson
Geoffrey R. Mallory
David C. Wilson

Contents

Appendixes

The Authors

David J. Hickson is professor of international management, and was formerly professor of organizational analysis, at the University of Bradford Management Centre, England. He worked in administration and qualified professionally in corporation administration (ACIS) in 1954 and in personnel management (AIPM) in 1958. He moved into research at the University of Manchester Institute of Science and Technology in 1958, where he received the master's degree by research (M.Sc.Tech) in 1960. Since then his principal research has been at the University of Aston, Birmingham, England, on organization structure; at the University of Alberta, Canada, on intraorganizational power; and at the University of Bradford on strategic decision-making. A constant theme has been cross-national comparison.

Hickson is founding editor-in-chief of the research journal *Organization Studies* and was a founder of the European Group for Organizational Studies (EGOS). He holds an honorary doctorate from the University of Umea, Sweden (1974), and was a Fellow of the Netherlands Institute for Advanced Study in 1982–83. He has published in numerous research journals and volumes of contributed papers and is joint author or editor of *Organizational Structure in its Context* (1978), *Organizations Alike and Unlike* (1979), *Organization and Nation* (1981), and *Writers on Organizations* (1983, new edition).

Richard J. Butler is senior lecturer in organizational analysis at the University of Bradford Management Centre, England. He received his B.Sc. degree in engineering from the University of Southampton (1962), his M.Sc. degree in management from the University of Loughborough (1968), and his Ph.D. degree in organizational behavior from Northwestern University (1973).

Butler's main research activities are in decision-making, voluntary organizations, and the government regulation of industries. He has published articles on these topics in a number of journals. He has also held positions in industry and at the University of Otago, New Zealand.

David Cray is assistant professor of human resource management in the School of Business at Carleton University, Ottawa, Canada. He received his B.A. degree from New College and his M.S. and Ph.D. degrees from the University of Wisconsin, all in sociology. He is currently involved in studies of the allocation of control between Canadian multinational subsidiaries and their American parents. He is also pursuing his interest in decision-making through the study of the impact of new data handling techniques on decision-making in the pension fund industry.

As a member of the European Group for Organizational Studies (EGOS), Cray maintains a research focus on international business strategy and the problems of organizations that must operate in conflicting cultural environments. A further project examines the impact of performance measurement on strategic choice in professional sports.

Geoffrey R. Mallory is assistant professor in the School of Business, Carleton University, Ottawa, Canada. He received his B.Sc. degree (1975) in management and administration from the University of Bradford Management Centre, England, and his M.A. degree (1976) from the University of Leeds. He is completing his Ph.D. on the topic of elapsed time in decision-making.

Before graduating as a mature student, Mallory held industrial positions in timber marketing and systems analysis, and he subsequently joined the decision-making project at the University of Bradford as a research assistant, becoming research fellow and lecturer.

While decision-making is his principal research activity, Mallory's master's dissertation was a critical assessment of autonomous work group practices, and his current interests are the development and impact of expert systems in organizations.

Mallory is a member of the European Group for Organizational Studies (EGOS) and the American Sociological Association.

David C. Wilson is a lecturer in organizational behavior at the University of Warwick and was formerly senior research fellow in organizational analysis at the University of Bradford Management Centre, England. He received his B.A. (1974) and M.A. (1975) degrees from the University of Leeds in management studies and his Ph.D. degree (1980) from the University of Bradford in organizational strategy. His principal research activities have been on strategic decision-making and power in organizations and he has concentrated in particular on longitudinal methodologies in the study of decision processes. Currently, he is the joint director of a research project investigating strategy and structure in British voluntary organizations, which forms a part of his future research efforts in the areas of corporate strategy and organizational change.

Wilson is a member of the European Group for Organizational Studies (EGOS) and is editorial assistant of the journal *Organization Studies.* He has published in numerous research journals and volumes of contributed papers. During 1985, he was Visiting Professor of Organizational Analysis at the University of Uppsala, Sweden.

Top Decisions

*Strategic Decision-Making
in Organizations*

Part I
Making Decisions

1

The Dynamics of Decision-Making

An electrifying decision

Alwyn Williams, Production Director of a leading British chemical company, Toxicem (names here are fictional but the story is not), had for some time pondered over the unused capacity for high-pressure steam in its plant. The boiler wastefully required fuel sufficient for high-pressure steam, yet all they needed and produced was low-pressure steam. In times of energy conservation, and rising energy costs, he and the engineers in the plant felt that this high-pressure potential should be used. He gazed from his window in the executive suite of offices overlooking the smoking, fuming chemical works, casting around for some action he could take, and unaware of the events he would unleash if he did.

The most likely possibility was for the company to use the steam to generate its own electricity. This would be sensational, for the state-owned electricity generation and distribution boards had a *de facto* monopoly and although the small print of legislation did allow others to generate electricity this was on such terms, with the economic and political calculations weighted so much against it, that few had ever tried. Despite this, Alwyn was intrigued by the possibility.

The first chance for him to act occurred when the firm was visited by the National Industrial Fuel Efficiency Service. Oblivious of the struggle this would initiate, he asked their opinion on electricity generation. They reported that it would indeed be feasible, given a boiler capable of even higher pressure than the existing one, a view which accorded with that of several chemists and engineers on the staff.

However, even with this support from both outside and inside the firm, Alwyn could not make any further move immediately, for capital expenditure would be needed to replace the existing boiler and to add a turbo-alternator, and capital funds were stretched. So he bided his time. He knew that his case would be strongly opposed, he was sure of that, so right timing was essential.

This was because Giles Robinson, the Purchasing Director, was as much against do-it-yourself electricity generation as Alwyn was for it: 'I thought that this project was ludicrous. No one could give any facts and figures which supported electricity generation. Nobody knew enough about the problems and the technology. . . .' Giles was regarded as something of a 'whizz-kid' who had achieved comparatively rapid promotion by securing favourable supply contracts. He would not see mis-spent (as he saw it) on turbo-alternators or anything else, and could be a formidable antagonist for Alwyn.

Production expanded, the plant steadily used more steam, and without any action on the part of Alwyn this raised the question of buying a new boiler. By coincidence, the National Coal Board then circulated an information sheet to industrial users of coal, Toxicem being one, which offered low-quality coal at a low price to firms with boilers that could burn it. Here was a chance for Giles to negotiate another good contract. Under his lead, Toxicem bought as its new boiler one that could use the cheap coal, but, incidentally, could also raise steam to the pressure needed to drive a turbo-alternator for electricity generation!

Alwyn and his supporters were overjoyed. Giles's eye for a good contract had played right into their hands. As Alwyn put it, 'this boiler was certainly capable of eventually producing electrical power with the addition of an alternator. The idea was, at least, a feasible reality . . .' However, they kept quiet about that, and appeared to approve of the new boiler for its other features. Once more they bided their time.

That time came when, after a year, the limit of even the new boiler was being reached; unless, of course it was to be operated at the higher pressure of which it was technically capable. Alwyn and his supporters now made their first direct move to obtain the funds needed for a turbo-alternator. They put the case for do-it-yourself electricity to the Managing Director.

Their proposals brought instant protests not only from Giles, but also from Tom Delaney, the Development Director. The issue was put to the Capital Control Committee in a series of meetings, and both parties wooed the Accounting Department because a clear financial assessment could be decisive. However, Accountancy were non-committal, and the Committee arrived at no conclusion other than that there was insufficient information for a decision one way or the other.

Giles and Tom vigorously maintained not only that the technical and cost considerations were against any such thing, but also that the 'proper business' of a chemical company was chemicals, and that of the public electricity industry was electricity, and the two should not be tangled. They too sought backing outside Toxicem, finding it at both national and regional levels in the electricity industry, where there was general hostility to private generation, and where authoritative judgements were given that it would be impossibly costly. In particular, suggested charges for reconnection to the public supply should Toxicem's generator break down (a contingency that Alwyn had to reckon with) appeared prohibitive. This certainly meant that the Capital Control Committee would pursue the matter no further. It seemed that Giles had won the day.

Sparked off

Not long afterwards, the Managing Director announced his impending retirement! Alwyn and Giles were prime candidates to succeed him. Alwyn realized that Giles's success over the electricity issue had reinforced Giles's 'whizz-kid' image, and that unless he, Alwyn, took some conspicuous action he could be at a disadvantage.

He set out to scrutinize all the memoranda, reports, documents, and calculations that the debate had produced. In a month he had found a critical error, if it was an error, in the charges suggested for any reconnection to the public electricity supply. The charges looked far too high. The figures had been obtained for Toxicem by a turbo-alternator manufacturer from the antipathetic electricity industry, who at the very least might not have troubled to follow through to guard against misconceptions. Alwyn wrote to the Confederation of British Industry (CBI) about this question of relationships between private industry and state monopoly, he told the Toxicem Capital Control Committee, and received a reply from the CBI specifically stating that Toxicem had been assuming charges about five times higher than those indicated to the CBI when they approached the electricity industry at national level!

Giles felt the ground shifting beneath his feet. The whole dispute reopened, and it did so entwined with a succession struggle of an intense and increasingly personal nature.

The protagonists threw the issue to and fro for nearly a year. Calculations and assertions succeeded one another, but because figures had to be based on hypothetical assumptions about steam pressure, generator output, and so on, no 'real cost' emerged. For those involved, and no one in senior management could entirely escape, Toxicem was no longer the same place to work in. The memoranda arguing for and against became ever intrusive in the carpeted corridors of the executive suite. The daily stroll from office building to canteen building for lunch, with the fuming pipes and tanks of the plant in the background, led not just to a comfortable meal but to yet more exchanges. The executives' dining-room became the scene for heated discussions, and for delicate decisions about where and with whom to sit as the arguments swayed back and forth between the tables.

Giles and Tom went back to the electricity industry to check the question of reconnection charges, and eventually brought their whole case together in a lengthy memorandum to the members of the Capital Control Committee. Its essence was that do-it-yourself electricity generation could only be justified by an unrealistically high assumption of future electricity needs; that whatever the starting assumption about reconnection charges, the electricity industry would retain the right to increase them radically so that Toxicem could be at their mercy, and higher quality, higher price coal would be needed. Alwyn, and the engineers supporting him, countered point by point with cost arguments, conceding only the trivial point that maintenance would cost more but twisting it around by saying that Giles's figure of £250 for this was too *low*! Suggesting that such a tiny cost might be *larger* had the effect not of admitting any serious oversight by Alwyn, but of questioning Giles's competence with figures even on such a minor item. Giles knew it: 'I saw the allowance of extra money for maintenance staff as a personal insult. It implied that Alwyn had no faith in Tom's and my calculations. He was trying to make us look incompetent.'

The Managing Director saw that it was up to him to settle the dispute somehow. It was becoming highly divisive, and clearly no agreed financial forecast was going to be reached. Informing the Capital Control Committee of what he was doing, he took a vote among all the senior managers. Having failed to sway the Accounting or other influential departments, Giles foresaw defeat: 'This played straight into Alwyn's hands. We knew that he had very strong support from the engineers and the electricians.'

Alwyn's case did receive majority support, the Capital Control Committee recommended it to the Company Board of Directors, and the turbo-alternator was bought. After six months of successful electricity generation, Alwyn was promoted to Managing Director!

Even though Giles and Tom went on protesting, claiming that the apparent financial savings were due more to inflation than to true gains, the decision once taken was the precursor to more. The first step made the next easier. Five years later, a second new boiler and second turbo-alternator were readily bought, Alwyn as Managing Director now having no difficulty presenting the case personally to the Committee and Board. (The tale of Toxicem is adapted from Wilson (1982) 'Electricity and resistance'.)

Problems, interests, and process at Toxicem

The alternatives of the decision at Toxicem were simplicity itself. They were just Yes or No. Either Yes to generating its own electricity or No to any such proposition. However, the making of the decision, that is arriving at a choice between Yes or No, was anything but simple. It swayed to and fro month after month, a *process* of decision-making ensuing from the *problems* raised by the matter for decision and from the *interests* which it entailed.

The problems

Although those on both sides of the argument were often adamant, this was due more to having to argue a difficult case with all possible vehemence than to confidence in the basis for the case. There was no accepted way of estimating the possible consequences of producing electricity, unlike the decisions on new products to which everyone was accustomed and where the basis in cost and sales estimates was agreed even if the particular decision was disputed. Nor could the duration of the consequences be foreseen. Would such a move be irreversible if the nationalized electricity industry put obstacles in the way of resuming full-scale supplies? Would an indefinite commitment have been made to generating electricity whatever the cost might become in future? Indeed, were the purposes of the company itself being changed?

Not only was there doubt over consequences, there was also the difficulty of coping with multiple sources of information and advice. Internally the production, engineering, buying, development, and accounting departments were closely involved throughout, as were the members of the Capital Control Committee, whilst from outside the company came the National Industrial Fuel Efficiency Service, the local electricity authority, the national Generating Board, the manufacturers of turbines and other equipment, and the CBI. Having to cope with so many heightened the complexity of the problem.

The interests

The decision was a contentious matter on which these parties exerted conflicting influences because of their opposed interests. Most obvious of the outside interests were those of the electricity industry in defending its control of supplies, of turbine manufacturers in a new sales opportunity, and of the CBI in encouraging private initiative. The two main protagonists turned for support to these interests externally, while internally they repeatedly added to the pressure by trying to win the support of other departments whose interests they tried to construe as supporting their own. In the end, despite the alliance against him of two directors, Giles and Tom, and their departments, sales and development, Alwyn as both works manager, and himself an engineer, was able to count on engineers throughout management to vote his way.

The process

From this combination of a complex uncertain problem and contrary influences came an uneven, oscillating process of decision-making. It began comparatively calmly as the idea of generating electricity was thought up by Alwyn and first considered by the Capital Control Committee, but then it became more and more political and personal as careers were seen to be at stake. Precipitating events heavily affected what took place, as when the visit of representatives of the National Industrial Fuel Efficiency Service gave Alwyn his first chance to gain support, and when the pricing of coal by the National Coal Board led to Giles recommending the purchase of a coal-burning boiler that incidentally added to the technical capacity to generate electricity and so strengthened Alwyn's position.

Bursts of action alternated with quiescent periods, whilst those concerned awaited the right opportunity at the right moment for their next move. A lot of the time of individual managers was taken up with investigations, recalculations, intermittent spasms of discussion along the corridors of the executive suite, and disputes over information from different sources – some of which commanded reasonable confidence, some of which did not. Taken as a whole, the process of arriving at the decision was an affair of spasmodic intense activity.

Games of manoeuvre

A case such as this, which so wracked top management, is exceptional, but it shows how all decision-making, to some degree, is a game of manoeuvre. This does not mean that it is a playful game, engaged in lightly, just for fun with no serious intent (Allison 1969). Toxicem shows that it is a serious business in its general consequences for organizations and all those connected with them, and in its specific consequences for some individuals. Yet it is seen as a game by those involved who see their moves towards each other as right or wrong, depending on the consequences and on their own positions.

An organization can be regarded as a collection of such games, an *'ensemble des jeux'*, (Crozier and Friedberg 1980) which are played one after the other and often more than one at once (Allison 1969), linked in a 'concatenation of manoeuvre' (March 1981) across 'bargaining zones' (Abell 1975). An organization is therefore less the result of deliberate design than it is the only partly intended accumulated result of decision-making games over the years.

Each game is known to those involved by its topic, which they label as 'our new product problem', or 'the question of the new department', or whatever. Usually topics are a particular crystallization of long-standing deeper and wider issues, such as sales volume or departmental responsibilities, which now and again become active as a matter of decision (Astley, et al. 1982), just as the decision on electricity in Toxicem arose from the wider issues of efficient plant operation.

The Toxicem case shows how decisions can be analyzed as a combination of both problems and interests, from which the process of reaching a choice arises. What can already be said about each of these aspects of decision-making, problems, interests, and process?

Decision problems

Streams of problems appear in organizations (Cohen, et al. 1972), so that life at the top can be a continual round of switching from one problem to the next. Comparatively few decisions have the kinds of implications that raise them to a strategic level, but those that have are notoriously full of *complex* problems. It may not be clear, for example, how much faith can be placed in estimates of cost or of working capacity, or what credence should be given to different recommendations and advice. It may not be known whether there may be other alternatives besides those being compared, and of those that are known it is not at all certain what the seriousness and extent of their consequences may be. There may be no accepted assumptions about cause and effect so that the probable effects of a decision cannot be foreseen (Thompson and Tuden 1964), and any decision is a high risk (Hage 1980).

If there are precedents then a problem is easier to handle: what was done before can be more safely done again, as long as no obviously disastrous consequences occurred last time. Moreover, it is well understood by those involved that one decision may reduce the alternatives open to consideration in the next, and so simplify and predispose it. The decision at Toxicem in favour of do-it-yourself electricity was understood to be a commitment that would affect subsequent decisions, so that, later on, the purchase of further equipment for the same purpose was decided without re-opening the whole question and reconsidering all alternatives afresh. Thus successive similar problems can be increasingly '*programmed*' along a narrower more recognized course with fewer alternatives, in a more and more routine way (Simon 1960).

Without clear precedents it is harder to know what to do. Different degrees of uncertainty may require different ways of working out a solution (Grandori 1984), but whatever the approach taken there is a tendency to play safe with the '*non-programmed*' decisions. When the consequences are obscure, caution is likely. The Toxicem Capital Control Committee did not know which way to turn when confronted with a proposal to do something which few others had ever tried to do and where there was no clear evidence that any had succeeded, so they played safe by avoiding any decision at all until the vote among managers demonstrated a majority in favour. They procrastinated until the power position clarified. This inclination for '*uncertainty avoidance*' (Cyert and March 1963), means that the small step is usually preferred to the bold stroke, and that the search for alternatives is 'simple minded' (Cyert and March 1963), because only simpler alternatives are considered which would not change the status quo very much.

It is necessary to cut problems down to a size that can be comprehended, by taking account of only a limited amount of information and advice (Simon 1960; Braybrooke and Lindblom 1963). While in an unreal, fanciful world all relevant information might be obtained and evaluated on every possible alternative, this '*rational deductive ideal*' (Braybrooke and Lindblom 1963) is in reality impracticable. It would swamp the working hours and mental capacities of those involved. So, in practice, most decisions are tackled in a piecemeal way, a bit at a time. Just a few possible alternatives are compared and if a marginal improvement can be made then that does for the time being, more remote imponderable ideal solutions being left aside. Aims are reduced to what seems feasible rather than what might be desirable. Whilst now and again problems do crop up that are so large and all-of-a-piece that they cannot be dealt with in this way (Schulman 1975; Lustick 1980), the constant tendency is to 'muddle through' as safely as possible (Lindblom 1959).

Decision interests

The 'bureaucratic politics' (Allison 1969) of decision-making implicate many interests, ranging from some whose stakes in any one decision are comparatively negligible, as were the stakes of the Fuel Efficiency Service in the Toxicem decision, to others who have a great deal at stake, as Alwyn and Giles and their departments had.

Those who represent these interests come and go, and are not all involved at once. Some are from within the organization, employed by it, and some are outside it and have other forms of contact with it. There is 'fluid participation' (Cohen, et al. 1972) both in decision-making and in the organization itself.

The individuals who come and go are unlikely to be manoeuvring just on their own behalf. Although Alwyn and Giles at Toxicem certainly pursued their own personal career ends, their viewpoints were rooted in their departmental interests: Alwyn expressing the viewpoint of engineers who professionally must strive for optimum energy utilization, and Giles expressing that of purchasing staff whose job it is to avoid wasteful purchases of equipment that later turns out to be of no use. The staff of a purchasing department can become suspicious of the enthusiasms of engineers, persuasively wrapped in technical jargon, which lead nowhere after the money has been spent (Strauss 1962). Thus individuals represent different interests from among the shifting coalition of interests that sustains an organization (Cyert and March 1963), a coalition that includes not only internal departments and divisions of many sorts but also owners, customers, suppliers, governmental and other public bodies, trades unions and others, depending on the organization.

These interests are there ready and waiting before any particular topic for decision arises, defining the objectives that anyone who becomes involved in decision-making on their behalf should pursue. The viewpoints of engineers and of purchasing staff in Toxicem preceded the electricity generation decision, and continued unchanged beyond it, ready for some future topic which would once again bring them out. In this sense the objectives of interests are answers lying dormant, waiting for questions to arise to which they can then conveniently fit. 'From this point of view, an organization is a collection of choices looking for problems . . . solutions looking for issues to which they might be the answer, and decision-makers looking for work' (Cohen, et al. 1972, p. 2). It is a 'garbage can' in which solutions and problems are churned around until solutions become attached to problems.

In this way decision-making proceeds by the *'quasi-resolution'* of *conflicts* (Cyert and March 1963) that are settled for the time being but will break out again another time. Despite intense conflict, a decision was ultimately made at Toxicem and was implemented, but the opposing viewpoints were not removed by it, and the last that was recorded of Giles, the loser, was that he was still looking for a chance to show that it had all been a mistake (Wilson 1982). Yet though conflicts persist within organizations, the organizations too persist, since interests are rarely pushed to a point where the whole disintegrates. An organization is an arena for decision-making games from which a range of interests benefit, and the continuance of the organization is necessary for them to be able to play at all. These are not life and death struggles but games for position within a system (Crozier 1976). One reason why the system is unlikely to fall apart, despite its 'schismatic tendencies' (Morgan 1981), is what the interests have in common. They are 'trustworthy'.

> A first principle of politics is that if everyone is rational, no one can be trusted. A second principle is that someone who never trusts anyone will usually lose, because although no rational person can be trusted, some people are innocent and can be trusted. Those who, by chance or insight, trust those who can be trusted will have an advantage over those who are unconditionally trusting. A third principle is that all players will try to look trustworthy even though they are not, in order to be trusted by those people who might become winners (by virtue of being willing to trust some people). A fourth principle is that the only reliable way of appearing to be trustworthy is to be in fact trustworthy. Thus all rational actors will be trustworthy most of the time (March 1981, p. 219).

The viewpoints expressed denote the '*logiques d'action*' of the interests involved (Karpik 1972; Weiss 1981) which guide what they do. Their logic of action may be to press continually for innovation, as did Alwyn and his supporters at Toxicem, or for stability so that efficiency can be improved, or for economies, or any of many other possibilities. These logics, or strategies of play (Crozier and Friedberg 1980), influence one decision after another until there is 'a pattern in a stream of decisions' (Mintzberg 1978) that becomes an overall *strategy* followed by the organization as a whole, whether or not recognized as such by its management.

Power

How big a part each interest plays in determining the decisions that go into forming a strategy depends on its power, its potential to influence the outcome. Decision-making 'may be understood as a political process that balances various power vectors' (Pettigrew 1973, p. 265). Power is unequal between interests, and the influence they then actually exert differs from decision to decision so that those who dominate one may be relatively peripheral to another (Hinings, et al. 1974). Because influence differs in this way, Giles of Toxicem was well advised to watch for another chance which might be more favourable to him.

The hierarchy of an organization means that those at the top have power that those lower down do not have, and then among those at the top there are differences between those representing different specializations such as finance or research, or distribution, and so on. The power of those at the top rests in the approval by societies of all political colours and all economic conditions of hierarchically structured organizations in which the elites have authority, or rightful power, to allocate resources, as did the directors and the Capital Control Committee of Toxicem. On the other hand, the exercise of that authority in decision-making is constrained by the influence of interests both external to the organization, such as a distant head office or a regulating government department, or a major customer or client; and internal to the organization, such as the departments for which Alwyn and Giles spoke. These internal interests derive their influence from the expert knowledge, the prestige, or the financial or material resources which they control (French and Raven 1959), if they can use such bases of power to cope with some uncertainty that confronts the organization (Crozier 1964). In a business such as Toxicem, the sales department may be able to ensure orders despite an uncertainly fluctuating market; the research and development department may keep the firm ahead of competitors; or the maintenance engineers may deal with unpredictable breakdowns that interrupt work (Crozier 1964). The favourable effect of coping with uncertainty upon power is maximum when other conditions are also favourable, namely that those who cope are centrally placed in the workflows of the organization and cannot easily be replaced by anyone else (Hickson, et al. 1971; Hinings, et al. 1974). And power feeds on itself, for power can be used to acquire resources which enhance power, as when Alwyn became Managing Director and so was in an even better position to push through subsequent decisions.

Decision-making processes and outcomes

What happens on the way to the making of a decision, or choice, is a response to these problems and interests. If the risks are high and the conflicts many, the 'trajectory' (Hage 1980) followed by the decision topic as it moves from person to person and from meeting to meeting is rarely swift and straight. It is hesitant and broken. It zig-zags to and fro, pauses whilst further information is sought or disputes are resolved, and may *'recycle'* again and again (Mintzberg, et al. 1976) in the way that the Toxicem Capital Control Committee went over their problem time after time. The whole process may pass through phases with different characteristics, as did Toxicem's which passed through a relatively rational deductive or 'synoptic' (Braybrooke and Lindblom 1963) phase to begin with, to a more personally politicized phase when Alwyn reopened the question (Wilson 1982). The focus of attention may change as influential interests emphasize first this and then that. There will be *'sequential attention to goals'* (Cyert and March 1963) because a decision is likely to impinge on more than one of the aims of the organization and its constituent interests, and these aims are too many and too complex to be attended to all at once, so first one and then another is brought to the fore, in sequence.

Outcomes

It is possible for the outcome to be exactly what somebody wants, as it was at Toxicem, but it can also be something different from what most people (or anyone) anticipated at the outset (Allison 1969). In this latter sense the decision-making process can be both disjointed along the way and disconnected from the result, the process of moving towards an outcome being partially 'uncoupled' from the outcome (Cohen, et al. 1972; March and Olsen 1976) because interests have their 'solutions' (or preferred outcomes) ready beforehand, pending an opportunity to attach them to a problem whether or not the course being followed had seemed to lead in that direction. For the same reasons it is unlikely that the outcome will be optimum and fully satisfactory from anybody's point of view. Alwyn was fortunate to get all that he wanted and Giles unfortunate to lose so completely, for their usual experience, like everyone else's, would be a decision that neither thought was good enough but each realized they would have to live with, at least until something better could be achieved, it being all that could be done in the then current circumstances. Incrementally arrived at, little by little as the problem clarifies and the interests emerge, this outcome would be neither wholly satisfactory nor wholly sufficient, but *'satisficing'*, a term coined from both (Simon 1960). Such an outcome will do for the time being, and is good enough to get by, for decision-making is not about searching for the sharpest needle hidden in a haystack, but for a needle sharp enough to sew with (March and Simon 1958).

Rules

There are rules defining everything, from who has what formal authority, to how arguments are to be presented; from what may or may not be used as evidence, to how far an advantage may be pushed; and what is fair play. These *'rules of the game'* (Crozier and Friedberg 1980) are the social norms governing behaviour in an organization. Thus Alwyn of Toxicem could not bypass the Capital Control Committee and go straight to the full Board of Directors to get the money he wanted. He could not attempt to persuade that Committee's members without going through the procedure of submitting written memoranda and reports, and these had to have the leavening of figures regarded as proper for such a case. He could not directly present his claim to promotion, but he could advance it via the process of deciding upon electricity generation. It was when conduct at lunch and at large began to transgress the rules on acceptable limits that the Managing Director acted to bring that decision process to a conclusion.

These rules may be so informal that the players in the game observe them hardly realizing they are there, or they may be formalized in memoranda and manuals of procedures and organization charts and constitutions. They ensure that decision-making proceeds 'neither at random nor at leisure. Regular channels structure the game. Deadlines force issues to the attention of busy players' (Allison 1969, p. 708).

Thus the players are interested both in the outcome and in any changes in the rules that affect their position in the future. One decision may fix rules for the next, so that each decision-making game proceeds within rules built up by some prior 'metagame' (March 1981), within a wider system of rules. 'The power and influence in any system is bounded by a super-system that sets limits upon and restricts the room for manoeuvre within the sub-system' (Abell 1975). The rules therefore substantially fix the differential distribution of power for any one occasion of decision-making, though they may be altered by it. They fix not only what should be done during decision-making but, over and above that, what kind of game it is (Crozier and Friedberg 1980). They become inherent in the language and thought of those involved, who tend to take them for granted along with the distribution of power (Clegg 1975). Power works within rules that power itself frames.

Differences in decision-making

The overall impression of decision-making given by the published mixture of research and imagination is therefore of games of manoeuvre characterized by obstacles, power, and muddle. Those who are involved represent the strategic *logiques d'action* of interests which can influence what goes on and its outcome. The rules of the game, and the human limitations which restrict attention to information and to viewpoints within practicable limits, enable the complexities of problems and the politicalities of power to be handled. Although the trajectory of the topic as it moves towards a decision may meander and even double back on itself, a satisficing incremental outcome will eventually be reached that few may wholly like but most can live with.

Although those involved in decision-making games mean business and are not there merely for the fun of it, the word 'power' can give an erroneously distasteful impression of what they are about. The power which they necessarily wield is of itself neither good nor bad: that judgement should be of the ends for which the power is used, and of the ways in which it is used. Power is the wherewithal to get things done. It is itself morally neutral.

The tale of Toxicem is an exceptionally vivid history in which the power of alliances of interests is plain to see. Its use as a grounding for ideas throughout this chapter may have misleadingly implied that it is typical, but it certainly is not. It does show that decision-making can be frayed and fractious, but it is exceptional in its degree of personal conflict.

To balance the tale of Toxicem, the story of a decision in another industrial firm to invest in new plant is more ordinary and far shorter to tell. This large British company, a world leader in its field, was replacing existing plant with a new process it had itself pioneered, and was deciding where one of its new plants should be located to give access to the Scandinavian and perhaps Western European markets. The possibility of siting the plant not in Britain but in Scandinavia was discussed by the overall Board of Directors, and then by the Board of the appropriate Division. Reports from departments – marketing, finance, technical and others – were called for, and a co-ordinated set of working parties was set up to examine different aspects. The assembled information was synthesized by a steering committee, and Sweden became the most likely location. Central and local government and unions in Sweden were approached with the aid of Swedish consultants, and finally the main Board decided to go ahead with a substantial investment in that country.

This was a straightforward case of the making of what was in financial and market penetration terms quite a big decision. It is a management textbook example of a synoptic process in which proper expertise was drawn in and correct information gathered until together they pointed to the best choice. Anything quite so smooth and controlled as this is not the norm, but it may not be as far from the norm as were the events at Toxicem. What it does show is how different two decision-making processes can be. What it does expose are the limits of the view of decision-making that research has so far achieved and which is synthesized here. It is a lively and insightful view which is a credit to those who have contributed and whose names have been mentioned, but more is needed, as indeed more understanding is always needed in any field of endeavour.

Description

More needs to be said about decision-making because the very liveliness and penetration of what can be said has led to a neglect of so much that is rudimentary and even simple. Most vitally, systematic *description of differences* is minimal. The composite picture yielded by research over the years is insightful but still general. Yet the making of decisions must surely differ from occasion to occasion. The managers at Toxicem, for instance, do not have the same harrowing experience every time they try to make a decision, nor do managers and administrators in other organizations. There must be big differences both within and between organizations. What are they?

Indeed, there is 'a relative paucity of hard data about organizational decisions' (Bass 1983, p. 172), and there are innumerable questions that have no answers, or answers based on very little evidence, though whether answers could ever be 'hard' is another matter.

Answers could be attempted, however, to questions such as what kinds of major decisions are commonplace and what are the rarities? Which ones are the most consequential? How many different interests are usually involved? Which of these interests are most (and least) influential, and over what? Can top management be outweighed? How long do decisions take? Do meetings delay them?

Most important, is it possible to find ways of comparing one process systematically with another so that differences and similarities of these kinds can be described? Is it possible then to group processes so that similarities and differences can be readily understood and explained?

Classification and explanation

If the processes of reaching decisions arise from the problems and interests inherent in those decisions, can the making of decisions be classified in terms of problems, interests, and processes? In other words, is the making of one decision so different to making another that it is not possible to do more than gaze fascinated at endless confusion, or can the essentials of decision-making be grasped more simply?

What makes the making of a decision follow a particular course? If different decisions follow different courses, then why? Is there any explanation why the Toxicem experience was what it was and not something different? Assuming that the reasons for what occurred can be found in the nature of the problems and interests contained in the decision, then does this mean that the nature of the matter in hand is of more significance for what is to happen than is the kind of organization in which it happens? If so it matters little whether a decision is occurring in, say, a public sector or a private sector organization. It will be made in much the same way. An investment decision, for example, would follow a similar process in both a private firm or a state-owned corporation. Alternatively, the kind of organization might have the greater significance. All decision-making in a business firm might be similar, and all that in a health service organization similar, but what happened in each would be quite dissimilar to what happened in the other. Even though decisions in both were on the same topic, such as budgets or departmental reorganization, they would be made in distinctly different ways.

The aim therefore is twofold: first to describe decision-making; second to explain this *process* of arriving at a choice in terms of the features both of the *matter for decision*, its problems and interests, and of the *organization* in which it occurs.

The Bradford studies

There has not been sufficient research to go on trying to answer such basic questions. Systematic comparisons of large numbers of decisions have been needed. Of course, there have been notable analyses of particular cases (for example, by Cyert, Simon, and Trow 1956; by Allison 1969 and 1971; and by Pettigrew 1973), but they have not had nearly enough follow up by comparative research. There has also been work which brought together sets of cases that had been recorded separately by different individuals, namely the pioneering work by Mintzberg's et al. (1976) students in Canada, and the typically vigorous presentation of 13 cases from Scandinavia and the USA by March and Olsen (1976) and their colleagues. There has always been work with questionnaires, including Axelsson and Rosenberg's (1979) comparison of views of decision-making in 20 Swedish organizations, and the 64 mailed questionnaires returned to Stein (1981a, 1981b) from unspecified American managers. But difficulties of comparison remained, samples were small, and the meaning of these mailed questionnaires is doubtful.

Signs that more substantial comparative research might be practicable came when Quinn (1980) achieved appreciable depth of understanding by talking to managers in nine business corporations, when Drenth, et al. (1979) widened the scope dramatically to 103 cases, though they reported only the influence of various levels in the hierarchy, and when Nutt (1984) analyzed 73 cases in health-related service organizations.

So the Bradford studies of decision-making, which are the substance of this book, were begun, early in the 1970s. Their aim was to examine more widely than hitherto, across a range of different decisions in a range of different organizations, what happens as managers and administrators at the top face the problems and the interests of the day. Using a mixture of retrospective case histories and records of concurrent decision-making, a (comparatively) large data base was built up which made possible an analysis of differences and similarities. From this a classification could be derived, and explanations formulated. A sustained effort, lasting more than a decade, was made to extend the boundaries of what is known and understood about strategic decision-making by applying comparative analysis to processual data.

Coverage of decisions and organizations

As many different kinds of decisions in as many different kinds of organizations as possible had to be covered, to the limits of what research funds and time allowed. In all, senior executives collaborated in the study of 150 cases of decision-making, in 30 organizations scattered across England.

Many of these organizations were world or national leaders in their fields, in either the private or the public sectors, and most were of considerable prominence. They were relatively large, the largest having 57,000 employees, but ranging down to one with only 100 employees; most were towards the smaller end of the distribution so that they were in line with the sizes of organizations generally in economically developed nations. The middle (or median) size was 2,600 employees. Each was approached by a letter to the chief executive, after selection from organizations listed in published directories. The choice aimed at a spread across the private and public, and goods and services sectors, to reflect the diversity of contemporary organizations. However, inclusion in the study was ultimately self-determined, since it depended upon the willingness of

Table 1.1 Thirty organizations studied

	Manufacturing (11)	Size (employees)
Public (2)	Construction equipment	2,000
	Chemicals B	1,800
Private (9)	Metal components	6,000
	Textiles	1,300
	Chemicals H	1,200
	Paints	300
	Tool components	750
	Friction products	2,500
	Glass	34,000
	Brewery J	4,500
	Brewery T	100
	Services (19)	
Public Commercial (3)	Air transport	57,000
	Electricity	9,000
	Water	6,000
Public Non-commercial (8)	Health Service B	4,500
	Health Service L	8,000
	Municipality	14,000
	Police	6,500
	Polytechnic H	1,900
	Polytechnic L	1,000
	University L	1,200
	University S	2,800
Private (8)	Insurance B	500
	Insurance R	22,000
	Bank	2,700
	Credit company	4,000
	Housing loans	7,600
	Road transport	200
	Industrial research	250
	Entertainment	100

managements to spend considerable personal time giving information about cases that had occurred recently enough to be within the memory of central participants, and in three cases to permit their being followed as they happened. Of the managements approached, two-thirds joined in the study.

There were 11 manufacturing organizations (two public, that is government-owned, and nine private) and 19 services (11 public, both commercial and non-commercial, and eight private commercial), as shown in table 1.1. Five cases of decision-making were studied in each organization, giving a spread across manufacturing and public and private services. There were 45 decisions in private manufacturers (plus ten in public manufacturers), 40 in public services such as health and education (plus 15 in commercial public services such as utilities), and 40 in private commercial businesses such as finance.

The five decisions were chosen jointly by the researchers and the executives in each organization to cover as great a diversity of subject matter as possible. In four organizations, each of the five decisions was on a different category of topic, such as a new product or service, or a reorganization, in 18 organizations the decisions covered four different topics, in seven organizations three topics, and in one organization only two topics. This means that though in a few organizations there is more than one case of one particular kind, for example two new product decisions or two reorganizations, in almost all the organizations a wide variety of decisions are covered. It is impossible to say exactly how representative they are, since no one knows what sorts of decisions are taken in what sorts of organizations, but they are as diverse a coverage as has been achieved and can reasonably be taken to be the most representative to date. They certainly included every *kind* of decision that had occurred, within active memory, in each organization, so that they show the full *range* of decisions which were occuring when the processes of decision-making took place, from the mid-1960s to the late 1970s. In general, they show what it is that is being decided in the organizations of our time, and what are the preoccupations of top managers and administrators (see list in Appendix A).

Phases of fieldwork

The challenge was to find a way of getting descriptions of cases covering the same features in each so that comparisons could be made, but requiring no more than the information necessary to the purpose so that the largest possible number of decisions could be studied. The answer was evolved by trial and error during the earlier years of the research. Over the period of fieldwork, 1974 to 1980, and with a concentration of work in the last three years, three overlapping phases emerged. To begin with, very voluminous accounts of each case were compiled, but then as experience showed the feasibility of doing so – and less and less time and money for research were forthcoming – the information obtained was pared down to a form that could be readily covered in interviews.

In phase one, the making of two decisions in each of three organizations, a utility, a university, and the manufacturer we have called Toxicem, was recorded in detail. In each of the organizations, one decision was followed as it happened, and one was traced back historically. This was done by a researcher spending many hours each week in each organization for between two and three years, talking with executives in their offices and over lunch, interviewing them, and searching files and documents. These six cases are reported more fully than they are in this book in Wilson (1980) and Wilson (1982).

As the members of the research team gained experience and were able to pare down what was needed, the second and final phases of research relied upon interviews to obtain first-hand inside reports from managers and administrators who had been present at the time, for example managing directors and function directors in firms, vice-chancellors (the equivalent of president) and deans in universities, management team members in health districts, and chief officers in local government. These lasted from an hour or two up to several hours of interview, discussion, lunch or after-work drinks, and tours round the premises, sometimes all in one session and sometimes over more than one visit. The second phase used two or more principal informants per case and covered one-third of the cases, and the final phase covered the rest of the cases with one principal informant each. Other managers and administrators would often come in, or be telephoned, to add to what the main informant could say. Those interviewed were *informants*, that is they gave information about what had happened and not about themselves or their opinions. As this and subsequent chapters will show, they talked about the departments involved, whether there were periods of inactivity, which interests were influential, whose was the final authority, and so on – information which was minimally biased by personal perspective.

The reliability of the interviewing was checked in two ways. In two manufacturers and a health service organization, feedback presentations were given to the informants, usually with their managerial colleagues also present, and this corroborated the researcher's understanding. Then information gained by interviewing was compared with that from the six cases studied intensively in the first research phase by interviewing executives in the same organizations about the same cases and then comparing their accounts with the fuller versions already obtained. It was found that the essentials of problems, interests, and processes could be gathered by interview in an outline narrative of main events and participants, and by the answers to a series of questions about what happened (see Appendix B on methods of research), without it being necessary to discover every incident or who said what on every occasion (though copious accounts were often given). The hindsight story that is forthcoming in interview is the same in main events and characters, just less cluttered with detail. The main pathways of the process are recalled and less attention is given to what became byways and dead ends.

Over the total period of research, several hundred executives talked to members of the research team. They were the principal informants, plus the many more who came in and out of interviews, and there were many more again in the three organizations where the six cases were covered in great detail in the first phase of fieldwork (see also Appendix B).

Subsequent chapters

The chapters that follow use this copious material and the results of its analysis to build up a picture of what happens in decision-making, and to examine why it happens. They look first at the *complexity* of decision problems, secondly at the *politicality* of decision interests, and thirdly at the *processes* of decision-making that ensue. As a result of what is found, a classification or *typology* of decision-making is then proposed, and through a comparison of similarities and differences between organizations, an answer is suggested to the question which matters most for what happens, the *matter for decision* or the *organization*.

2

Problems and Complexity

The process of making a decision, of getting from the first signifying that a choice is there to be made to making the choice, can be understood as a response partly to the problems raised by the subject of decision and partly to the interests implicated by it. This chapter looks at some aspects of the problems.

There could hardly be a decision without problems, and the problems raised by the making of strategic decisions are greater than most. For instance, would the building of an industrial plant abroad rather than in the home country lead to strains in future between the distant local management and head office? Would the net transport costs of a plant abroad be greater or less, when lower costs in transporting finished goods to the customers are set against greater costs in transporting raw materials? In a public corporation, what else would be affected by merging several departments into one? Would the benfits of this rationalization be outweighed by slower or less effective work in other respects? In a hospital service, could the resiting of certain medical ancillary functions have long-term implications that are not yet apparent? Would alternative provision for patients be adequate? Might the ordering by an airline of 'next generation' aircraft be premature, committing capital which is then not available later should some unforeseen change in passenger demands or aircraft design occur between placing the order and the delivery years afterwards of the new planes? Or will delay in ordering mean having to fly old aircraft in the distant future in competition with other airlines which did re-equip? Problems and yet more problems.

It is these problems and the headaches they bring that create the *complexity* of a decision. Complexity has many sources, not neces-sarily evident all together or in any one decision. One source is the *rarity* of the matter for decision. If the decision is unusual, even outside all previous experience, then the problems encountered in the making will be the more novel. It will be especially difficult to know what to do about them. Another source is *consequentiality*. Possible consequences may be radical, or serious, or widespread, or long-term, or any or all of these, and the more they are, the more complex are the decision-makers' problems.

Then there are the consequences the decision may have for subsequent decisions in the future, in a word its *precursiveness*. It may constrain future options in ways that were neither foreseen nor intended. And, of course, there is the complexity inherent in sheer numbers, not the figures in financial calculations though they are always there, but the numbers of interests (and individuals) that become involved in one way or another. More *involvement* means more different kinds of information and advice to be made sense of from more different quarters.

What strategic decisions are about

These are some of the sources of complexity in the making of strategic decisions. They cannot be discussed any further without knowing what strategic decisions are. What makes decisions strategic? What are they about? Are they positive or negative, a yes decision or a no decision?

What makes strategic decisions strategic?

The decisions which are the subject of this book are those made at the top about the bigger matters. These strategic decisions are not wholly different from all others, moving on a rarified plane unique to themselves, but are towards one end of a continuum, at the other end of which are the trivial everyday questions. To say that this chapter and this book are about strategic decisions is a convenient way of indicating which end of the continuum is in mind.

A strategic decision is one in which those who are involved believe will play a bigger rather than a smaller part in shaping what happens for a long while afterwards. This is a relative judgement, relative to the organization in which the decision is being made, for although research to be discussed in this chapter suggests a distinct consistency between organizations, it is not impossible for what is a big matter in one to be less weighty in another (Wilson 1966). A

strategic decision is likely to shape what happens because it has some
or all of certain features to a greater extent than do other decisions.
First, it is about something that does not come up very often. It is
more rare and non-routine than most (Hage 1980) and therefore
comparatively novel (Wilson 1980). There will be few if any direct
precedents for it, yet it is likely to set precedents for subsequent
decisions (Mintzberg, et al. 1976). Second, it commits substantial
resources (Mintzberg, et al. 1976). Third, it sets off 'waves' of lesser
decisions (Mintzberg 1979) and so is comparatively organization-
wide in its consequences (Wilson 1980). In short, it is relatively
unusual, substantial, and all-pervading.

The topics of decision

Strategic decisions have been thought to be about many possible
matters, but exactly which matters has been screened from outsiders
because organizations just do not publish lists of 'This Month's Top
Decisions'! There are some published research cases (e.g. Pettigrew
1973; March and Olsen 1976; Mintzberg, et al. 1976; Quinn 1980);
and now and again an example is blazoned by the public news media
when a scandal is exposed or a board room battle breaks out. Until
now, there has been no knowing just how unbalanced an impression
is given by this appearance of cases here and there with no
connection between them. Probably the impression has been more
sensational than typical. The large number of cases covered by the
Bradford studies is a chance to form something approaching a more
balanced view.

At first sight, some of the decisions did not seem to be very
strategic, but when understood from the insider's perspective they
took on a greater significance. For example, one of the District
organizations of the National Health Service was treating a change
to a new method of food preparation with great deliberation, even
though only a few employees in one hospital were affected. It
became clear, however, that this was a crucial matter because the
system, if decided upon, would be used in a new thousand-bed
hospital – with sweeping effects on work and pay.

More obvious in nature was what was called 'the last decision' in a
private company, whether to accept or to resist a takeover bid by a
competitor. There were also decisions the other way around,
whether or not to buy subsidiaries, and there were merger decisions

in the public sector such as whether to combine previously independent colleges and to integrate previously independent airlines. There
were decisions in both the public and the private sectors whether to
locate multi-million pound plants in Britain or abroad, and there
were internal restructurings, such as the insertion of a regional level
between branches and head office in a national financial institution.
There were decisions to launch new products or new services, and to
re-equip with new production technology and computer technology.

To get a general view of what the 150 decisions were about, the
numbers dealing with different *topics* were counted. Altogether, the
decisions were found to have covered ten categories of topic. A topic
is simply the 'label attached by those involved' (Hickson, et al. 1985)
to what is going on. It tells what the decision is about, such as a new
product or a new division, or raising capital or negotiating a merger.
Most topics are the focus at a particular time of longer-standing and
deeper *issues*, an issue being 'a persisting problem or opportunity'
(Astley, et al. 1982, p. 373). Thus a long-standing issue in a firm of
just how far to go in foreign markets will surface in the particular
topic of whether to locate a new plant abroad. Issues of the
utilization of energy and equipment lay beneath the decision in
Toxicem, described in chapter 1, to use surplus energy to generate
electricity.

Retrospectively, the topic label becomes the choice made, the
decision on 'the Swedish plant' or 'the generating of electricity',
whereas at the time it may be less specific since it may not be known
for sure which way things are going.

The 150 topics were classified by two members of the research
team into the ten categories, shown in table 2.1 in order of
frequency, according to what the decisions were about as denoted by
their 'labelling' during interview by the executive informants. It
would be possible to have more categories than ten. The technology
category, for example, could be split into decisions about equipment
alone versus those about buildings, and the control category could
be split into plans and budgets alone versus decisions which included
data-processing facilities. However, splitting the categories any
further would make the number of decisions in some of them too
small for comparative purposes.

Since topics were labelled by the choices (decisions) made and not
by the considerations when making them, nor the difficulties of their
implementation, nor their consequences, few ambiguities were
encountered when classifying them. A decision to launch a new

Table 2.1 Topics of decision

Topic Category	Number of cases	Examples
(1) Technologies	23	Equipment and/or premises e.g., whether to invest in new machinery and buildings, buy 'new generation' aircraft, close geriatric wards.
(2) Reorganizations	22	Internal restructurings, e.g., whether to insert regional level between branches and headquarters, merge departments, change overseas branches into subsidiaries ('domestication' in host nations).
(3) Controls	19	Planning, budgeting, and requisite data-processing, e.g., what the five-year 'strategic plan' or annual 'business plan' are to be, whether to purchase a computer.
(4) Domains	18	Marketing and distribution, e.g., whether to bypass wholesalers and distribute direct, introduce 'no-charge' banking, standardize a name for all branches of the company.
(5) Services	16	New, expanded, or reduced services, e.g., whether to launch a novel form of inter-disciplinary university degree, to increase municipal housing, to decrease European air services.
(6) Products	12	New products, e.g., whether to launch a new beer, a new glass-impregnated cement, or to generate electricity.
(7) Personnels	12	Job assessment, training, unions, e.g., whether to make a first productivity agreement, to use consultants to regrade all staff, to resist unionization.
(8) Boundaries	11	Purchases of, and mergings with, other organizations, e.g., whether to buy a subsidiary company, to merge colleges.
(9) Inputs	9	Finance and other supplies, e.g., whether to raise funds by a share issue, or (local government) by a lottery, or to change the sources of supply of components.
(10) Locations	8	Site and sites dispersal, e.g., whether to build a new plant abroad, to move company's principal offices, to reduce dispersal (by closing branches).
Total	150	

product, for example, which was labelled as such by the executive informants because it was a choice between no new product and alternative variants of a new product, would have included market and financial considerations. However, it would not have been labelled as a market or a monetary decision, because these were not seen as the primary choices. A market decision would be one where domain of operation was the primary choice, from which consequences for products might then flow.

Which are the more frequent topics?

The decisions defined by managers and administrators as being strategic include just about every possible subject (see table 2.1). Almost anything can loom up and take on significance for the organization in the eyes of those at the top, not just the computer installations or product launches or investments that have attracted most attention from journalists and researchers. Most frequent were decisions to re-equip, rebuild, or reorganize, the 23 'technologies' topics and the 22 'reorganizations'. Next came the making of plans, the fixing of budgets, and commitments on the requisite electronic data-processing, all 'controls' topics; and 'domain' or market-type decisions on price, distribution, and image. New 'services' and 'products' decisions were not such a high proportion as might have been supposed, together rather less than a fifth of the total. From the varied 'personnel' topics, for example complete staff regrading or unionization, the numbers drop through 'boundary' topics on takeover bids and similar moves, to 'inputs' of money or materials and finally to the eight decisions on 'locations' of major plants or corporation headquarters. Decisions on location do not happen often since most organizations stay put most of the time. The different categories of topic are discussed in greater detail in chapter 5.

We tabulated elsewhere (Butler, et al. 1979/80) the topics covered by published smaller-scale case research on processes. Table 2.2 contrasts our own and four other larger scale comparative studies which cover 124 British, Dutch, or Yugoslavian cases, 73 American and Canadian, 25 Canadian, eight Scandinavian, and five American. Using the set of ten categories of topic covered in the 150 Bradford studies cases as the criterion, it may be seen that comparative research on decision-making has had an uneven empirical grounding.

Table 2.2 Topics covered by comparative research*

| Topic category | Cases ||||||
	150 British[1]	124 British Dutch Yugoslavian[2]	73 American Canadian[3]	25 Canadian[4]	8 Danish Norwegian[5]	5 American[6]
(1) Technologies	23	70	17	8		
(2) Reorganizations	22	19	4		3	3
(3) Controls	19	17	16	2		
(4) Domains	18	⎫	7	4		
(5) Services	16	⎬18	15	5	2	1
(6) Products	12	⎭		2		
(7) Personnels	12		7	2	1	1
(8) Boundaries	11			1		
(9) Inputs	9		5			
(10) Locations	8		2		2	
Unclassifiable				1		

*Entries are numbers of cases. The allocation of cases from the other five studies to topic categories is based on the published details: for the study by Nutt (1984) there may be some unreliability due to difficulties of interpreting brief case details.

Researchers responsible:
1. Bradford team
2. Drenth, et al. (1979)
3. Nutt (1984)
4. Mintzberg, et al. (1976)
5. March and Olsen (1976)
6. March and Olsen (1976)

There have been gaps in the range of decisions covered. Even in these larger studies, very few decisions have been included on domain or market, personnel matters, boundary changes by take-overs or mergers, inputs or location. There has been a concentration upon decisions about new technology/investment, controls (especially electronic data-processing), reorganization, and services and products. Fortunately, this can be seen to have been a bias in the right direction since judging by the distribution of the Bradford cases these do seem to be among the most commonly strategic topics.

In the systems terms of outputs and throughputs, there is a notably even distribution of topics among the 150 Bradford cases, 46 being outputs topics (about products, services, and domains), 54 about throughputs or organization functioning (technologies, personnels, and controls), and 41 about the form of the organized system itself (reorganizations, boundaries, and locations). Inputs from the external environment, of which there are only nine cases, do not bulk large as a strategic concern; and as six of these are financial and only three are about physical supplies, the latter especially appear not to be of major concern for organizations. By contrast, the prominence of organizational topics indicates not only their importance but suggests also the importance of research and teaching on organizational problems (Hickson, et al. 1985).

Therefore, it is not just an organization's external world and outputs to that world which are strategic for the organization, but also internal questions such as reorganization or personnel problems. Moreover, these kinds of topics are strategic for all kinds of organizations for what is strategic in one organization tends to be so in others too. Only one difference can be detected between organizations in the proportions of decisions made on each topic.

We had supposed that private enterprise might be especially occupied with new product decisions, compared to the public services such as health, education, police, water and electricity, which are denied free choice of what they do for they must provide their respective services and must do so to specified publics. But there is no evidence for this, as table 2.3 shows. Public services have about the same number (11) and proportion (20 per cent) of new outputs decisions as private manufacturers (11 or 24 per cent), the implication being that the public services are as alert to the possibilities of new services as private enterprise is to new products. The only noticeable difference is in reorganizations decisions. There may be a tendency for the public services to undertake more reorganizations (again 11

Making Decisions

Table 2.3   Outputs and reorganizations decisions as a percentage of all decisions in different kinds of organizations

Organizations	Organiza-tions	Total number Decisions	Topic categories Outputs (products or services)	Reorganiza-tions
Private manufacturing	9	45	11 (24%)	4 (9%)
Public manufacturing	2	10	1 (10%)	1 (10%)
Total manufacturing	11	55		
Private service	8	40	5 (12%)	6 (15%)
Public service	11	55	11 (20%)	11 (20%)
Total service	19	95		

decisions, 20 per cent of their total). If so, this tendency is shared with private services such as transport and finance (six decisions, 15 per cent). So it is likely due not to the peculiarities public ownership, but to the managers of all services being inclined to think that they can be bettered by reshuffling the organization that provides them, whereas manufacturers keep their eyes on the product and are less inclined to look behind them at their organization itself.

Negative as well as positive

Decisions are normally thought of as positive. 'Yes, we will reorganize our departments'; 'yes, we will make a five-year strategic plan.' But are they *all* positive? Do decision-makers never say no?

There are, of course, the 'might have been' decisions, though to call them decisions is misleading. These are the topics that never were, the underlying issues that never surfaced as topics for active decision-making. They remained latent, either because the powerful wished to avoid them being made explicit or because the weak dared not raise them, and the time for them to surface never came. Perhaps they included the issue of whether the aims of the business were acceptable at all, or whether public funds should be spent on giving such a service, but who can know? These 'non-decisions'

(Bachrach and Baratz 1962) never became identifiable topics for decisions.

However, of the topics that did surface and were studied, not all denoted positive decisions. The great majority, 138 out of 150, were positive in the sense that it was intended that something should be done rather than undone. These were decisions to buy subsidiaries, to buy new equipment, to issue new shares, and so on. Thus decisions that are seen as being strategic are mostly positive, judging also by other research which is virtually exclusively on positive decisions (e.g. March and Olsen 1976; Mintzberg, et al. 1976). Not all are positive, however. Twelve (8 per cent) out of 150 cases were negative, either maintaining the status quo or intending negative action. Seven were decisions to preserve the status quo, to do nothing: for example, not to make a takeover bid, not to relocate the company's headquarters, or not to enter a market. Five further cases were decisions on negative action: for example, to close retail shops or to close hospitals. Though this proportion seems at first sight quite small, on reflection it seems remarkably large if it is suspected that executives are inclined to forget what was not done, or to avoid telling it because it does not make a good story, and so probably over-represent the positives and under-represent the negatives. That 8 per cent should nonetheless be negative suggests that negatives are a more important element among strategic decisions than has previously appeared to be so.

Strategic topics

It was said earlier that strategic decisions can be thought of as lying at one end of a continuum, at the other end of which are the more trivial decisions. However, the strategic ones would not all be at exactly the same point. Some would be more strategic than others. These would be the more novel, the more consequential, the more precedent setting. Which topics are the most so and which the least?

Rarity

A close indication of novelty is given by *rarity*, the frequency with which similar decisions recur (Butler, et al. 1979/80; Hage 1980; DIO

International Research Team 1983). The executives interviewed commented on how often decisions of the same nature as the case under investigation arose in their organizations. This does not mean how frequently decisions in the same topic category occur, for instance that decisions on the product range recur year after year as they do in some manufacturers, or that reorganizations are always coming up in hospital services and utilities. It means how far similar matters arise within a topic category, for instance successively similar product questions as compared to a completely novel product idea, or departmental reshuffles on a similar scale within a service organization as compared to an unprecedented restructuring.

Scored on frequency per year (see Appendix C), with the majority tending to occur much less often than once a year, the rarest, most nearly unique decisions included Toxicem's do-it-yourself electricity generation, and a long-established financial institution's first ever reorganization of its point of customer contact by introducing minimum staff 'mini-branches'. Among the relatively common recurring decisions were these same two firms respectively switching to a new source of raw materials, and altering interest rates (the latter a decision that happened relatively often, but being in the largest institution of its kind was of national economic significance).

Table 2.4 ranks topic categories by the mean rarity of the decisions in them, showing that it is successive environment-orientated decisions that are most nearly the same, whereas organizational decisions present the most novel challenges since any one is rarely the same as anything previous. The environment-orientated domains, products, and inputs decisions rank 8, 9, and 10, the most similar from one instance to the next, whereas reorganizations and locations decisions rank 1 and 3, many being unique. A decision to reshape the organization's structure or to relocate its premises is most unlikely to occur in the same way again, whereas one new product launch may be much like another, strategic though each one is. A curiosity is the novelty of services decisions, in second place: though one product launch may be much like another, each new services decision is more likely to be novel compared to its predecessors, and indeed a university launching a one-off new form of degree cannot do the same again and a state electricity board committing supplies to an enormous new coalfield is unlikely ever to have the chance again – both will launch new services, but not like these services (Wilson 1980; Wilson, et al. 1985).

These relatively rare reorganizations, new or changed services,

Table 2.4   Rare and common topics of decision

Topic category	Rank order	Rarity Topic mean *(Likely number of* *occurrences per year)*
		Most rare
Reorganizations	1	.14
Services	2	.29
Locations	3	.34
Personnels	4	.52
Technologies	5	.53
Boundaries	6	.69
Controls	7	1.15
Domains	8	1.42
Products	9	2.20
Inputs	10	2.93
		Most common

and relocations decisions will probably be the most difficult to handle since there are unlikely to be clear previous examples to look to. At the bottom of the table, a new product or a change in the source of financial inputs may be vital, but something similar has been experienced before and therefore people know how to handle it. handle it.

Consequentiality

The most strategic of the topics are also likely to carry greater commitment and consequences. Four indicators of consequences go well enough together when analyzed by topic to form a tentative rank order index of topic *consequentiality*, the four being the *radicality* of the consequences, the *seriousness* of the consequences, the *diffusion* of the consequences and their *endurance* (see also Hickson, et al. 1981, p. 181). They are respectively ratings by executive informants of how radically a decision 'changed things', and of its seriousness if 'things went wrong' (e.g. loss of sales and reputation if a new product failed, or public accusations of inefficiency in local government if reorganization were unsuccess-ful); a count of the number of kinds of criteria by which the correctness of a decision was judged (e.g. costs, morale, market share) with more criteria indicating that more diffuse aspects of the

Table 2.5 Consequential topics of decision

Consequences	Overall Consequentiality		Radicality		Seriousness		Diffusion		Endurance	
Topic category (in order of overall rank)	Overall rank	Mean rank order	Rank order	Topic mean (on five-point rating)	Rank order	Topic mean (on five-point rating)	Rank order	Topic mean (number of criteria affected)	Rank order	Topic mean (horizon in years)
Locations	1	2.0	3	3.4	1	3.7	2	2.6	2	10.0
Products	2	2.2	1	3.6	2	3.6	1	3.3	5	7.6
Reorganizations	3	3.5	2	3.5	8	3.0	3	2.4	1	12.3
Technologies	4	4.5	5	3.3	5	3.5	4	2.1	4	8.6
Controls	5	5.7	9	2.6	2	3.6	4	2.1	8	7.0
Domains	6	6.5	3	3.4	7	3.2	7	1.8	9	6.2
Boundaries	7	6.5	6	3.1	6	3.4	7	1.8	7	7.2
Personnels	8	6.7	8	2.9	2	3.6	7	1.8	10	3.6
Services	9	7.0	9	2.6	10	2.8	6	1.9	3	8.8
Inputs	10	7.7	6	3.1	9	2.9	10	1.5	6	7.3

organization were touched by its consequences; and 'how far ahead did people look' when making the decision, anticipating how long its consequences would endure (details are in Appendix C).

Table 2.5 shows the means, and rank orders of the means, for all ten topics on each of the four aspects of consequences, the topics being listed in order of their overall ranking shown in the first column. Each topic is placed in this overall ranking by the mean of its four separate rankings. Caution is due, because some topic categories do not contain many cases (see table 2.1), only means are compared, and absolute differences may be small. Of course, there should not be large differences since all the decisions are more or less strategic and all topics tend relatively to be radical and serious, to have diffuse numbers of consequences, and to have long enduring consequences. On the last mentioned criterion, endurance, the horizon of those concerned – how far did they 'look ahead' to enduring consequences – averaged 8.1 years over the 150 cases and in one case was as long as 20 years. Strategic decisions are seen as choices for the long term.

However, although the rankings on the four aspects of consequences are not at all perfect matches, they accord well enough to be looked at together for a view of which kinds of decisions are probably the most consequential of the consequential. The most radical weighty matters with the most diffuse and enduring consequences appear to be locations, products, and reorganizations decisions which rank first, second and third in the table, whilst services and inputs decisions (ninth and tenth) appear less likely to wrinkle brows.

Products decisions are understandably highly consequential for they are the *raison d'être* of manufacturing organizations which stand or fall by their consequences in the most visible way. Thus product launches in American big business too, such as IBM's decision to give heavy backing to a new form of computer (the 360), and Ford's decisions to back the Pinto model (a success) and the Edsel model (a failure), are rightly seen as having been strategic 'high risk' decisions (Hage 1980) because they committed the future. So do relocation and reorganization decisions, as the American executives who talked to Quinn (1978) also realized. Relocation and reorganization decisions have exceptionally enduring consequences (means of 10.0 and 12.3 years), and are highly consequential generally in the sense that they are imponderable in their ramifications. Executives pointed out that the consequences of some of these decisions could never be traced or evaluated, so how could anyone ever be sure whether they had 'worked'?

Yet despite this, reorganizations have only the eighth place in the seriousness ranking, executives often explaining that there was 'no money involved' or 'little economic impact'. This exemplifies the well-known tendency to emphasize visible and therefore monetary factors, which also showed up in the frequency of profits, costs, return on investment, and sales returns among the criteria by which decisions were judged.

Decisions on personnel topics are curious in that they do not bring so much radical change nor diffuse nor enduring consequences (eighth, seventh, and tenth places), so from these points of view they are not of the greatest consequence, and yet they are seen as relatively serious (joint second place). So the consequences of decisions such as the re-evaluation of a large proportion of jobs, or an attempt to deter union control, can be serious. Personnel decisions at a strategic level are not to be taken lightly.

The consequentiality of topics often contrasts with their rarity, implying that although both aspects are strategic they co-vary only slightly. A decision which is consequential need not be rare, and vice versa. The most obvious in this are the products decisions, highly consequential (table 2.5) but not at all rare (table 2.4), for although they are highly consequential they are no strangers to those concerned. Whilst they are vital, they have happened before and will do so again. The outputs of service organizations are the reverse, decisions on services being rare but comparatively inconsequential for the fate of service organizations does not rest so heavily on the success or failure of any one output. Probably the most tricky of all are decisions on relocation and reorganization which are highly consequential and novel as well, never having occurred before in the particular form; they stand high in both tables.

In summary, the chances are that:

(a) *inputs* decisions will be *least consequential, and least rare.*
(b) *services* decisions will be not very consequential, but rare.
(c) *products* decisions will be highly consequential, but not rare.
(d) *locations* and *reorganizations* decisions will be *both highly consequential and rare.*

Hence the more strategic among the strategic seem likely to be locations decisions (for example, where to situate major new manufacturing plants, whether to move an entire corporation headquarters through which all work from branches is funnelled, whether to change policy on branch dispersal); reorganizations decisions (for example, whether to change the hierarchy by inserting a regional level between branches and headquarters, or to change the division of labour by amalgamating or dividing departments); and products decisions (whether to launch new products).

Precursiveness

A further criterion of a strategic decision is that it sets precedents. Subsequent related decisions can be taken more readily, as was the decision in Toxicem to purchase additional equipment for electricity generation following the first decision to do so. Consequentiality as it has been defined here covers something of precedent-setting in the diffusion and endurance of consequences, for as they widen and extend, so they open up or close off further possibilities. The concept of precedent-setting, however, is expanded by the idea of *precursiveness*, the extent to which a decision initiates parameters within which subsequent decision-making is constrained (Mallory and Cray 1982). Since it sets constraints that were not there for it to follow, it is less constrained than its successors. Precursiveness is implied in Simon's (1960) computer analogy of programmed and non-programmed decisions, but the parameter-setting precursor does not necessarily programme how a subsequent decision should be taken, but sets constraints as to what the decision may be. Whereas programming sets the steps to be followed to reach a decision, precursors set the range within which a decision must come, as when a budget sets cost limits for other decisions or an investment in new plant sets design limits for subsequent new products.

Comparing 41 cases classified as precursive with 107 classified as less precursive (of 150 cases, data were missing on two), the presumption that precursiveness is a strategic characteristic is supported by the precursive cases being more enduring in their consequences. The difference is not a huge one – their consequences are foreseen as lasting on average a good ten years as against about seven years for the less precursive decisions (means 10.6 and 7.2: F ratio 9.2, probability 0.003, degrees of freedom 1,145) – but it is in the expected direction, and precursiveness and endurance do correlate (0.24: 99 per cent confidence level).

However, there is no obvious division among topics of decision into those which always set parameters for decisions that follow and those which never do. It cannot be said that the setting of a budget is always more precursive than a commitment to a new product or service, or the other way round. Only boundaries decisions seem proportionately more often precursive. Takeovers of subsidiary companies or mergers, which are typical boundary decisions, make commitments that afterwards constrain decisions on investment or supplies, or marketing, so that resources flow towards (or away from) the new part of the organization.

Complexity

Sources of complexity

This chapter can now return to where it began, to the complexity of the problems raised by the making of a decision. If the process of getting to a decision is to be understood and explained, part at least of the explanation must be the complexity of the problems faced, and the features which have been described as making a decision strategic also make it complex. The *rarity, consequentiality*, and *precursiveness* that lift decisions to a strategic level do more than that as far as managerial decision-makers are concerned. The difficulty that confronts them is not that the decision is strategic, but that it presents complex problems. Locations, reorganizations, and products decisions raise more problems than do, say, inputs decisions, for the latter are not only less strategic but also less complex. The complexity of the supply, market, financial and international considerations involved in deciding in which country to locate a large new manufacturing plant, for example, far exceeds those pertaining say, to decisions between limited and familiar sources of monetary or material inputs.

Greater or lesser complexity figures prominently in the decision-making in all kinds of organizations. In German firms that were either buying or selling industrial capital goods, such as building, shipping, and aviation equipment, and computer software, a single complexity factor was isolated in the decisions to buy and sell (Kirsch and Kutschker 1982, pp. 474–5). In Swedish schools and colleges, it typified the decisions of academia (Axelsson and Rosenberg 1979).

Uncertainty

The complexity of juggling with a variety of considerations is compounded by the uncertainty of their consequences. The more radical the consequences, the greater the problems of assessing the risk; the more serious the consequences, the greater the fear of a mistake; the more diffuse the consequences, the less easy it is to envisage their ramifications; the more enduring the consequences, the hazier the distant future into which they extend. Indeed, there are times when organizations, or rather those who run them, 'do not know what they are doing' (Cohen, et al. 1972, p. 11), for an organization is 'an open system, indeterminate and faced with uncertainty' (Thompson 1967, p. 13). 'For many organizations the causal world in which they live is obscure. . . . It is hard to see the connections between organizational actions and their consequences' (March and Olsen 1976, p. 12). There may be disagreement on what causes what and therefore on what the results of a decision will be (Thompson and Tuden 1964). Executives are often not at all sure whether what happens is as a consequence of what they decided or is nothing to do with it, and not surprisingly they disagree on what follows from what. They turn to past experience as the best guide, but trying to learn from the past is not easy, for even when something of a similar nature has been dealt with before, 'History can be reconstructed or twisted' (March and Olsen 1976, p. 12) in the light of differing and unclear goals (McMillan 1980). Facts can cease to feel as factual as they once seemed to be.

To return to the tale of Toxicem, told in chapter 1, that do-it-yourself electricity decision was enveloped by uncertainty, for there was no agreed information on what the costs of generating electricity were likely to be, and no experience of private electricity generation which could be turned to for guidance. Even so, it must not be thought that all strategic decisions are so uncertain, for in the same firm a decision to make a new chemical, here called 'bluestuff' (Wilson 1980; Wilson, et al. 1985), was reached with much greater surety. Though there were severe technical problems in handling a corrosive chemical under high pressure, so that a special Development Committee including outside consultants was formed and met continually during what came to be called 'fortnights of afternoons', when its members pushed aside their other work, there was adequate information about everything else. Growth in world demand for pigments manufactured with bluestuff was already known, the current market price was known, and sales and financial projections could be made. There were published reports and articles and Toxicem's own model laboratory process and pilot plant to rely on, as well as the expertise of the consultants, and the assurance that competitors were already successfully in production. Compared to the electricity decision, everyone knew what they were doing with bluestuff.

Complex involvements

A further source of complexity, in addition to rarity, consequentiality, and precursiveness, is *involvements*. The more parties that become involved in the process of making a decision, the more complex the problems are to those who are drawn in on behalf of each party. As the numbers involved, or about to become involved, build up, so it becomes more and more taxing to remember who has yet to be asked and who was asked and what they said, who may know what, which meeting expressed which views and which committees have yet to report, what is significant and what can be ignored. It is simpler to decide by oneself, for the more others get in on the game, the more complex it becomes. This is due to the different 'contexts' from which they view it so that it becomes a 'multi-context problem' (Kirsch and Kutschker 1982, p. 454) as the ways of looking at it multiply. There are more fingers in the pie to allow for in the mixing.

We have stressed elsewhere the sheer numbers that come in and out of the process of making a decision during the months or years it takes to reach a conclusion (Kenny, et al. 1985). There is 'fluid participation. Participants vary in the amount of time and effort they devote to different domains; involvement varies from one time to another' (Cohen, et al. 1972, p. 1). This involvement, which Hage (1980) calls 'extensity of participation,' though the word participation is not used here because of its prior associations with formal consultation and human relations, is both internal and external.

Internal subunits

The division of labour in organizations creates sub-units of many kinds, by whatever name, so much so that organizations can be regarded as 'interdepartmental systems' (Hickson, et al. 1971), and their power studied in that light (Hinings, et al. 1974). They are so subdivided that it has even been argued that it would be useful to regard them as 'schismatic systems' always about to disintegrate (Morgan 1981). These sub-units become involved in decision-making in many ways. In industry, sales departments prepare surveys, accounting departments supply cost estimates, research and development committees make recommendations, and the personnel manager has a talk with the managing director about morale. In a Health Service District, doctors from different hospitals sit on a committee with nursing and medical ancillary and administrative representatives, and each puts their case. In government, the array of departments and agencies involved in the American President's decision to blockade Cuba during the 1962 nuclear missile crisis was described by Allison (1969) in his 'bureaucratic politics model' of decision-making.

External organizations

We have called the external organizations which appear in decision-making 'organizations-in-contact' (Hickson, et al. 1978). These may be the suppliers who are telephoned to see whether they can change what they make to fit a possible new product, or important customer firms who are consulted about whether they would take the new product, or banks, or trade unions, or departments of government such as the Department of Industry or the Treasury, and many more. Pressure groups can make themselves felt, as in the Netherlands when the advent of a political pressure group in decisions on supplies of coffee for a Dutch retail chain forced compliance with public opinion (Hofstede 1980). So, too, in the public water authority included in the Bradford studies, when anglers opposed a proposal to extract water from a river, and environmentalists pressed a local municipality to question the effects of a plant to treat sewage (to be precise, the possible smell).

James Callaghan, a British Prime Minister of the 1970s, may have been prone to become involved in person on behalf of the top decisions of major corporations. When Ford's were considering where in Europe to build a plant, Henry Ford II was invited to lunch at 10 Downing Street, where Callaghan attempted to press Britain's attractions (Dunkerley, et al. 1981). When British Airways were deciding whether to order the new Boeing 757 or the European

Airbus, Callaghan visited the President of the American Eastern Airlines to intensify pressure on them for a parallel order for the 757 (which would use British Rolls-Royce engines), without which Boeings would not launch the new model.

Numerous involvements

The many involvements in Toxicem's electricity decision, from internal engineers to the external CBI, have already been described. Comparing two less extraordinary cases, the decision in the same company to produce the new bluestuff chemical brought in, over a period of almost four years' consideration, five main departments, production, research, development, sales, and accounting, as well as several outside organizations, including market research consultants, potential customer firms, likely competitors, and insurance companies. In a District of the National Health Service, putting together a first ever five-year strategic plan brought in, during less than a year, the financial, orthopaedic, obstetric, paediatric, pathology and several other medical and ancillary units, and the higher Regional and Area levels of the Health Service's national hierarchy.

Some units may be drawn in once only in the course of the making of a decision, as when the CBI provided a single item of cost information for Toxicem, but most, and especially the internal sub-units, are involved continually, and sometimes continuously, throughout.

This complexity of involvement is brought home by summing across all the Bradford cases. There were 1,021 internal and external units named as involved in the 150 processes of decision, or in other words about seven main units per decision, ranging from a handful in some instances to as many as 20 in the case of one manufacturer's new product. Yet this is a substantial underestimate of the complexity experienced by the centrally involved managerial elite, for it does not indicate the frequency of interaction of each, nor does it indicate the number of individuals interacting. Clearly, the involvement of a single department, for example, can mean the involvement of numerous individuals. There are many more individuals, in and out, than the number of internal sub-units or external organizations counted here.

Classification by interests

To make comparisons across cases of the large numbers involved in decision-making, it was necessary to find a way of classifying them. The units (rather than individuals) listed by executives as being involved, and whose involvement is recounted in the chronologies of events, were classified by their 'interests' in the functioning of the organization in which the decision occurred. The interests of these internal sub-units and external organizations are the origin of the ever present politicality of decision-making that is discussed later. The classification derives from that proposed by Katz and Kahn (1966), and rests on the assumption that both insiders and outsiders have interests of varying magnitudes in what is going on. Internal departments and sections of whatever kind have 'bureaucratic contracts' of interest with their organization, analogous to the interests of external organizations which are frequently tangible in written agreements and obligations. Thus production-type units have a fundamental interest in the organization continuing to transform inputs into outputs so that their capabilities are utilized, and similarly, research departments have an interest in the organization being innovative, but this is of less matter to maintenance or personnel departments whose prime interest is stability so that the working of equipment and the employment of people can be maintained. In the same way, external suppliers have their interest in the inputs function of the organization, customers in the outputs, unions in the employment, inspectors and auditors in the standards observance, and competitors in the performance (Hickson, et al. 1985).

The resulting classification included 14 forms of interests, eight internal and six external, as shown in table 2.6. The first is transformation, signifying the interest that production and equivalent functions in service organizations, like nursing in hospitals, have in the organization sustaining its work of transforming inputs of resources or people into outputs. As already mentioned, engineering and personnel sections have a similar interest in stable operation to occupy equipment and employees. Accounting, inspection and the like are concerned with conformity to certain requirements, whilst complaints and equivalent sections are concerned with adjudication.

Table 2.6 Classification of interests

Primary interest in the organization	Examples of interest units
Internal	
Transformation	Production department (small tool manufacturer); transport department (haulage company); nursing staff (health authority)
Stability	Engineering department (car component manufacturer); maintenance section (electricity board), personnel department (chemical manufacturer)
Conformity	Accounts section (chemical manufacturer); quality control section (brewery); inspector (bank)
Adjudication	Liason section (local government); complaints department (water authority); claims section (insurance company)
Innovation	Design section (brewery); research department (glass manufacturer); development section (research and development organization)
Acquisition	Procurement section (airline); purchasing department (chemical manufacturer)
Domain	Marketing department (haulage company); sales department (textile company); advertising (paint manufacturer)
Autonomy-devolution	Divisions (finance company); departments (university)
External	
Inputs	Suppliers of materials and/or finance
Outputs	Customers and clients
Employment	Trade unions
Public standards	Factory inspectorates (heavy equipment manufacturer); foreign government (glass manufacturer); local government (building society).
Private standards	Auditors (bank); trade association (building society); shareholders (brewery).
Comparative performance	Competitors

Innovation by the organization is the obvious interest of research departments, whilst its domain is equally obviously the concern of marketing and related units. Self-sufficient divisions are interested in the autonomy permitted them by the organization's formal structure.

The reasonings for the groupings of external organizations in contact are more self-evident. They include the conformity that interests both the government factory inspectorate and a trade association, for instance, the first being concerned with conformity to public standards of working conditions, and the second with conformity to the industry's own norms of accepted practice.

This classification is not free of ambiguities and unsolved difficulties of definition. Is the interest of a personnel department that an organization shall give expanded rather than stable employment? Does the interest of competitors lie in the destruction of a particular organization, or in its survival in a condition that compares unfavourably with themselves? Nevertheless, classifying by similarity of interest is a rationale for grouping units that is pertinent to their involvement in decision-making, and that encompasses both internal and external units, and it is therefore more appropriate than some more extraneous criterion even if that were better defined. It is an attempt that is unavoidable if the 1,021 units involved in the 150 cases of decision-making are to be grouped to find out which kinds are most involved and which are least – and which exploit that involvement most influentially. (This last is the subject of the following chapter.)

Crude though the classification is, it arrives at 14 different kinds of interests, and even this is both a further sign of the complexity of strategic decision-making at the top, and another underestimate of it, for there are many more viewpoints and nuances than it suggests.

Complex interests

The numbers of interest units of each kind involved in all 150 cases are given in table 2.7, listed from the category with the largest number down to that with the least. For example, 186 accounting, quality control,and inspection units that had conformity to requirements as their primary interest were involved, more than one per decision on average, but at the foot of the table only 14 purchasing or similar departments were recorded in only a handful of decisions. Involvement usually denotes a direct contact, anything from phone

Table 2.7 Involvements of interest units

Typical interest units* (primary interests in brackets)	Involvements (number of interest units in 150 cases of decision-making)	
(1) Accounting, quality control, inspection (conformity)	186	(18%)
(2) Production and equivalent 'workflow' departments (transformation)	131	(13%)
(3) Auditors, trade associations, shareholders (private standards)	112	(11%)
(4) Government departments and agencies (public standards)	108	(11%)
(5) Self-sufficient divisions, etc. (autonomy/devolution)	101	(10%)
(6) Supplier firms (inputs)	79	(8%)
(7) Sales, marketing (domain)	70	(7%)
(8) Maintenance, personnel (stability)	51	(5%)
(9) Competitors (comparative performance)	45	(4%)
(10) Customers, clients (outputs)	43	(4%)
(11) Trade unions (employment)	35	(3%)
(12) Research, design departments (innovation)	25	(2%)
(13) Liaison and claims departments (adjudication)	21	(2%)
(14) Purchasing (acquisition)	14	(1%)
Total	1,021	(100%)

*External interest units underlined.

calls or a visit, to taking part for months in continual discussions. But this is not always the case. Involvements also include units listed by executives as having affected decisions when there may not have been direct contact, for example when a market decision was affected by a competitor who naturally enough was not asked about it but whose reactions were considered, and whose personnel may have been communicating indirectly on the grapevine, whether they intended to or not. Further, since the informant's viewpoint was being taken, if the informant wished to include a general category such as 'competitors', or 'customers/clients', when there were no identifiable main competitors or customers to specify, that was accepted.

Omnipresent in decision involvement are the already mentioned conformity interest units who top table 2.7, and appear in almost every decision-making process, for what decisions do not involve accountants and their kind somewhere along the line? Corresponding external organizations whose interests too are in standards are high on the list at third and fourth places, this last being government departments, for most decisions at this strategic level go beyond the formal boundaries of the organization in their implications and many touch the interests of the state. Equally, very little can be decided that does not in some way involve the core 'workflow' departments such as production in manufacturing and nursing in hospitals which stand second in the table.

The internal research, design, complaints, and purchasing departments in the bottom three places are specialized on such narrow areas of competence that they feature only in those few decisions at this level which are directly pertinent to them. Low down in eleventh place are the trades unions, whose marginality to what goes on at the top we have discussed in detail elsewhere (Wilson, et al. 1982) and will examine again in this book.

The picture as a whole reaffirms that amid the complexities of multiple interests, managerial decision-makers have to be externally orientated. Though their decision-making is hardly ever exposed to the mass media, they are not locked away from the outside world in its other forms. That outside world manifested in trade associations, state factory inspectorates, suppliers, customers, competitors, unions and many others, often glimpses what is under way, for 41 per cent of all the involvements are of external interest units (those underlined in table 2.7). Managers and administrators are constantly compelled to look both ways, inwards at their fellows yet also outwards at changing sets of outside interests.

Does that mean that external interests have a great influence on the outcomes of decision-making? Is government influential? Has management lost control in its own house? In short, does being in on the process mean influencing the outcome? These questions will be discussed in the next chapter.

Quasi-decision making

The complexity of rare, consequential, precursive and highly involving problems is not always as fearsome as it might at first seem. Surprisingly often, the problems are more symbolic than real – though symbolism has another reality of its own – and the process of making a decision is something of a charade because the decision has effectively already been made. Although the game has to be played out, its result is hardly in doubt. Perhaps it happens that one choice is overwhelmingly attractive to all involved, with no realistic alternative. Perhaps a dominating chief executive has already made up his mind, and he has a reputation for not changing his mind very easily. Perhaps both evidence and power combine, a dominating chief executive, or other powerful parties, persistently paying attention to some evidence and to nothing else. When questioned, executives agreed that decision-making often felt like this. On a four-point 'openness to alternatives' scale (see Appendix C), it was obvious to some or all that 'the decision had already been made' in 40 cases out of 124 where data were available, and only in 57 cases was the decision so wide open that there was no hint of the prior closing off of possibilities.

It is startling that so many strategic decisions are not all that wide open, and that those who are in the know are aware of this. But it confirms the supposition that a lot of decisions are 'simple-minded' (Cyert and March 1963) in so far as all sorts of more speculative alternatives are closed off and a comparative few which are not so different to what has been done before are weighed up. To attempt more would be beyond human capacities, or beyond what prevailing circumstances – including the balance of power – would permit.

Yet if the outcome is in some measure a foregone conclusion, why waste time and effort on 'decision-making'? Perhaps because the foregone conclusion may not have been apparent right at the start, even though it became apparent early on. Perhaps because even if it was apparent to some, many others still needed convincing. Or because though it may have been apparent it was indistinct and needed to be better defined and to be checked against cost or other estimates, just to be sure. *Quasi-decision making* – the making of a decision which some know has already all but been made – is a normal part of the game.

From complexity to politicality

The level of *complexity* describes the nature of the decision-making problems as they are experienced by those involved. This complexity has many aspects, each of which may contribute to the characteristics of a decision. Particular attention has been paid here to *rarity*, *consequentiality* (radicality, seriousness, diffusion, and endurance of consequences), *precursiveness*, and *involvements*.

Taking the 150 Bradford cases altogether, three patterns of association between the different aspects of complexity can be seen. First a precursive decision, which sets parameters to constrain those that follow, is likely to cause greater changes and those consequences are likely to endure longer, as the idea of precursiveness suggests they should (r precursiveness . radicality = 0.3; precursiveness . endurance 0.2; both at 99 per cent confidence level). Second, since widespread consequences touch more interests, a decision with more diffuse consequences is likely to involve more diverse internal and external units (r diffusion . involvement and diversity of involvement both = 0.3; beyond 99 per cent confidence level).

Third, among the elements of consequentiality itself, the greater the changes wrought by a decision's consequences the more serious they are likely to be, as would be expected (r radicality . seriousness = 0.4; beyond 99 per cent confidence level), and all the other elements of consequentiality are mutually though weakly associated except for seriousness and endurance. However, these links are not enough to warrant the summation of the indicators of complexity into a single measure. The four principal aspects of complexity remain distinct. Any one decision tends to have some but not all, to be high on some and not on others. How far this is because the stuff of which strategic decisions are made is inherently shifting and shapeless, difficult to get to grips with, and how far it is because adequate data are still not available, is impossible to say. Complexity, the essence of decision, itself stays complex.

Do the numerous difficulties endemic in the most complex strategic decisions, shown here often to be location, reorganization, and product decisions, lead to their being handled differently? In other words, does the complexity of what is in hand explain, partly at least, the course of reaching a decision? This is a question which cannot be answered until the politicality of decisions is examined too.

Politicality

Politicality is the obverse face of strategic decisions. Since decisions are made among people by people for people, they are a welter of action, interaction, and counteraction. Each step in a process of dealing with complex problems is also a move in the political game of manoeuvre. Hence, if a complex decision has widespread potential consequences, so those consequences can also implicate many interests. As information is garnered from many quarters to cope with complexity, so also further interests become implicated. Whilst that information is sought and supplied, so also selections are made of whose information is relevant and whose is not, and whose information is influential and whose is not. So to the uncertainty is added the not knowing how much influence will be brought to bear and in what direction. Hence the highest risk decisions can be those likely to 'upset the power equilibrium' (Hage 1980, p. 109), and even in the making of a none-too-complex choice of computer equipment for a British retail firm, described by Pettigrew (1973), politics were of the essence of the decision.

This pervading politicality is the subject of the following chapter.

3

Interests and Politicality

Interests in the arena

Who decides? This variant of the famous question 'who governs?' asked by Dahl (1961) prompts this chapter, because who decides must shape the process of decision at the same time as it is shaped by the complexity of the problems encountered. The process of decision-making is a response to politicality as well as to complexity. The involvement of interests that heightens complexity is the opportunity for the exercise of influence in the pursuit of objectives. How far that opportunity is taken ranges from the slightest touch upon what is decided to stamping the shape upon it.

Influence is brought to bear in an arena jostling with interested parties of all kinds, as we have already seen. Hence 'organizations are best conceptualized as political bargaining systems' in which the bargaining and conflict primarily occur in 'specific decision-making spheres' (Bacharach and Lawler 1980, p. 213). Influence is exerted from all quarters, inside and outside the organization. The contest at Toxicem over do-it-yourself electricity evoked influence both from the contending internal departments and from external interests which they drew in to support them. The comparatively textbook decision in another firm to build a new plant in Sweden was influenced from a similarly wide spectrum of sources, though in this case they were not drawn in to support opposing contestants but to add to a gathering consensus. A range of internal departments, from engineers to lawyers, were all very influential, and at the same time Swedish consultants and Swedish local government had quite a big say on personnel, building, and legal questions.

In the world of public services, a controversy about buying a body scanner for a National Health Service District escalated until it attracted external intervention. Although the District was big enough to cover a medium-sized industrial city and its far-flung metropolitan surroundings, a scanner capable of taking three-dimensional pictures of the whole body was at the time a relatively costly as well as a novel piece of technology. It was costly in absolute terms, but even more so in that it demanded an unprecedentedly large commitment on one single item, when there were numerous other current claims. The state-financed Health Service suspended purchases of scanners when questions about their effectiveness arose – at a time when some Districts in the more prosperous South had already got scanners but before the Northern District in question had acquired one. The matter grew from one concerning mainly internal medical interests to one about regional equality, and about private versus state action since a proposal was made that the money be found locally by a fund-raising campaign. Influenced from outside by the press and by citizens' groups, a decision was taken both to buy a scanner and to try and raise the money by a campaign circumventing state sources (which was successfully done).

Different interests

The source of the objectives of the internal interest units in each decision is plain enough. It lies in the division of labour, the splitting up of who does what, and the division of authority, the splitting up of who legitimately has power over whom.

> The starting point of the political model is the existence of differentia-tion. An organization is conceived as being made up of separately identifiable groups differentiated both horizontally and vertically, according to a division of labour and a division of authority which has its source not only in the organization but also in society as a whole. These differentiated groups may just as easily have conflicting as coinciding interests and values. It is now a commonplace that organizations, *per se*, do not have goals. What we call goals are the products of a process of interaction and negotiation within the organization, and indeed across organizational boundaries (Walsh, et al. 1981, p. 133).

This quotation refers to internal groups, or units, but recognizes that there are also interests from beyond an organization's boundaries in the decisions taken within them. An organization is dependent upon others for materials, money, information and every other kind of resource, and others are dependent upon it (Pfeffer and Salancik 1978), and either way these outsiders too have a stake in what may happen.

All these therefore have an *interest* in the decision-making game, because they have a stake in its outcome. What is to be done, or at any rate what is intended shall be done, may affect their own futures. 'Organizational politics involve the efforts of interest groups to influence decisions that affect their positions in the organization' (Bacharach and Lawler 1980, p. 79) – a statement which applies as much to external interests as to the internal interests which its authors had in mind. The values which define objectives 'are not free floating, idealistic positions. . . . Individuals and groups will tend to adopt values which fit with material interests' (Walsh, et al. 1981, p. 138).

As already noted, interests in a decision are rarely pressed to a point where the arenas for decision-making are themselves destroyed, that is, where the organization disintegrates. Most interests, most of the time, get enough out of an organization to keep it going. Indeed, '. . . we need not assume that decision preferences represent naked self-interest: many times they do, but not always. . . . Decisions about new products or services may have a healthy mixture of what various groups think is best for the organization and best for the interest group . . .' (Hage 1980, p. 55).

The objectives of an interest group or unit as to the outcome of any one decision-making process are the expression in that situation of its longer-lasting interests. Interests are relatively constant across decisions, whereas objectives are particular to a decision and may change from one to another. This distinction between interests as persisting, and objectives as changing from occasion to occasion, is appropriate to the study of decision-making and avoids other difficulties of definition (Lukes 1974; Benton 1981). Constancy of interest is detectable in the '*logiques d'action*' (Karpik 1972) which, pursued by an influential interest unit or alliance of units, can repeatedly sway successive decisions so that they have a theme in common and the organization can be held to be following a 'strategy' (Mintzberg 1978). For example, interests in business organizations may pursue production logics of action, emphasizing the volume of output more than anything else, or profitability logics, emphasizing immediate gains, or 'puissance' logics, which seek monopolistic or oligopolistic market positions, and so on (Karpik 1972).

External interests, in examples from Sweden, show the clients of a construction company always stressing price and reliability whereas its competitors in the industry were not interested in these criteria but in its viability and conformity with the norms of the industry. Likewise the medical association was interested in a municipal hospital upholding professional standards, whereas local politicians were more interested in the number of people it could treat, that is they were interested in its capacity and size (Rhenman 1973, p. 38).

Interests and *logiques d'action* are there ready and waiting for whatever opportunity may come along. They can change, of course, but they are not reappraised every time something comes up; it is the objectives for the particular situation that have to be worked out, and which may sometimes surprise others who are not able to anticipate what may suit an interest when some fresh topic arises. So it is that a whole range of possible interest units awaits any decision-making game, poised to be drawn in, or to push in, as occasion offers. It is in this sense that the solutions are there before decision problems ever arise, awaiting a chance to influence outcomes in pre-desired directions (Cohen, et al. 1972).

The decision-set

These multiple influences have long been taken account of by regarding organizations as social artefacts sustained by 'coalitions' of multiple interests (Cyert and March 1963). Mintzberg (1983) has separated the internal and the external interests, and postulated eight different kinds of internal or external coalition according to the pattern of power within each. Whilst this perspective draws attention to the fundamental character of organizations, the term 'coalition' can mean either every interest concerned with an organization, which in a firm includes shareholders, managers, workers, suppliers, customers and everyone else, or it can mean particular alliances within this entirety (e.g. Bacharach and Lawler 1980, p. 48; Hage 1980, p. 122; Pfeffer 1981, p. 154). The ambiguity persists because it has not been quite clear when and where these interests come to life, so to speak. Where can they be found at work? The answer is in the influencing of strategic decisions.

However, every interest does not influence every decision. Each decision is influenced by a specific sub-set. This '*decision-set*' (or 'constellation of interests' (Astley, et al. 1982, p. 373) is akin to the 'organization-set' (Evan 1971; Aldrich and Whetton 1981) of surrounding organizations that embody standards for and have expectations of any given organization. The decision-set similarly is the surrounding interest units, but it is both more precise in that it means the set of interest units which exert influence upon a particular decision, and wider since these are internal units as well as external organizations.

Thus the decision-set is those interest units from among the overall organizational 'coalition' of interests which influence a decision. Within the decision-set there may be particular alliances, in the other sense of the word coalition. The decision-set is the visible face of power that materializes – metaphorically – in each decision-making process, changing expression from process to process. 'When operating with a political model of an organization, utilizing an active concept of power, the natural focus of interest is the decision making process. Power is exercized in attempting to ensure that one's objectives are embodied in the decisions made in the organization' (Walsh, et al. 1981, p. 134).

Politicality and influence

The decision-set of interests brings the politicality into decision-making. *Politicality* is the degree to which influence is exerted through a decision-making process upon the outcome. 'If politics is the study of power in action' (Pfeffer 1981, p. 7), then in this context that means *the exercise of influence in decision making*' (Hickson, et al. 1985). Influences come from all directions. Many may be anticipated because of known interests, but others are more surprising because the implicating of an interest had not been foreseen. Each interest has something to gain and something to give, however little, and in the exchange influence is created, so that organizations have been called 'markets for influence and control' (Pfeffer and Salancik 1978, p. 24). Politicality arises in the approved influence of recognized departments or authority figures, as well as in less official or even underhand influence, so the term includes both (and not only the latter, as in Mintzberg's (1983 p. 172) use of the term 'politics').

Timing

The timing of an influence attempt is vital if it is to succeed in accomplishing anything. In a municipality, a proposal for a new source of funds, a lottery, was pushed through at the end of the summer holiday season when some councillors and officials were still away and others may have been less alert than usual, and this probably accelerated a favourable decision. At Toxicem, Alwyn and his supporters did not put their argument for the equipment needed to generate electricity until the time came when some action on the plant was needed in any case since its limits were being reached at the current steam pressure.

Timing is vital because everyone cannot attend to everything that is going on day by day in a working organization, and cannot be everywhere at once (March and Olsen 1976, p. 45). Time, as different to timing, is scarce in busy lives at the top. Since 'every entrance is an exit somewhere else' (March and Olsen 1976, p. 47), the judgement of when to pay less attention to one decision-making process, in order to give more time to another, becomes critical. Leave it too long and the game may have reached a point when minds are sufficiently made up and commitments entered into so that the outcome is beyond being influenced in a different direction. Attempt to influence too soon, and a decision which looks fairly settled can be reopened later by the emergence of interests which were not taken into account. The tactics of committee attendance are a common example of this: the chances of sitting through a meeting at which nothing of interest to you occurs, when a lot of other things need time and attention, have to be weighed against the risk that if you stay away, opinion will harden without your being able to influence it so that next time it is too late to have your say.

Influence

If the exercise of influence is power in action, it is not the same as power. Power is the capacity or ability to *attempt* to influence, as most definitions imply but do not quite say (Miles 1980, p. 165 lists some of the definitions that abound). 'Politics refers to the active influence process, but power is latent, referring to the ability or capacity to influence' (Miles 1980, p. 184), or more clearly, to attempt to influence. For the capacity may not achieve anything. It is a capacity made up of sources, or bases, of power, such as the control of finance or other possible rewards, or expertise and know-how, or personal charismatic qualities, or authority which is the legitimized or rightful power to make choices for others and to give consequent instructions to them (e.g. French and Raven 1959). But authority, for instance, does not necessarily mean influence. There are strong chairmen and chairwomen and weak ones, strong managing directors and weak ones, strong bosses and weak bosses. In other words, some exert a lot of influence and some only the bare minimum consonant with retaining office at all, and when they lose even that they are a joke, or a liability to be concealed. Conversely, influence can be based on sources other than authority, so those who are influential need not be in authority, as will be seen later in the dispersal of influence around the decision-set far beyond those whose right it is to make the final choice. In decision-making terms, whilst 'Authority refers to the formally sanctioned right to make final decisions' (Bacharach and Lawler 1980, p. 44), other power sources are much more widespread. The influence of the interest units in a decision-set is the measure of the effectiveness of those sources in the decision-making, for influence is effective power.

The influences of the interest units in the Bradford studies were represented by ratings on five-point scales from 'a little influence' to 'a very great deal of influence' (Tannenbaum 1968, Tannenbaum and Cooke 1979), in the same way as Hinings, et al. (1974, p. 30) measured the influence of internal sub-units in each of a range of areas of decision (see also Appendix C). In the Bradford studies, however, influence was rated in the vividly explicit context of given cases of decisions. Executives attributed influence during an interview about the particular case, after having described the story of what had happened. How and why the influence had been exerted was known to both interviewer and interviewee. These ratings therefore denote the extent to which an interest was taken into account in the course of arriving at a decision, as recalled by one or more managerial informants who were centrally involved at the time. They denote influence as it was felt by those subjected to it, rather than as those who attempted it may have erroneously imagined, or hoped, it to be.

Internally generated politicality

The internal interest units in a decision-set derive their influences from their situations within an organization. These units can be divisions of a firm, or committees of a municipal government, or any other kind of unit that acts sufficiently as a unity to exert influence, but the commonest are formally defined departments. Since these are set up to specialize, their specialization may put them in a position to deal with uncertainties that beset the organization (Crozier 1964), in effect shielding other sub-units from the consequences.

> If organizations allocate to their various subunits task areas that vary in uncertainty, then those subunits that cope most effectively with the most uncertainty should have most power within the organization, since coping by a subunit reduces the impact of uncertainty on other activities in the organization, a shock absorber function. Coping may be by prevention, for example, a subunit prevents sales fluctuations by securing firm orders; or by information, for example, a subunit forecasts sales fluctuations; or by absorption, for example, a drop in sales is swiftly countered by novel selling methods. By coping, the subunit provides pseudo certainty for the other subunits by controlling what are otherwise contingencies for other activities. This coping confers power through the dependencies created (Hickson, et al. 1971, pp. 219–20).

Any appropriate resources may be used to cope, such as having expert know-how, including know-who, having crucial information, or having access to funds, perhaps even having prestige in the outside world which can be especially important in universities (Pfeffer and Salancik 1974).

This is one reason why people twist and turn politically to defend the area they work in from encroachment by others, and to stop either their sector of uncertainty or their means of coping with it becoming so routine that either they have nothing uncertain to cope with any more, or the way they do it becomes so obvious that others could be substituted for them and do it instead (Crozier 1964; Hickson, et al. 1971, pp. 223–4). 'Non-substitutability', and some 'centrality' of position within the workflows of the organization, are two conditions of the 'strategic contingencies theory' explaining how

Table 3.1 Influence of interest units

Typical interest units* (primary interests in brackets)	Influence (means of five-point ratings for all involvements)	Rank order	Involvements Rank order
Liaison and claims departments (adjudication)	3.6	1	13
Sales, marketing (domain)	3.4	2	7
Customers, clients (outputs)	3.3	3	10
Production and equivalent 'workflow' departments (transformation)	3.2	4	2
Self-sufficient divisions, etc. (autonomy/devolution)	3.0	5	5
Research, design departments (innovation)	2.9	6	12
Accounting, quality control, inspection (conformity)	2.8	7	1
Auditors, trade associations, shareholders (private standards)	2.8	8	3
Maintenance, personnel, etc. (stability)	2.7	9	8
Supplier firms (inputs)	2.7	10	6
Government departments and agencies (public standards)	2.6	11	4
Purchasing (acquisition)	2.6	12	14
Competitors (comparative performance)	2.5	13	9
Trade unions (employment)	2.3	14	11
Overall mean (excluding General Management)	2.9 (SD 1.4)		
All internal interest units combined (=599)	3.0 (SD 1.4)		
All external interests units combined (=422)	2.7 (SD1.4)		
General management:			
Chief executive level (=121)	4.3		
Other general management entities (=94)	3.4		

n for each category of interest units = number of involvements in table 2.7.
Total n = 1,021 ratings of interest units + 215 of General Management = 1,236
*External interest units underlined.

effective power, or influence, is acquired (Hickson, et al. 1971). They mean that influence is precarious. On the one hand, those who have influence can'manoeuvre to protect and enhance the position that gives rise to it, using their resources to get more resources (Pfeffer and Salancik 1974; 1977) so that the resourceful get powerful and the powerful get resourceful. On the other hand, at any moment a change in what is uncertain, the advent of a rival, or a shift in the flows of work through the organization, can pull the contingencies on which their influence rests from under their feet (Hinings, et al. 1974, pp. 41–2).

The politicality of decision-making is due to this rise and fall of the influence in it. Those at the top, and those not at the top, of the influence scale across the Bradford studies' 150 cases are given in table 3.1. This shows the mean ratings by executives of the influence of each of the 1,021 interest units that were involved in the decisions. The units are classified in 14 categories of interest affinity as described in the previous chapter. Those underlined are external to the organization.

The classic prominence of sales and production, each both co-operating and vying with the other, can be seen immediately in the table where they are second and third among the internal units. These two categories cover not only interest units in manufacturing firms, but also those in services of many kinds. Sales includes the customer services department concerned with promoting the services offered by a bank, and distribution departments: production includes, for example, nurses in hospitals, and the transport department of a haulage firm. Their placings in the table confirm in influence terms the systemic prominence of these main functions in all forms of organization. Sometimes one and sometimes the other has the edge. Whilst in these varied British organizations, sales is just ahead on those decisions which involve it and Perrow (1970) found the same in American firms, Hinings, et al. (1974) found that it was production which was consistently foremost in small Canadian and American breweries and packaging manufacturers.

Occasionally sales or production can be outweighed by 'adjudication' interests, in the few decisions in which these do become involved. Often they do not, but when they do they make a difference in what happens for they are top of table 3.1. They are at first sight an extremely mixed group of units, yet as they have resource allocating and co-ordinating functions inside or outside organizations, they are classified as having a common interest in 'adjudication' by finding ways around problems and applying regulations. Examples are the Development Committee heavily influencing a university budget decision, its influence being given the highest possible rating of 5 on the five-point scale, a Priorities Committee influencing a National Health Service District radiography decision (also rated 5), and the Discipline and Complaints section of a regional police force influencing a policy decision in favour of more civilian (non-police) employees (rated 3).

Lower down the scale in table 3.1, maintenance engineers do not have as much influence upon these strategic decisions as Crozier (1964) thought their equivalents had in French tobacco factories. However, the influence of the French engineers was at a routine level of organization, far below strategic decisions which were all centralized in Paris.

Weakest of all internal interest units are purchasing departments, in the comparatively few decisions in which they are involved. Strauss (1962), too, found this many years before in English firms where purchasing sections were striving to counter the more powerful persuasions of engineers as to what should be bought. Even in Toxicem where purchasing had company director status in the person of Giles, one of the two prime contenders in the electricity dispute, he and his department eventually lost the argument. This poses the question of how far the qualities of an individual, notably personality, can transcend his or her organizational situation and exercise more influence than someone else could have done? There is certainly not enough evidence to rule out this possibility, which could be more likely in organizations where the formal hierarchy is not so steep as it is in a business firm, but Giles's experience suggests that it is unwise to pin too much upon personality. Despite his vigour and his 'whizz-kid' reputation, he could not rise above his weak power base in purchasing and overcome Alwyn and the production engineers. Personalities without power bases are ultimately powerless.

Externally generated politicality

The world of organizations is largely made up of other organizations with which they are interdependent for goods of every kind, from materials to information (e.g. Wamsley and Zald 1973; Benson 1975; Pfeffer and Salancik 1978). Through this vibrating 'interorganizational resource-exchange network' (Hickson, et al. 1981, p. 166) run vertical, horizontal, and symbiotic interdependencies (Pennings 1981, p. 434) in which power accrues to those least dependent upon others (e.g. Jacobs 1974; Pfeffer and Salancik 1978; Hickson, et al. 1981). The influence of one organization in the strategic decision-making of another is explained by, in effect, projecting externally the strategic contingencies theory used above to explain internal influence: an organization which does something for others that is useful to them, which they cannot readily find a substitute for (there is more or less of a monopoly), and which is centrally situated in the interorganizational network, influences their decision-making.

We have caricatured elsewhere the 'paralytic organization' (Butler, et al. 1977/78; Hickson, et al. 1978), a public service utility so enmeshed with powerful outsiders – a single dominant supplier, customers it had no choice but to serve, a single source of capital, large competitors who prevented any switching into their fields, and so on – that it was 'immobilized by a balance of power . . . tipped sharply in favour of external interests' (Butler, et al. 1977/78, p. 52). Here was an instance not so much of influence upon decisions but of powers which ensured that there were hardly any strategic decisions to make, similar to the situation in the tobacco factories that Crozier (1964) described.

External interests which influenced decision-making in other organizations are underlined in table 3.1, where a conspicuous phenomenon is *internal–external* influence *equivalence*. The external counterparts of internal departments tend to appear at much the same point in the table, that is to have much the same degree of influence upon decisions. Four pairs can be seen. Customers and clients are in a powerful third place next to their internal counterparts, sales and marketing, which are in second place. Auditors, shareholders, trade associations and the like which set requirements for an organization are next to the accounting and other internal units whose job it is to check how far requirements are met. Suppliers are just above their weak purchasing counterparts. Weakest of all are the trade unions which do not have an exact internal counterpart but have some affinity to personnel which, grouped with maintenance in terms of broad type of interest, are weakest but one among the internals.

Reasons for this pronounced feature are difficult to pinpoint, but there is an intuitive sense to it. It may be explicable by the strategic contingencies theory. For example, major customers are in themselves something of an uncertainty, since their behaviour can be a critical contingency for an organization which is dependent upon them and whose decisions they influence. If in a business firm the sales department copes with that uncertainty, then its influence is in effect drawn from that of the major customers and equivalent to theirs, the rest of the organization being dependent first upon the customers and then upon the sales department. So it can be suggested that internal–external influence equivalence arises from serial dependence of the organization, first upon external interests and then upon the internal specialisms that are functionally equivalent to them and deal with them.

Among the six categories of external interests, from the influential customers and clients down to the less influential auditors, suppliers, government departments, competitors, and lastly trade unions, governments and unions are most in the public eye. How strong or how weak are they? How far does their influence reach into the corridors of decision?

Governmental influence

On the whole, governmental influence is surprisingly weak (see also Hickson, et al. 1985). In Britain, national departments and agencies, and also city and county local governments, average only eleventh place on influence in table 3.1. Here is the symptom of government in a pluralistic society wrestling with a recalcitrant economy whose decision-makers do not leap to do its bidding. The influence it exerts on what they decide is on average less than that of most of their internal departments, implying that an organization's own interests are very much first among the considerations, governmental interests taking a back seat. Among the external pressures, the influence of customers or clients is again well ahead of governmental interests, implying that market-place survival, success in the field of operation whatever it may be, takes priority over any governmental desires.

An efficient totalitarian government relying less on cajoling and more on force will be in a stronger position, of course, and organizational decision-makers will find themselves much more hemmed in. A change in a society in a totalitarian direction will slice away their alternatives, as the giant Dutch firm Philips found under German rule during the Second World War. Its alternatives in what it could make and what people it could employ were reduced until it was collaborating in military production and in using forced labour, whatever its original intentions may have been (Teulings 1982).

However, the normal Western European government relies on means such as subsidies and regulations, and propaganda and nationalization. It may also sponsor work that has long-term indirect effects. In the leading manufacturer referred to earlier where it was decided to invest in Sweden, a decision was made to commit huge sums to the development and testing of a radical new product that could not have occurred but for government action, years previously. A state research laboratory had been established where an employee, who incidentally was not British, found the solution to a technical problem which for decades had baffled researchers and firms throughout the world. The manufacturer bought the patent rights and decided to develop the product. Private enterprise exploited what public initiative had opened up.

This case was unusual. The 150 Bradford cases show that in Britain, governmental influence is usually exerted through the appropriate channel among a set of channels evolved to connect government with particular sectors of activity. Strategic decisions in the Health Service are influenced by the Department of Health, in the universities by the University Grants Committee, in industry by the Department of Industry, and in public utilities by the Departments of Environment or Agriculture and by local governments with interests in the services provided. Intervention other than through these specialized channels is rare, and conspicuous personal moves by a Prime Minister, such as those by James Callaghan (mentioned in the previous chapter) are rarer still.

Though table 3.1 shows that government in a state such as Britain does not have the influence to order everything to its own liking, it can still have fingers in a great many pies. Influence from governmental sources was reported in as many as 40 per cent of the decisions studied (60 out of 150). The first impression, therefore, is of weak but extensive influence. However this general impression is superficial and rather misleading. There are more subtle features which are more notable.

Since an ideological reason for state ownership is to subject organizations to greater governmental influence, differences would be anticipated between the decision-making of nationalized (state-owned) industries and services, and those which are privately owned. Is decision-making in public industries and services beset – or maybe stimulated – by governmental influence, whereas private enterprise decision-making is blithely free of it?

Before the findings are examined, it must be remembered that the nationalized organizations depend on the state for their financing, a power base that is latent behind every decision made. It gives government an ultimate stranglehold. Government can sell them off or close them down.

Thus, it is unexpected, and may be surprising, to find that the amount of governmental influence reported in the decision-making of the state-owned business organizations is no greater than in those that were private. If anything, it could have been less, though the difference, if any, appears negligible, and nothing much should be read into it. The mean rating of the influences of national government departments, and of agencies such as the Health and Safety Executive and the Monopolies Commission, was 2.5 (on the five-point scale) for nine instances of influence in the decision-making of three state-owned organizations, against 3.0 for 17 instances in 13 privately-owned organizations. The three public organizations were an autonomous division manufacturing products different to that of its parent corporation, a subsidiary company also making products different to those of a parent that had been reluctantly taken into a form of public ownership because of its economic difficulties, and a large service organization that was a household name in Britain and beyond. The 13 private organizations ranged from manufacturing to brewing and financial services.

The comparison is of the influence ratings of all reported instances of government department or governmental agency involvement in the decision-making in comparable business organizations. This excludes three private firms where there were no such involvements in any of their five cases of decision-making and therefore no ratings of governmental influence: it was not meaningful to equate no rating with nil rating numerically. Also excluded are eight non-commercial public services in health, education, the police, and local government; and two public utilities and an industrial research association.

However, although the *amount* of influence exerted by any one department or agency upon any *one* decision does not differ on average between public and private business, government influences a much *greater proportion* of the decisions of nationalized concerns. Switching from the influence of interest units to the number of decisions influenced (irrespective of amount exerted), 15 cases of decisions were studied in the three state-owned organizations, five in each, and among these eight showed governmental influence, that is 53 per cent. Eighty decisions were studied in 16 privately-owned organizations (the 13 where governmental influence was reported, and three where there was none), only 15 of these decisions showing any governmental influence, that is 15/80 or 19 per cent. Hence there was governmental influence on nearly three times the proportion of decisions in nationalized industries and services as in private business. Again caution must prevail, since the numbers in the nationalized industries are small, but the proportionate difference strongly supports the assumptions and periodic complaints of public sector managements that they encounter government at every turn whatever they do. *In nationalized businesses, government does not exert a greater amount of influence on any one decision, but it exerts influence on more decisions.*

A striking example of intrusive but ineffectual governmental influence in the public sector is provided by two decisions that coincidentally were virtually the same, and so make an apt comparison: one in a nationalized manufacturer and one in the leading private manufacturer that has been mentioned before. Each chose to site a substantial new plant in Sweden and committed the required financial investment. The private firm went ahead with this major commitment, which created employment in Sweden and not in Britain, with no interference from government. From the British Government that is, for the Swedish Government was of course positively influential (ratings of 2 for Swedish national government and 5 for local government). The nationalized corporation, by constrast, was caught between two governments pulling in opposite directions. The Swedes were again very positive (with an influence rating of 4), but on the other side were the British Treasury and Department of Industry (both also rated 4) striving to retain capital investment and employment in Britain. The state-owned business had to contend with them whereas the private business did not. Yet the decision also shows that once the financing and terms of operation of nationalized organizations are arranged, the British

Government influences but does not determine even their strategic moves, for in this case the investment went to Sweden despite the efforts of the Treasury and the Department of Industry to stop it. A similar case, where the French Government delayed but eventually did not stop foreign investment by the nationalized Elf oil corporation, is reported by Bauer and Cohen (1983).

The obverse to this should not be missed. If government influences any one decision in a state business no more than in a private business, that also means there are times when it *can* influence a decision in a private business just as much! Private business cannot exclude government from its deliberations.

So public/private differences are relatively small. Indeed, they are by no means the feature of governmental influence. There is a much more vivid contrast which cuts across the decision-making of both. Governmental influence is far greater when its departments and agencies intervene or threaten to intervene specially, than when routine subsidies and regulations are applied in the ordinary way. This applies equally to the public and private sectors, as table 3.2 shows.

In this table, the nine instances reported of governmental interest units exerting influence in the decision-making of state-owned businesses are compared with the 17 instances in private businesses, both divided into instances of routine support and regulation versus particular interventions. If every decision in each organization were influenced by one governmental interest unit, for example, the table might show ten units influencing ten decisions in, say, two organizations (all five cases studied in each of the organizations), and the entries would neatly correspond along the rows in an immediately self-evident way. As life is not so tidy, there is no such correspondence, first, because not all decisions are influenced by a government department or agency, and second, because some decisions are influenced by more than one such unit. So, for example, in the first row under the hearing 'routine support and regulation', there are *five instances of influence* (the Department of Trade influenced two decisions, and the Department of Industry, the Health and Safety Executive, and the National Enterprise Board influenced one each), which give a *mean of 1.2* (on a five-point scale), in *five decisions* (here it does happen that each decision was influenced by one unit only) among the ten cases studied in *two state-owned* business organizations.

Table 3.2 Governmental influence in public and private business

Government department or agency influencing a decision	Influence rating	Decisions influenced	Organization
OVERALL MEANS			
	State-owned businesses:		
9 interest units	mean 2.5 8 decisions		3 organizations
	Private businesses:		
17 interest units	mean 3.0 15 decisions		13 organizations
ROUTINE SUPPORT AND REGULATION			
	State-owned businesses		
5 ie Department of Trade (twice) and of Industry, Health and Safety Executive, National Enterprise Board	mean 1.2	5 decisions, i.e., new products and factories, massive re-equipment	2 organizations
	Private businesses		
12 ie Department of Industry (10 instances), Health and Safety Executive (2 instances)	mean 2.4	11 decisions, i.e., new products, buildings and plant, and one factory closure	9 organizations
PARTICULAR INTERVENTIONS			
	State-owned businesses		
Specialist ministry	5	Major reorganization by merger	Transport service
Specialist ministry	4	Reorganization of personnel	
Treasury	4	Siting of plant in Sweden	Manufacturer
Department of Industry	4 mean 4.2		
	Private businesses		
Treasury	5	Change in interest rates	Financial institution
Department of Environment	5		
Department of Employment	5	Productivity agreement	Insurance company
Arts Council	4	Budget and programme	Entertainment service
Monopolies Commission	3 mean 4.4	New credit service	Finance company

Comparing first these routine instances, the influence attributed to the five departments and agencies involved in the decision-making of the two state-owned businesses was weak, the mere 1.2 rating, and that of the 12 units involved in the larger number of decisions in nine private businesses was no higher than a mean of 2.4. It is again noticeable that when decisions are classified in this way, government may even have less overt influence in the decision-making of state organizations than in private business, if there is any material difference at all; but that is not the significant point. The conspicuous feature is the relatively low influence *irrespective of ownership* of the Department of Industry when giving grants towards new industrial and commercial developments, of the Department of Trade when a nationalized service concerned with purchased equipment abroad, of the Health and Safety Executive concerned with pollution, and of the National Enterprise Board which at the time held shares in firms on behalf of the state and in one case approved expansion in the firm's manufacturing capacity. All these are instances of relatively routine subsidizing and regulating of business. Whilst for state policy they are evidence that governmental action of this kind does have some effect, they show that it is far from decisive. It is merely a contributory level of state action.

Beyond it is a further and more vigorous level of action. The instances of particular intervention shown in the lower section of table 3.2 average very high influence indeed in *both* state and private businesses, the means being respectively 4.2 and 4.4. These are occasions when a department or agency deliberately influences a particular decision in a particular organization as far as it can. Among the state businesses, major reorganizations with repercussions beyond Britain were successfully influenced; and efforts were made to prevent investment in Sweden though these were unsuccessful, as already described. Among the private businesses, key interest rates were successfully influenced in the direction of government policy, and the Department of Employment influenced an unusual 'white-collar' productivity agreement in a world leader insurance company at a time when government was attempting to push such agreements in the direction it wanted. The Arts Council directly affected an entertainment organization's programme by the terms and size of its financial grant, and the threat of Monopolies Commission action constrained a finance company's move into a new credit service (Hickson, et al. 1985).

The case of the unsuccessful effort to prevent a nationalized manufacturer investing in Sweden rather than in Britain shows that it is necessary to interpret these cases of attributed high influence in conjunction with the outcome of the decision-making. It is possible for a decision to go against highly influential government interests, either because they lack absolute power or because they come to accept or tolerate the opposite view. Influence on this scale appears to be of two kinds:

(a) *constraining*: where the influence of the government department or agency is taken into account in framing an alternative or alternatives acceptable to them, as, for example, with the insurance company's productivity agreement approved by the Department of Employment, and the entertainment organization's programme shaped to fit likely Arts Council financial support.

(b) *indicatory*: where the influence of the government department or agency is exerted in favour of a specific alternative. Although the governmentally favoured alternative will probably win the day, it may fail to do so as happened in the case of the investment in Sweden.

However, it is clear that specific non-routine governmental interventions can and do have an effect; and that this can be just as great in the private sector as in the public sector. At first sight government looks weak, but even though its influence may be outweighed by the many other influences on a decision, and even though it often cannot dictate to its own (as the Swedish case shows), it can be a force to be reckoned with on those occasions when its departments and agencies intervene in certain situations.

From this comparison of public and private sectors, three remarkable inferences can be drawn. First, government does not have any special ability to 'call the tune' for any one decision even in its own nationalized corporations, though it does influence a larger proportion of their decisions. Second, government influence does penetrate the privacy of private enterprise, albeit as a lesser influence among greater internal managerial influences. Third, government is most effective in this form of influence, both in public and private sector organizations, when its departments and agencies intervene in particular circumstances beyond the usual run of subsidizing and regulating.

Union influence

The situation of trades unions at the bottom of the pile, so to speak, turns upside down the image given to them by the British and international media. Press and television reports fix on the dramas of strikes and of disputes over national economic policy, but whether or not the unions actually influence decisions escapes them. There have been indications that the unions' position is by no means as strong as it appears to be (Edwards 1978; Heller, et al. 1977) and their influence on strategic decisions, which we have examined in detail elsewhere (Wilson, et al. 1982), affirms this.

First, what is not there. There is not a single case of pay among the 150 strategic decisions. This may be because such decisions have been routinized in national negotiations, whose outcome binds the employing organizations in which therefore there are no decisions of any consequence to be taken. Or it may be because executives do not see pay as strategically shaping the course they are pursuing, but as a cost along the way. Probably it is both together, the one leading to the other, for organizations reflect the institutionalization of industrial relations (Brown 1980).

Furthermore, unions are *not* involved in 121 of the 150 decisions, despite the extent to which their members' pay and job security can be affected by new products and 'domains' or by policy changes and related decisions. These kinds of topics continue to be wholly managerial prerogatives (Wilson, et al. 1982, table 1). Even in the 29 decisions when unions were said by executives to have had an influence, it was mostly slight, as their average in table 3.1 shows. It was usually rated 'little' or 'some' that is 1 or 2), as in the case depicted in figure 3.1. In this decision by an engineering firm to open a new plant, which would have consequences for the Union's present members and its future membership, the AUEW (Amalgamated Union of Engineering Workers) shared with a Finance House the position of least influence, in an executive's judgement; it is a moot point whether the AUEW saw itself differently, but if it did so then it would have had an inflated view of its own significance. This decision-set graph, developed from Tannenbaum's (1968) 'control graph', also happens to show how averages such as those in table 3.1 obscure variation, for it reveals a decision in which marketing had less than its average overall influence, and an equipment supplier had more, not surprisingly given that this particular decision topic was about a new plant.

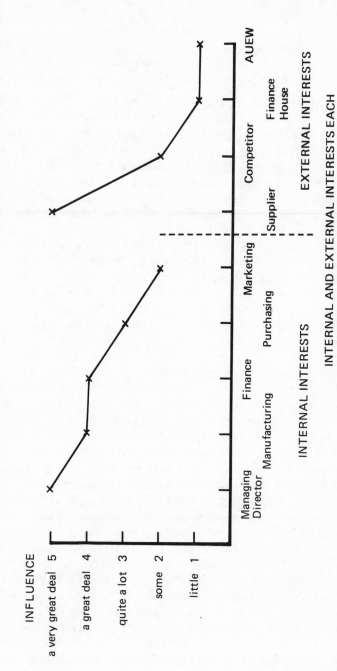

Figure 3.1. DECISION-SET GRAPH
A rating of the influence of interest-units in a Decision to open a New Plant in an Engineering Firm.

Source: Wilson, et al. 1982, p. 329.

However, there were nine strategic decisions in which unions exercised substantial influence (represented by ratings of 4, 'a great deal', and in one case 5, 'a very great deal'). These are shown in table 3.3.

> In three of these situations, the union just defended its members' interests without attacking the decision itself, and the decision went through. In three more, it resisted outright the decision that was being made . . . and lost. That leaves three decisions only, of 150, in which the unions had it more or less their way. These were the transport service's reorganization, the health service district's policy on radiographers, and the police force's change of staff appraisal system. At first sight it seemed that union power won the day. A second look gave a different interpretation. In each case the management were either not averse to the union view, or positively wanted the same! In short, the unions only 'won' when there was no one to beat (Hickson, et al. 1985).

It may be objected that if management anticipates strong union opposition on an issue it avoids anything which might bring the issue to the surface, and never embarks upon decision-making at all.

Table 3.3 Nine cases of high union influence

Highest union influence ratings	*9 Decision topics*	*Organization*
4	Reorganization of personnel	Air transport
4	Merger of departments	Municipality
5	Increase radiographers	NHS District
4	New catering programme	
4	Amalgamation	Polytechnic
4	Creation of Boards of Studies	
4	Resist unionization	Credit company
4	Change staff appraisal	Police Force
4	Policy on travel	

Source: Wilson, et al. 1982, p. 329.

There is no direct evidence here to either confirm or deny that possibility, yet if it were so, no hint of it was picked up in interviews and discussions, and it is strange that no case was found where management 'miscalculated' and really effective union influence did arise. It seems far more likely that unions have a merely reactive role in a limited range of decisions which they influence only as one among a number of stronger influences (Wilson, et al. 1982).

Their image in the public mind, which can be shared superficially by those executives whose days are taken up with union matters (Wilson, et al. 1982, pp. 338–9), probably comes from their influence on the specifics and speed of implementation *after* decisions have been made. Koopman's (1983) report of Dutch decisions that cut the labour force suggests the same. These questions of implementation are important to individual trade union members, but relative details from the perspective of organization-wide strategy.

Political mix: heavyweights and lightweights

It is plain from the trade union and government examples that involvement does not mean influence. Obviously it is possible to have interests implicated, and representatives actively engaged in the decision-making process, and yet to affect it hardly at all. This is apparent whether it is looked at as the numbers of interest units involved, as it was in chapter 2, or as the proportion of 150 decisions in which each *kind* of interest unit is involved. The kinds of interest units most often involved are also involved across the broadest range of decisions (r involvements . breadth of involvement $= 0.9$; $n = 14$ categories of interest units as in table 2.6).

Table 3.1 shows not only influence but also the rank order placings of the categories of interest units on involvements from table 2.7, so that the rank order placings on influence and on involvements can be readily compared.

The differences are startling. Some go up and some go down. Some are widely involved but when involved are not very influential; and some are influential when involved but are not involved often. Up in influence compared to involvements (by five places or more) go sales and marketing, research and design, and liaison and claims internally, and customers and clients externally. All these customer- or market-orientated units tend to be highly influential when they are involved, though often they are not involved. Down (by five places or more) go accounting, quality control and inspection, and both the external 'standards' interests, the Goverment departments and agencies and the auditors, trade associations, and shareholders. These whose influence is less than their involvement, so to speak, are frequently drawn in to provide or check information, their frequent involvement giving an illusion of influence. But their influence is less than may be imagined. The setting and checking of financial standards, or of quality standards for products, is not of itself an influential activity, nor is routine governmental aid or regulation as was found earlier, nor are the counsels of trade associations, nor even the possible wishes of shareholders. Accounting departments exemplify this. During the intense electricity decision in Toxicem, accounting shrank from attempting to exert influence and managed to sit on the fence despite efforts from both sides to tip it off. As Hinings, et al. (1974, p. 39) wrote of the accounting departments in the firms they studied: 'They kept records of everything and sent reports to and collected information from everyone . . . but took no action on this themselves and hence influenced no one.' Indeed, had they tried to act they might have got nowhere: the dramatic events recorded live by inconspicuous cameras during a cliff-hanger decision at the top of the British Steel Corporation in the early 1970s, and shown publicly on television, revealed the Director of Finance vainly trying to prevent a multi-million pound investment which the Chairman and other interested parties were swaying the Planning Committee and Board towards, almost regardless of cost and output calculations, for non-financial strategic reasons. He was certainly not sitting on the fence, but for all the influence he exerted he may as well have done. It should be said on his behalf, perhaps, that the subsequent decline of the steel industry implies that he was right!

This is not to say that Accounting and related departments and others such as quality control are always powerless. Of the 14 interest groupings in table 3.1 they are in seventh place, just above the middle of the ranking, and in table 3.4 which divides groupings simply by their being in the upper or lower halves of the rankings on involvements and on influence, accounting, etc. just get over the edge into the frequently involved and frequently influential category in the bottom right-hand box. These are the *internal heavyweights*, production and equivalent, sales, and accounting and equivalent, the

Table 3.4 Heavyweight and lightweight interest units*

	Involvements Infrequent	*Involvements Frequent*
	Fringe lightweights	*External lightweights*
Influential Infrequently	Trades unions Competitors Purchasing Maintenance, Personnel etc.	Auditors, trade associations, shareholders Government Departments and agencies Suppliers
	Fringe heavyweights	*Internal heavyweights*
Influential Frequently	Customers, clients Research, design Liaison and claims	Production, and equivalent Sales, marketing Accounting, quality control, inspection Divisions

*External interest units underlined. 'Frequent(ly)' = rank order placings 1 to 7 on table 3.1, and 'infrequent(ly)' = placings 8 to 14.

main functions in organizations which always have to be reckoned with in any strategic decision, plus relatively autonomous divisions and the like. They are central to the making of most decisions, almost always involved in the action at some stage and almost always influential.

They contrast with the *external lightweights* in the top right-hand box, often involved but not much of a force to be reckoned with in most decisions, the auditors, trade associations and shareholders, governmental interests, (though these can be effective in selected situations, as has been shown), and suppliers. On the left of this simple matrix are those that are less often involved, so that by comparison they are on the fringe of strategic decision-making. Bottom left are those whose interests are implicated in fewer decisions but can be very influential when they are involved, the *fringe heavyweights* such as customers and R and D, and top left are the *fringe lightweights* whose infrequent involvement and weak influence means they are of little consequence for strategic decisions, including the unions and purchasing departments.

The typical political mix in a decision-set of interests over the course of decision-making, as suggested by what happened in this large number of decisions in a diversity of organizations, is therefore a central bunch of internal heavyweights from the central functions of production or equivalent, marketing, and finance, joined by external lightweights such as trade associations or government departments or suppliers whose influence does not challenge that of the central internal functions. Now and again, in some decisions only, this core of internal influence is matched by that of a fringe heavyweight such as a major customer or the research department on topics where they are directly relevant. Fringe lightweights, such as unions or the maintenance department, do not disturb this pattern, though in a small minority of decisions the actions of competitors are given greater weight than this average fringe position suggests and may be the instigators of what is decided.

Balance of power

As the main heavyweights are *internal*, and going back to table 3.1 it can be seen that most *external* interests are in the lower half of the influence ranking, it seems that the balance of power is safely tipped internally. Sometimes not even a remote headquarters, external to a particular subsidiary but with ultimate control over it, can overcome unified internal resistance, as in one case where a subsidiary was pressed by its divisional headquarters to market a 'super glue'. The glue complemented its other products, but the subsidiary demurred, fearing that injuries to glue users, and law suits, would damage its public image, and contending that any profits would be too small to be worthwhile. The argument went on for over two years but eventually the subsidiary's Managing Director, armed with a specially commissioned report, went in person to the USA, and stood his ground on the negative decision not to sell this type of product.

This tipping of the balance internally is confirmed by the average influence ratings for all internal and external units combined (3.0 and 2.7 at the foot of table 3.1). There is certainly no external dominance, and the difference, if any indicates internal control.

Yet internal control is not impregnable. Although on average only a third or so of the total influence brought to bear is from external interests (over 150 cases, the mean influence per case attributed to external interests is 39 per cent), and is less (28 per cent) if the general management categories at the foot of table 3.1 are included,

Table 3.5 Five cases of dominant external influence

Decision topic	External influence (%)	Number of interest units		External interest units (influence ratings on five-point scale in brackets)
		Internal	External	
Interest rates (financial institution)	65	6	5	Financial Institutions' Association (5); the British Treasury (5) and Department of Environment (5); investors (suppliers) (3); borrowers (customers) (2)
Share (one-third) in another company (chemicals division)	69	3	7	The other company (5); companies holding the other shares (4, and 4); two suppliers (3, and 3); group head office (2); County Council (4)
Amalgamation of departments and colleges (polytechnic)	70	3	6	Other colleges (3, and 2); unions (4, and 3); Student's union (3); owning municipality (1)
Company name (construction equipment manufacturer)	81	2	8	Other subsidiaries of the same corporation (5, 3, and 1); customers (5); competitors (5); consultants (4); suppliers (1); group head office (1)
'Take Home' division (brewery)	90	2	10	Owning corporation head office departments (5, 5, 4, 3, and 3); other large subsidiaries of the same corporation (4, 4, 3, and 1); marketing consultants (3)

there are nevertheless 20 exceptional decisions out of 150 where it was 50 per cent or more (range = 0–90 per cent). In most of these it was not much above 50 per cent, and in any case too much precision should not be read into these gross attributions of influence, but in table 3.5, five cases of greatest external intervention where it clearly dominated are singled out.

Taking as an example the last case in the table, where it was decided to set up a special 'Take Home' division in a brewery to concentrate on sales of beer not drunk on the spot in a pub, the extraordinary figure of 90 per cent external influence is calculated from the sum of the ratings of ten external interest units as a percentage of the ratings of all units which are two internals plus the ten externals.

These five cases of overwhelming external influence, from 65 per cent to 90 per cent, all heavily implicate the interests of outsiders. The second and third are boundary topics where it was decided to extend the organization to incorporate others partly or wholly. One of these was a decision to join in a tripartite commitment by three public sector and private sector corporations to buy equal shares in a fourth company with which they were all interdependent. This decision in a large autonomous chemicals division, aimed at ensuring a buyer for its own byproducts, was heavily influenced by its partners in the venture and by the subsidiary-to-be which was in favour, much more than by the environmentally defensive local government County Council (table 3.5). The other boundary case, the amalgamation of various departments and colleges, primarily teacher-training units, into the polytechnic of a municipality, was among the examples of high union influence in table 3.3, and preceded the decision on Boards of Studies in the same polytechnic that also appears in that table and is dealt with again later in the chapter.

The other three cases are domain-orientated, or domain-originated, in a marketing sense. The first in the table is in effect a price change decision, namely a decision by a major financial institution, which makes loans to a mass public, to reduce interest rates. This was the decision discussed earlier that was nationally significant because it impinged on government monetary policy and had strong governmental influence behind it. Fourth in the table is a decision to change a variety of overlapping names for different subsidiaries and branches of a company into a standard form, a decision risking the allegiance of established customers in the hope of a more definite market image in general. Finally there is the case of 90 per cent external influence no less, where the head office of a brewery's owning corporation and its sister subsidiaries pressed it to set up a new product-type division to control its sales through supermarkets and shops, alongside its long-standing geographically-based organization distributing to the traditional English pubs, to help counteract retail bulk-buyers in this field who were in effect playing off one subsidiary against another.

The feature of these five extreme cases is the large number and variety of interests in each, the percentage of external influence increasing down the table with their numbers. The influential externals can be other organizations in the same group, or of the same kind (private or public), or customers, suppliers, consultants, sometimes even government departments and unions. However, it is remarkable that 'HQ' did not play a leading influential part, although these were major externally-orientated decisions: all organizations except the financial institution were ultimately subject to some other body, which for this purpose was classified as external to them, yet only the decision in the brewery was heavily influenced by head office. Whatever subsidiary units are authorized to do, they can do without interference.

So whilst on the one hand strategic decision-making does not often veer out of the control of internal management interests, tugged from their grasp by outsiders, they must always be aware of external influences present or imminent, and in the most externally implicating decisions they can find themselves outweighed. In none of the cases in table 3.5 were they flatly opposed to these outsiders, whose objectives they shared in some degree, but direct conflict can occur. It is probably typified by the take-over bid situation, of which, out of 150 cases, there was one instance 'on the receiving end'.

This was 'the last decision' mentioned before, where a decision was taken to try to resist takover. The attempt was too little and too late, for a large investor rapidly acquired the bulk of the shares (and an influence rating of 5 compared to 1 each for several internal management interests) and changed the management, ending the research team's contact with the firm with data collection completed just in time!

The involvement of external interests increases the potential politicality of a decision, if only because it means that the total number of interest units involved is likely to be higher (r number of involvements with influence ratings of external interest units as a percentage of the sum of ratings of all interests = 0.4, at 99 per cent confidence level). But it also affects the balance of power inasmuch as it is likely to be less a balance and more an imbalance, with both more strong and more weak units appearing in the decision making arena (r range of influence ratings with percentage external influence, as above, = 0.3, also at 99 per cent) (Cray, et al. 1983). In other words, in decision-making that involves major customers or suppliers, or perhaps government departments, or other significant external interests, influence is more polarized between a few strong interests such as this external party and the internal heavyweights, who dominate the process, and the rest of the departments and any other outsiders who have much less say. The latter departments and outsiders may not want much of a say, of course. The decision may not concern them very much, and they may readily leave it to production, sales, and finance (by whatever name) to sort it out in conjunction with the main external interest.

Pressure

Politicality is heightened when some decisions are 'leaned upon' more than others. That is, they are subjected to greater influence from the interests in the decision-set, irrespective of whether these are internal or external. This *pressure* is not the same as conflict, for all the pressure may be in the same direction, but it means treading carefully since in such a situation conflict is the more difficult to overcome should it occur. There are more 'heavyweights' in the decision-set, and a lot of influence is being brought to bear. The pressure being exerted on the course of a decision is shown in the mean of the influence ratings of all the interest units involved, including the general management categories shown at the foot of table 3.1.

Some decisions attract a great deal more influence than do others, so there are high-pressure decisions and low-pressure decisions, the extremes being a high-pressure case where the influence exerted was as high as a mean 4.5 (on the five-point scale of influence) and a low-pressure case where the mean was only 1.6 (mean of 150 means = 3.1, standard deviation 0.6).

The contrast between decisions under higher pressure and under

Figure 3.2. HIGHER AND LOWER PRESSURE

Decision-set graphs of ratings of the influence of interests units in two decisions: a decision in a Municipality to enter on joint financing with the Health Service of a Home for the Aged (higher pressure), and in a Brewery not to launch a new brand of beer (LOWER PRESSURE).

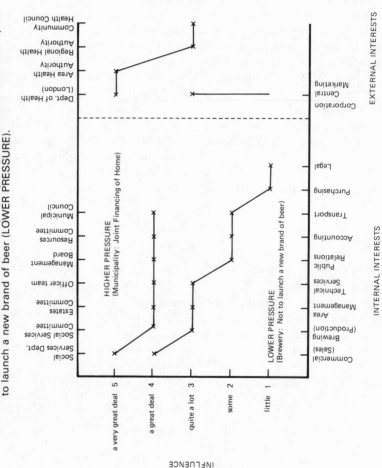

lower pressure is illustrated in figure 3.2. It juxtaposes on the same graph the influences attributed to the interest units involved in a decision in a municipal authority and in a decision in a brewery, the first being higher pressure and at the top of the graph and the second being lower pressure and at the bottom of the graph. Internal interests are shown to the left of the graph and external interests to the right, both plotted left to right from greatest influence to least.

The pressure in the decision-making of the municipality was both high (mean of 11 influence ratings = 4.1), and balanced. It was balanced in so far as there was high influence from internal and external sources, and a series of ostensibly equal internal influences indicated by the level line against 'a great deal of influence' (there is always an indeterminate risk of an informant getting a 'response fix' and persisting unthinkingly with the same rating, in this case 4, but even if this were so here, the influences were certainly adjudged on the high side). The decision was an example of a smooth process with no dissent, all interests having complementary objectives and using their influences to those ends. It was, however, delicate, for it was an interorganizational collaboration between local and national public sector organizations, each very much in the public eye, the municipality and the National Health Service. They agreed to finance jointly the building of an old people's home. Building such a home was a humdrum matter, but the joint financing was unique for the municipality and exemplified a new direction for the NHS. The influential central government Department of Health (rated 5) had to approve, as did the organizationally autonomous NHS Regional and Area levels (rated 3 and 5). The body giving voice to the views of the local populace, the Community Health Council, also did so. Within the municipal authority itself, the nature of local government decision-making shows up in the influences of the succession of committees which worked on or pronounced upon the matter, from the municipality's team of senior officers to the elected council and its specialist social services, estates, and resources (finance) committees (committees and boards were treated as distinct interest units whenever the executives saw them that way).

The lower pressure process (mean of 10 ratings = 2.4) arrived at one of the negative decisions referred to in the previous chapter. It was another example of disagreement between corporation head office and a subsidiary company, similar to the super-glue case. The management of a brewery decided not to launch a new premium

beer, which would have been picturesquely called 'Old Joe Bitter'.
In an industry with long product life-cycles, 'Old Joe' would have
been a rare event. However, market research, and small-scale trials
of a specimen beer in one area, suggested that a new line might not
do much more than take sales from the company's established main
brand, and detract from a coming move into the growing lager
market, so the idea was postponed, if not abandoned, despite
pressure from the owning corporation's central marketing department to go ahead. Their comparatively high influence (rated 3) could
not outweigh the combination of the subsidiary's internal departments (ranged along the bottom of the graph) all of which were
either hesitant or against the idea, including the two 'heavyweights',
commercial (or sales: rated 4) and brewing (or production) with its
associated area managements and technical services (all rated 3).

It might be expected that the most consequential decisions would
draw the most influence, each of the interests involved striving to
influence a far-reaching decision in its favour. In short, consequentiality would elicit pressure. There are occasions when that
happens, but no general tendency of that kind. The general explanation of pressure must be that, as influence arises from interdependence, the coming into a decision-set of highly interdependent
interests means that each is then inevitably highly influential, for
without it the decision would go differently. In the case of the old
people's home, the agreement of the several Health Service bodies
was vital to the municipality's decision, for without the Health
Service's money there would be nothing to decide – or at best a
status quo decision to do nothing. Similarly with the 'super-glue'
case that has been mentioned, also high pressure (mean 4.2), where
subsidiary and headquarters were bound together interdependently
and headquarters were unable to get such a glue on to the British
market when the subsidiary refused to co-operate. Thus high interdependence of interests in the decision-set means high-pressure
influence upon the decision.

Cleavage and contention

Politicality – the exertion of influence through a decision-making
process on its outcome – has its origin in *cleavage*. Cleavage is the

differences between interests that are built into an organization; the extent to which they are 'non-convergent' (Bacharach and Lawler 1980). As said earlier, interests and objectives are not the same. Objectives are more decision-specific and shortlived than interests, and are formulated in the context of a particular decision-making process. Even if interests differ, objectives in a particular decision for particular reasons may not. That is, cleavage of interests does not equate with *contention* of *objectives*.

To repeat Pettigrew (1973, p. 265), decision-making 'may be understood as a political process that balances various power vectors'. Contention does not necessarily mean outright conflict, for the proverbial 'bone of contention' may be dealt with peaceably enough by compromise or by fiat of higher authority before anything as overt as is implied by the word conflict breaks out. Contention of objectives is a propensity for conflict, just as cleavage of interests is a propensity for contention, but whether each occurs depends on how the topic for decision takes shape and is processed. The fewer and starker the alternatives, the more likely there is to be conflict, Hage (1980, p. 122) suggests.

There is high contention in almost exactly half of the 150 cases. From interview case notes, the objectives of the interest units were categorized by the research team from strong support for the eventual decision (+2) through qualified support (+1), neutrality (0), qualified opposition (−1) to strong opposition (−2). An interest unit 'wanting to be kept informed' or 'interested in how things would turn out' was assumed to be neutral, for example, and those which seemed to have done no more than present standard departmental viewpoints were put down as plus or minus 1. A comparison was made by taking the *range* of differences in objectives between the interest units influencing a decision as a measure of contention, so that if interest units with +2 and with−2 objectives were involved the decision scored as highly contentious, 4, whereas if the objectives of all units were the same (nil range) it scored 0. Seventy-six decisions scored 3 or 4, which shows that strategic decision-making is a pretty contentious game.

Although the two decisions portrayed in figure 3.2, the old people's home and 'Old Joe Bitter', have a geriatric verbal coincidence(!), they differ in contention as well as in pressure. As has already been described this difference is not what casual first thoughts might presume: the high-pressure decision-making in the municipality was not contentious. Although politically delicate, it had a unanimity of objectives within and between both municipality and the Health Service, which is summarized in the first contention plot in figure 3.3. The plots in the figure symbolize, visually, the degree of contention, showing which interest units broadly supported or opposed the eventual outcome of a decision-making process. An uncontentious decision appears with all plus signs, whereas a contentious one has a flattened out 'U' shape with opposed interest units at either end since they are arranged by objectives plus to minus from left to right, with those more or less uncommitted in the middle.

The unbroken row of plus signs on the first plot in figure 3.3, the old people's home case, all in favour of joint financing, includes the municipality's crucial management team of executive officers and social services department and committee, each deeply involved, and all the crucial Health Service bodies, outsiders to the municipality, every one giving firm +2 support.

Not so with 'Old Joe', the case headed 'Moderate contention', where the contention between the brewery's own objectives and those of the owning corporation's central marketing department is summed up in the unanimously + or at least neutral stances of its internal units, as against the −2 for the frustrated central department (care is necessary in interpreting the signs on the plot in this case, for as the decision was negative, not to launch the new beer, a plus sign means support for that and a negative means opposition to it, that is favouring new beer). This internal unity accords with some tendency across all cases for differences internally to be lower when there is more external influence exerted (*r* contention among internal interest units and percentage influence of external units = −0.3, at 99 per cent confidence level), a predictable standing together in the face of external threat (Cray, et al. 1983).

With the old people's home collaborative financing not being contentious, and 'Old Joe Bitter' being moderately contentious, the third plot shows a decision that was more highly contentious, ranging all the way from +2 to −2 objectives. As part of a process of amalgamation of smaller colleges into larger units in British higher education in the late 1960s and early 1970s, the polytechnic decision shown earlier to have been heavily externally influenced (table 3.5) had brought together a number of departments and colleges,

Figure 3.3. HIGHER AND LOWER CONTENTION

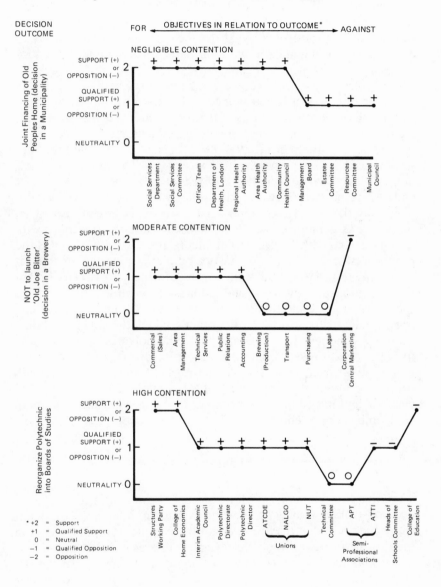

DECISION
OUTCOME

FOR ← OBJECTIVES IN RELATION TO OUTCOME* → AGAINST

* +2 = Support
  +1 = Qualified Support
   0 = Neutral
  −1 = Qualified Opposition
  −2 = Opposition

including a college of education and a college specializing in home economics and similar subjects. After the first few years the central polytechnic administration realized that this supposed integration was no more than nominal, especially since these colleges and the central campus were separated, and they set up a working party to examine the problem. The working party recommended an entire reorganization of the polytechnic into boards of studies (or faculties) within which the two colleges were to be included so that their affairs would be discussed and determined within a uniform structure along with those of all other sections of the polytechnic. As the contention plot shows, this was a 'hot potato', a classic story of academic 'politicking' (Butler, et al. 1977/78) over sub-unit autonomy. Support within the central polytechnic was mixed. The directorate were more or less in favour, the heads of schools more or less against (+1 and −1 respectively), whilst the college of education (−2), supported by the ATTI (Association of Teachers in Technical Institutions), an association of academic staff concerned not so much with the change but with ensuring its members' representation, fought the proposal which it saw as drastically diminishing its degree of autonomy. Moreover, the college was unwilling to risk its exceptionally good playing fields and gymnasium facilities, on which its special reputation in athletics and gymnastics depended, being laid open to allcomers. However, the other college, the college of home economics, hoped that integration into the polytechnic would raise its status, and so was equally strongly in favour (+2), it too having employee associations on its side, in this case three trades unions also concerned about representation. The proposal went through – but was last said not to be working well, partly because of the hours of staff time spent attending Boards of Studies meetings!

Who decides?

The inherent politicality of decision-sets of interests at this level of decision-making is evidenced by the exertion of influence, consonant with objectives that may or may not be in contention, derived from the prevalent organizational cleavage of interests. It is omnipresent in the making of strategic decisions any of which may threaten the existing disposition of resources and upset the pattern of power (Hage 1980, p. 109). It may be regarded as at its highest when decision-set pressure is high, that is when many interests, especially external interests, are influential; and when there is contention between objectives.

Because of politicality, there is not so much 'the decision' but 'the deciding'. For this reason, the question 'who decides', with which this chapter began, may not be the best question. At its face value it is too easily answered. In the 150 Bradford studies cases, the lowest level at which a final choice was formally authorized, that is at which a strategic decision was taken, was divisional level in a large organization. The level of authorization ranged from there, upwards through chief executives and boards, councils, and the like, to the quarter of all decisions that were ratified, if nothing more, above the organization itself in some higher governing body. It is a truism that decision-making among interests at the top will be formally concluded centrally at the very top.

The better question to ask is, 'who influences the deciding?' That is the question that this chapter has been answering. The deciding of the outcome is influenced by a wide variety of intraorganizational and interorganizational decision-sets of interest units, some large, some small, most including both recurrent internal heavyweight units and an external lightweight or two, plus some others of varying influence. There are occasions when government can be decisively influential through one of its departments or agencies, and many occasions when it cannot. Trades unions cannot. No one is all-powerful. No single senior executive can 'move mountains with a memo' (Donaldson and Lorsch 1983). Decision-making at this level is less the 'dialogue' which Mayntz (1976) sees as going on between echelons and more a hubbub of pressure and contention.

Yet to describe it as 'organized anarchy' (Cohen, et al. 1972) is going too far. There is a hand on the steering, despite the tumult, which gives a feeling that things are, most of the time, under control. Table 3.1 has at its foot two means of influence ratings that have not so far been made use of. These are for general management at the pinnacle of an organization, namely the chief executive, and also a broad category including function director equivalents and high level committees and boards such as the Working Party and Academic Council in the polytechnic Boards of Studies case, and the Management Board and Social Services Committee (of municipal councillors) in the old people's home case. When executive informants rated influence they often singled out these two levels, including individual chief executives, for example the polytechnic director in the third contention plot, figure 3.3, and if they did so this was accepted, so that there are 121 ratings for chief executives and 94 for other general management entities. The two influence means are 4.3 for chief executives, and 3.4, the first being much higher than the mean for any interest unit category and the second being the third highest in the table. Hence when all is said and done on behalf of all the multifarious interests, the most influential of all are the general management who have ultimate authority in an organization. Their influence matches their authority and is sustained by it. It is an influence that is probably at its peak in the early formative and closing conclusive phases of decision-making (DIO International Research Team 1983, p. 10). It is an influence that adds substantially to the internally tipped balance in most decision-sets.

Since there are no rule books, in these British organizations anyway, which say who should or should not be involved in the making of a strategic decision, or when, custom and practice are loose enough to leave considerable initiative with the ultimate top management as to whose contribution is recognized and to what extent. They are final arbiters of who is in and who is out. They are not above the politicking, for it takes place around them and they take part in it, but if what is going on appears to be getting out of hand they are able to make a decisive move, as the Managing Director of Toxicem did to end the open conflict between Alwyn and supporters and Giles and supporters. By personifying the organization, they ensure a bounded politicality that holds the participants and the politicking within bounds.

Yet theirs is not a dominant position in the processes of making strategic decisions. A chief executive may exert more influence than any one other source of influence but he does not have more influence than everyone else combined, nor more than sub-alliances of interests, especially external interests. He has a hold that is open to challenge. There is not a single hegemony over the managerial pluralism of internal and external interests, but a *malleable constrained domination*.

The politicality of the decisions within this regime, together with their complexity, shape the ensuing *processes* of making decisions, so it has been argued. If so, then should there not be typical configurations of complexity, politicality, and process? Should it not be possible to trace connections between them in such a way as to find which kinds of decisions are most likely to be made in which ways? If there are, and if it is, then first the stuff of process must be understood. Differences in process must be described before they can be explained, and it is to this that the next chapter turns.

4

Decision-Making Processes in Action

Making the process

Strategic decisions are not made in a moment with a snap of the fingers. They take time, usually quite a lot of time. Individual managers and administrators may snap their fingers at stages along the way, and make crisp personal decisions on what shall be done next, but these are decisions on moves in the process of reaching a strategic decision, not the decision itself. That is the outcome of a stream of activity, and sometimes inactivity, over a period. People have to talk, in meetings and corridors and offices, files have to be looked into, investigations have to be made, reports have to be written, those whose interests are implicated have to be asked or told or listened to, things have to be waited for, and other things which crop up have to be attended to so that making the decision gets pushed aside.

We have argued that this process of making a decision is a response to the problems and interests inherent in the matter for decision, a response to their complexity and politicality. It is set in motion, by those who have the power to do so, when they signify their recognition of a decision-making topic. They place it on the agenda of the board for the first time, or raise it in a discussion in someone's office, or call for a preliminary report from a department such as finance or research, doing something whatever it is that initiatiates movement towards a decision.

Thereafter those involved, some eager, some indifferent, some reluctant, respond to the complexity of the problems in a variety of ways. Perhaps they get estimates of costs or capacity from this department or that, perhaps they bring in outsiders such as customers or consultants, perhaps they set up working parties or project teams to thrash out the details. At the same time, they respond to the politicality embodied in the various interests, by clarifying the different objectives and working out compromises, by negotiating during drinks before lunch, by bringing together in committees the people whose views count (or, alternatively, by excluding them). Move by move, step by step, these and innumerable other actions accumulate into processes of fits and starts, of phases of rapid progress or of inertia, of clarity or confusion, welcomed or deplored as the case may be by those for or against the likely outcome as it emerges.

Clearly, if processes of strategic decision-making come from the attempts of managers and administrators to cope with the problems and interests in a decision, then processes must differ from decision to decision as the problems and interests change. Each process will have a character that may be similar to that of another or may differ from it.

How then do processes differ? In what respect do they differ? By what means can one be distinguished from another? How can they be told apart? Do different ways of getting to a decision have distinctive characteristics, and, if so, can their characters be described?

Phases of process

Other researchers have broadly agreed that the route towards a decision goes through three phases, a 'start-up' or 'identification' phase when the topic for decision is first recognized as such, a 'developmental' phase when the search is on for relevant information and the development of alternatives, and a 'finalization' or 'selection' phase when the choice is narrowed down and made (Mintzberg, et al. 1976; DIO International Research Team 1983). Each phase encompasses routines of activity, such as 'the recognition routine, wherein the need to initiate a decision process is perceived, and the diagnosis routine, where the decision situation is assessed', two routines said to take place during the start-up phase (Mintzberg 1979, pp. 58–9).

Most of the action is thought to be during the central developmental phase which lasts longest and has most conflict, as information and views are sought and attempts are made to set out alternatives

(DIO International Research Team 1983). During this phase, attempts to persuade others to change their minds, that is to change their 'preferred outcomes', are followed by bargaining if these attempts fail and different positions persist (Abell 1975, pp. 17–18). In extreme situations, even bargaining may be impossible, as in the Toxicem electricity decision, where once the announcement of the Managing Director's forthcoming retirement had convulsed the process is became so intensely and personally political that he himself had to step in and compel a conclusion by counting heads for and against.

The defining of phases and routines within phases does not by itself amount to an adequate description of how processes get from start to finish, since they do not happen in any foreseeable order. Routines can be repeated over and over again so that phases and whole processes turn back upon themselves. After what has been called the 'diagnosis routine' in the 'start-up' phase when, for instance, it may have been believed that the range of services offered by an organization needed to be reappraised, the balance of evidence and opinion might be found to contradict this first diagnosis so the process returns to the 'diagnostic routine' for a second look at the whole question. Hence there is no 'simple sequential relationship' in what happens (Mintzberg, et al. 1976, p. 252; Mayntz 1976; Witte 1972). One phase does not lead to another in a logical order, so that processes as a whole do not move steadily onwards phase by phase in an inexorable progression. They jump about. They hop to and fro. They turn back. Fresh information forces a rethink, something unforeseen happens which opens up a new alternative, powerful voices close off an otherwise attractive course of action. So there are rediagnoses, reconsiderations, reassessments, and people find themselves going through the same thing all over again. At the extreme, processes can seem to veer uncontrollably, and solutions can come before problems, in a veritable 'garbage-can' of problems, solutions, and participants, in which decisions are arrived at that appear to have little to do with the process of arriving at them, the choices being 'uncoupled' from the processes (Cohen, et al. 1972). Even if, as a management text might advocate, a problem is defined, relevant information is obtained, alternative solutions are scanned and evaluated, and a choice is made, these elements may not occur in this order and may recur more than once. The 'trajectory' followed by a process may bounce about like that of a molecule in a bubble chamber (Hage 1980, p. 110).

Incrementalism

The trajectory does so because decision-makers, it is believed, feel their way along as cautiously as they can, turning from side to side and circling back to get more information and avoid obstacles. The tentative feeler is more to be expected than the bold stroke. The moderate move on a modicum of information is more common than the brilliantly informed penetrating advance. This is forced by the impracticability of gathering all possible information on all possible alternatives so that it can be precisely evaluated in a smooth controlled process. To actually achieve the hypothetical perfection of that 'rational deductive ideal' would deluge decision-makers with prodigious indigestible information, so they do not attempt it.

Instead, they go through a process of '*disjointed incrementalism*' (Braybrooke and Lindblom 1963). They get as far as they can, little by little. Instead of trying to be fully informed, an elusive and awesome ideal which if realized would swamp them with data, they simplify decisions by examining only a few alternatives and contemplating only marginal changes. Rather than adjust means to ends, the logical ideal, they do it the other way round, adjusting ends to means by scaling the ends down to what the means make feasible. So processes shuffle along in an irregular series of small disjointed steps, not necessarily in an orderly sequence but each adjusted to the circumstances of the moment.

For administrators who are aware of this 'science of muddling through', working in accordance with its principles is not incompetence in decision-making, but a realistic adaptation to the difficulties (Lindblom 1959). Whilst it may be disjointed incrementalism, it is also 'logical incrementalism' fitted to a complex and political world (Quinn 1978). Even in industry, 'Good managers are aware of this process. . . . Properly managed, it is a conscious, purposeful proactive executive practice' (Quinn 1980, p. 58).

The general impression given by these perspectives on phases, which recycle, and movement, which is incremental, is of reiterative piecemeal processes. There is nothing in the results of the Bradford studies that questions this as an insightful impression which enlarges the idea of what happens beyond any facile assumption that all is rationally tidy; though it should not be allowed to lead to the opposite facile assumption that nothing is ever rational. There are guiding rationalities at work even if their results are not wholly rational, a point for later discussion.

However, there is more to be said of a process than that it is in some degree probably reiterative and piecemeal. Indeed, more has been anticipated in descriptions of decisions that were too indivisible to be handled incrementally (Schulman 1975; Lustick 1980), and by the advocacy of a process of 'mixed scanning' to give a longer view (Etzioni 1967). The possibility of aspects of processes other than their incrementalism was always envisaged (Lindblom 1969).

Process duration: the time it takes

The most self-evident further characteristic of a decision-making process is its duration, quite simply how long it takes to arrive at the conclusive choice. Decisions can be taken so unexpectedly quickly that they catch people napping, or the process can stretch out for so long that people wonder if any decision will ever be taken. But how quick is quick and how long is long?

To determine that it is necessary to define the beginnings and the ends of processes, an unwelcome necessity since it forces the cutting out from organizational histories of periods of time. In effect, it assumes that what is inside such a period is a decision-making process and what is outside it is not. This is uncomfortable since things are more gradual than that, especially at the beginnings of decision-making, yet also at its endings as the making of the choice slides into the implementation of that choice. Despite this, the marking out of slices of time cannot be avoided, accepting anyway that all research by whatever method takes samples and periods that are less than the whole of life and are, therefore, some inadequate vignette of it. To research is unavoidably to distort by selection and perception.

Recognizing and perforce accepting this, the Bradford studies are based on marking out periods from the 'start' to the 'finish' of a decision, that is from 'the first recalled deliberate action which begins movement towards a decision (when, for example, the matter is discussed in a meeting, or a report is called for) to the approved choice (when the decision and its implementation are authorized)' (Hickson, et al. 1985). Thus 'the decision process encompasses all those steps taken from the time a stimulus for an action is perceived until the time the commitment to the action is made' (Mintzberg 1979, p. 58), from 'first proposal' to 'final decision outcome' (Hage 1980, p. 117).

The 150 cases at this strategic level are found to have taken just over 12 months on average to reach an authorized decision. This is somewhat shorter but not out of line with the 70 weeks reported

Figure 4.1. THE DURATION OF STRATEGIC DECISION-MAKING: PROCESS TIMES OF 150 DECISIONS.

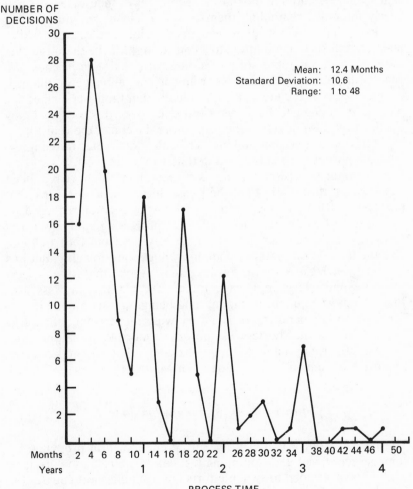

Mean: 12.4 Months
Standard Deviation: 10.6
Range: 1 to 48

PROCESS TIME
(rounding up odd numbers of months to even numbers)

from the mixture of strategic and tactical decisions studied in three Dutch organizations by the DIO International Research Team (1983, table 2).

The *process times* for the 150 cases are plotted in figure 4.1 which shows the time it took from the first recalled action that started movement towards a decision to the decision being formally made. Five peaks appear on the graph, at six months, a year, 18 months, two years, and three years. There is no firm explanation for this. It is as if managers and administrators keep notes in their diaries at half yearly intervals, reminding them to call a halt to any outstanding processes that have not yet arrived at a decision, and between whiles make no efforts to get matters to a conclusion! Maybe there is a clue there, in so far as there are conventions of thinking in periods of a year, or half a year, for example from one annual budget to the next or one season to the next. It is quite likely that thoughts such as 'six months is enough to have been dithering over this' or 'we really ought to get this one out of the way before the end of the year' shape the duration of decision-making. The calendar frames thinking, so periodic pushes are made to bring things to a close.

In general, decision-making is faster than might have been expected at this level. Published case histories of decisions that dragged on for very long periods, such as the decision recorded by Pettigrew (1973) on new electronic data-processing equipment in a British retail firm, which lasted for seven years from 1961 to 1968, give the impression that they commonly linger interminably, but this is not so. Such cases are rarities. Figure 4.1 shows that for a process to go beyond two years is exceptional. The majority are less than that, the most frequent or modal time being only six months.

On the other hand, there is a very wide range from shortest to longest. Whilst the shortest was not much more than a month, the longest was four years, a range matching that of the 25 cases recorded in Canada by the students of Mintzberg, et al. (1976).

Shorter processes; a municipal lottery

The fastest of all was not in an entrepreneurial firm propelled by some stereotypical desk-thumping task master, but in a polytechnic where it was decided to switch efforts into running short courses for industry by funding specialized posts for the purpose. Almost as fast was a decision in the popularly supposed turgid political bureaucracy of a municipal authority. This body held sway over an area in which 400,000 people resided in the North of England, a section of a much larger metropolitan conurbation. It had the usual structure of senior officials, 'directors', heading major functions, all subject to an array of committees composed partly or wholly of elected representatives, 'councillors', who belonged to political parties (some of this structure appears in figures 3.2 and 3.3 in the previous chapter where the same municipality's old people's home joint financing decision is described). Yet in the autumn of 1977, in not much more than a month, in the face of doubts on morality, a decision was taken to augment strained funds by launching a municipal lottery, one of the first in Britain. This opened up an entirely novel source of funds, the first that was not directly from local taxpayers or national government.

The decision originated when the leader of the council (that is, the leader of the controlling political party), who was ex-officio chairman of its powerful finance committee, met a lottery promoter whilst both were on holiday one summer in Devon in the South West of England. The leader became interested, one of his fellow councillors became enthusiastic, the promoter visited the municipality, and the proposal was put through the senior officials, and the council itself, rapidly in an August to October period when numbers of councillors were still away on holiday. Despite the qualms of the members of some churches, which cut across party lines, there was little outright opposition. The lottery was launched in December.

One of the reasons for the speed and fluency of this decision may have been that it proposed an alternative source of funds without precedent, and so was not bounded by the procedures that had been built up over many years of municipal administration to govern how decisions on raising money from taxpayers should be made. These governed the preparation and scrutiny of budgets and of each proposed change in the figures, institutionalizing the annual contest between political parties step by step. Further, this particular decision was backed by individuals who, given that it was not bounded in quite the usual way, were in a position to push it through or around procedures. It was the same with the fast decision in the polytechnic, where there were no procedures restraining the Rector, or chief executive, from declaring a new policy largely on his own initiative. What the procedures governed was implementation, regulating step by step the creation of each of the new positions that were to run the new short courses.

As the saying goes, 'where there's a will there's a way', true at least for determined authority figures who choose their moment to push something through rapidly. As the polytechnic and munici- pality show, they can do this in public administration as elsewhere, for particular kinds of organization are not noticeably faster nor slower than others in decision-making. If anything, it is the bypassing of normal procedures, and avoiding seeking fresh information, that saves time and speeds decisions, and that can be so in any organization.

Medium-length processes: boosting a bank

A typical one-year decision, just about the average length of process, was taken in 1971/2 in a savings bank whose management was attempting to move it up to cheque-issuing status, with the aim of turning it into an organization more like a 'real bank'. Most of the time that elapsed was taken up by meetings of a special working committee of its senior managers set up to consider the matter, and by internal preparatory work and discussions between the meetings. Though this bank was nationwide, it had traditionally operated only through counters inside the stores of retail chains with which it was associated, and in effect on a cash basis, since its customers could not write cheques on their accounts. In the early 1970s, its whole strategy was changed towards competing with what are known in Britain as the 'high street banks' on more equal terms, emerging from obscurity to advertise a broader range of services. To offer cheque accounts, it had to be a member of the national 'clearing house' system, through which the big banks clear centrally what each owes the other after millions of customer cheque transactions have taken place.

Thus the working committee had to weigh up the chances of the other banks admitting a new competitor, the cost of modernizing branches, the effects on staff, and the chances of success in moving out into a more conspicuous position and encountering the full force of competition. After nine months' deliberation they recommended going ahead, and shortly afterwards the Board agreed. Most difficulties were encountered not during the process of making the decision, but when implementing it, for just as much time was taken up negotiating 'clearing house' membership with the other banks, who were accustomed to a small select membership which they had no reason to open to a newcomer who might take business from them. Membership was eventually conceded, and a rare new entrant appeared on the British banking scene, the trend in which until this occurred had been to fewer and fewer institutions as the banks bought one another up.

The longest processes: a massive investment

The impression that organization and duration are not noticeably linked, if only because the time taken is affected by so many other factors, is reinforced by the most drawn out of all the cases in figure 4.1. Whereas the shortest decision-making process was in public administration, a municipality, the longest was in private enterprise, a dominant manufacturer in which it took four years to decide to make a massive investment in a new plant (Hickson, et al. 1985). The company had been responsible for the invention of a revolutionary manufacturing process which it was itself using but which was also being adopted by competitors around the world. The question was not so much whether to switch further to this process, for survival demanded that, but when and where and on what scale. In 1973 a Division Planning Committee proposed action, and discussions began, but then the uncertainties of demand after the oil price rise of that year caused the matter to be shelved. Two years later it was looked at again, cautiously, with government prompting, which urged the company to try and increase employment and pointed out the availability of a state grant to subsidize the reclamation of industrial wasteland for new building. The Division Planning committee, and a long succession of technical working parties and working groups, compiled and assessed information, and eventually in 1977 the Divisional Board and the General Board and its Planning Committee accepted a final report recommending the closing of certain existing plants and the building of a new one which would be the largest and most modern in the world.

About half the total process time was spent waiting in the hope that market prospects would clarify, and half was spent in and out of the numerous committees and working parties in a copy-book process of gathering and sifting information and arriving at a conclusion. So scrutiny, as we have elsewhere called it (Astley, et al. 1982, p. 363), the searching for and analyzing of information, costs time as Hage (1980, p. 12) thought it would. Indeed, the second longest case in figure 4.1 is from the same company, which again took the better part of four years to weigh up in a similarly comprehensive manner the prospects of a totally innovatory breakthrough in product use, which had eluded researchers everywhere for decades, before deciding to go ahead. Both these lengthy processes led to decisions that committed money, and both concerned topics on which it was possible to obtain substantial financial and technical data. The fast municipal lottery decision, by contrast, did not require any significant monetary commitment and required no information beyond what the lottery promoters already had about sales for other purposes or in other countries, and the fast polytechnic decision to run short courses for industry rested on the Rector's hunch and went ahead with no time-consuming market research.

Gestation

One of the most curious features of decision-making is not the time the deliberate process takes but what happens beforehand. There can be conversations and speculations long before any definite steps are taken towards reaching a decision, that is before what is usually thought of as the process of decision-making, as defined here, commences. Eighty-eight of 150 cases include this *gestation time* (Mallory, et al. 1983, p. 199; Hickson, et al. 1985), a period from the first-recalled mention of a potential decision to the onset of process time, when the topic for decision is forming behind the scenes. This or something like it had been called a 'pre-conception period' (March and Olsen 1976, p. 144), but this is inapposite since the conception of a topic has certainly occurred even though, to continue the natal analogy, those who between them are to give birth do not yet know what is coming.

The figure of 88 processes in 150 being preceded by an identified period of gestation is almost certainly too low, for when it comes to recalling the most distant remarks, and who may have mentioned something in the office over coffee, memories are stretched to the uttermost. It must be presumed that a number of informants forgot early incidents like this, which had they remembered, would have increased the figure.

So there is not the same confidence in the numbers and lengths of gestation periods as there is in process periods but nevertheless they seemed to average between one and two years, doubling the total duration of decision-making in this fuller sense.

Among the most protracted was the prelude to a decision in a paint manufacturing firm to bypass the longstanding wholesaler distribution system and sell direct to retailers. This was mooted now and again for something like 15 years, no less, before the risk was taken of overtly examining the question. After a change of ownership, a working party was set up to consider the idea, and this move initiated a process which ended in a decision in only three months, on the face of it quite precipitate, but less so given the prolonged gestation period which had slowly prepared the ground. The hesitation, if that is not too small a word, was due to fears that were such a deliberate process to end in a decision to sell direct, as it did do, the risk to sales and the hostility of the wholesalers might be underestimated.

Gestation periods, therefore, reveal the power to set decision-making in motion, or not to do so, a reason for not doing so being the hope that procrastination will allow feared obstacles to fade away. However, there can be no generalization that preliminary gestation periods usually or even always accelerate the subsequent decision-making processes by preparing the way for them, because gestation times and process times are not correlated. If gestation beforehand usually speeded process afterwards, the two would be negatively correlated, the longer the gestation the shorter the following process, but there is no such inverse relationship. It can happen, but need not. Of the three cases of contrasting process times that have been described, the municipal lottery, the savings bank's cheque-issuing status, and the manufacturer's new plant, it was not the fast lottery decision which had the longest prior gestation but the bank decision which had been on the cards for years.

Process interruptions: slowing things down

Unlike the fast uninterrupted processing of the lottery decision, most processes run into all sorts of interruptions and disruptions, as

Mintzberg, et al. (1976) found. As would be expected, these tend to lengthen process time (r disruption . process time = 0.3; beyond 99 per cent confidence level: disruption being a short scale of the extent of delays – see Appendix). This is a tendency, not a certainty, for a short process can be delayed and still be short, as was the planning of new hospital catering in a Health Service district when an unconnected national strike interrupted consultations with the affected unions; and a longer process can proceed virtually uninterrupted as did the innovatory product-use decision in a company mentioned earlier, the second longest process of all, which took longer not because of delays but because of careful sifting of information. Further, whilst the tendency is clear, it is at the same time small enough to indicate that delays are only one of the possible influences on the duration of decision-making.

Impediments and delays

Delays happen for all kinds of reasons. Nine reasons, that is nine kinds of impediments which cause delays in processes (r impedance . disruption = 0.7, beyond 99 per cent confidence) are listed in figure 4.2. They are arranged in ascending order of 'impedance' from least to most, that is the delays they bring are less and less controllable up the scale. Each decision process was scored by the highest point it reached on the scale, that is by the greatest impediment it encountered; but this is not a cumulative scale, and there is no presumption that a process has encountered all the impediments up to and including the point on which it is scored, although it can have done so.

The impediments which bring the disrupting delays range from incidental distractions through efforts to improve information, to coming up against resisting interests. The least impediment is nothing more than 'sequencing' (score 1), in effect waiting in a queue for the attention of executives preoccupied with other matters or moving up in an agenda or something equivalent. Impediments then escalate through 'co-ordinating', for example awaiting getting crucial people together at the same time and place; 'timing', for example the industrial investment decision referred to earlier awaiting market stabilization after the 1973 oil price rise before consideration of a possible new plant was resumed; the two facets of

Figure 4.2. IMPEDIMENTS TO THE DECISION-MAKING PROCESS

Of 150 decision-making processes, 42 had no
identifiable impediments of the kinds given below.
108 had impediments, as indicated. Each process is
placed on the scale at the point of its most serious
impediment.

NUMBER OF
DECISIONS

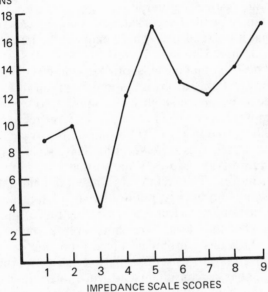

IMPEDANCE SCALE SCORES

The reasons given by informants for delays in decision
processes were coded on the following scale:

1. Sequencing; awaiting priority in the order of attention.

2. Co-ordinating; awaiting requirements becoming available.

3. Timing; awaiting an opportune time.

4. Searching; awaiting the obtaining or analyzing of data,
   either by direct action or by the action of other
   agencies.

5. Problem solving; awaiting, investigation of what is not
   understood.

6. Supplying; awaiting the availability of resources.

7. Recycling; awaiting reconsideration of what has already
   been gone over.

8. Internal resistance; awaiting the outcome of active
   internal opposition.

9. External resistance; awaiting the outcome of external
   opposition.

scrutiny, 'searching', such as analyzing costs or doing market research, and 'problem solving' where what is needed is available, but is assessed further, for example more testing of alternative designs, both of which the same company did through its many committees; 'supplying', that is waiting to be sure of potentially necessary resources before going further towards a decision; 're-cycling', that is reconsidering; and finally internal or external 'resistance', an interest getting in the way.

Nine kinds of impediment is a considerable number – and no claim can be made that it is exhaustive. There may well be more. Among the nine, the peaks in the graph in figure 4.2, from scale score four to nine, show that decision-making most often encounters delays due to searching for information, to investigations required to solve problems, to doubts over the availability of resources, to reconsidering once again what has already been gone over before (recycling), and to resistance either from inside or from outside the organization.

Most frequent of all, it is unsolved problems (scale score 5) or influential resistance (scale scores 8 and 9) that impede movement towards a conclusion. This reinforces the argument that both problem complexity and interest politicality shape decision-making processes, and corroborates Mintzberg's et al. (1976, pp. 263–4) suggestion that what they term 'interrupts' are due most often to 'new options', which raise further unsolved problems, or 'political impasses'. Unsolved problems set internal specialist departments or outside advisers, such as consultants, to work to try to clarify the situation. Influential interests, such as internal departments with strong views or externally a major customer or a head office, have to be reconciled, and that too takes time.

Of course, to those pressing for a decision which they believe will go their way, all impediments that bring delays are a frustration, whereas to others who fear that the choice will go against them, delays are a welcome relief, a respite, a chance to persuade their colleagues to change their minds. It is unfortunate to have to write of 'impediments' and 'delays' since both words carry a negative bias which implies that processes should not be delayed by impediments. But whether they should or should not be depends on the point of view of the participants in decision-making, and no point of view is intended to be conveyed here either way. It is just that no better words could be found.

Since searching for information can introduce delays into the process, it is also to be expected that the *more* who search, the longer the process will tend to be. More specialists preparing reports, more departments preparing figures, more external agencies preparing advice, mean it sometimes takes longer to reach a decision (*r* number of information units researching . process time = 0.2, at 99 per cent confidence). This affirms that scrutiny costs time, presenting managers and administrators with one of the constant difficulties of making decisions, whether to request more information knowing that to get it will take time, yet knowing that to wait for it may mean waiting too long. How much information is enough and how long a postponement of the decision is too long?

It seems better to spend time awaiting the results of scrutiny by the organization's own staff than awaiting the findings of outside experts. Executives have far greater confidence in the organization's employees who are familiar with the circumstances, and over whom they have some control, than they have in hired consultants, well-intentioned government officials, competitors with experience, or other external sources. As the saying goes, 'better the devil you know'.

Talking time: do committees slow things down?

Talking is the very stuff of decision-making, the activity that occupies most of the daily round for managers and administrators. There is talk on the telephone, talk in the hall way, talk around the office desk, talk over tea, and talk in meetings of every conceivable kind. Personal contact, the chance to talk, can be divided into informal and formal interaction. Informal interaction includes all the more casual forms of talking time, on phones, in offices, over meals, and so on. Formal interaction includes every size and shape of board, council, general committee (like an executive committee) and specialized committee (like a finance committee); and also relatively transient project groups, or working parties. That is, formal interaction covers all degrees of prearranged meetings by whatever name.

The very act of talking takes time, and it is therefore easily assumed that interaction protracts decision-making (Hage 1980, p. 121). The more chatter in the corridors of decision the longer it will take to get a decision. Across 150 cases, there is a little evidence for this; but it is slight and is only so for *in*formal interaction (*r* informal interaction . process time = 0.3, 95 per cent confidence). Obviously enough, longer processes are inclined to have more casual contacts and talks, but in itself that is only one factor in spinning them out.

There is not even that small an association between *formal* interaction and the length of processes. Formal interaction is common enough. Pre-arranged meetings, such as boards or committees or working parties, figure in all but four of the 150 cases, the average being between two and three such bodies. At the far extreme a budget review in a public utility, which was effectively also a major price decision, wound its way though 11 forms of meeting from a series of division level meetings to the central Policy and Resources Committee, the Corporate Management Team, meetings of divisional sections of the General Board on which representatives of the public sit, and the full Board.

Yet the number of forms of meeting, or committee, to use a convenient word in a very broad sense, through which a topic for decision passes is completely unrelated to the time taken to arrive at a decision (*r* formality . process time = 0.1, formality being the number of forms of committee in the process). *More forms of committee does not mean taking longer to make a decision.*

There must be care in interpretation here. This is the number of distinct committees, as in the decision which passed through 11 kinds, and not the number of times each met nor how long its meetings took, which are not known. Nevertheless, it does match the finding by the DIO International Research Team (1983) that passing a decision through a works council or through many managerial hands does not increase the time it takes in total: and it does imply that committees can speed things up as much as slow them down. Those who suffer in committees on long hot afternoons, and are inclined to remark that 'people lie as they sit in standing committees', and similar cynicisms, will feel incredulous at this implication. How can it be?

First, the time they personally spend in meetings about decisions must be separated from the time a decision process takes to reach an outcome. Individuals personally spending a lot of their time in meetings is not the same as a decision taking a long time, although the one colours the perception of the other. Committee members to whom life at times seems nothing but incessant meetings, understandably feel that these meetings slow down decision-making as much as their own work is slowed down. Not so, however. The approach of a regular meeting of a standing committee can actually prompt work to be done, such as a report, which might otherwise be left aside; and whilst delays can be caused by items on agendas being left over to subsequent meetings, or by committee indecision, it is also possible for a chairperson or an interested party to force a conclusion sooner than might otherwise have happened.

Second, the length of time for which a committee meets, which is the focus of attention for those who want to get out of the room, must be separated from the time it takes for a topic to pass through that committee and on to another. It is quite feasible for working parties, committees, and a board all to meet in quick succession, or for one to meet virtually continuously as did the Toxicem Development Committee which met during 'fortnights of afternoons' about the new chemical product 'bluestuff'. Several committees meeting one after the other during a few days or weeks can despatch a topic pretty rapidly, however drawn out the meetings of each one may be and however tiresome to their individual members.

Therefore it seems that the occasions when committees delay decision-making are offset by the occasions when they spur it on. The budget review cum price decision, which passed through 11 forms of committee, was completed in only six months, since it passed smoothly from one to another. In short, although a labour cost is incurred in individual member time, *scrutiny by committee costs no more decision time than any other way of doing things*.

This is, of course, an analysis within a set of British-managed and British-owned organizations in Britain, except for two. These two were the *British-managed* subsidiaries of *American-owned* multinational corporations, which in a detailed comparison we have presented elsewhere (Mallory, et al. 1983), seemed to be influenced by an American approach to management transmitted from afar. This impelled faster decisions with informally assembled working groups, compared to rather slower decisions in similar British-owned firms which had standing committees. Although it comes from only a small number of cases, this is an intriguing possibility, that the making of decisions by managements under British ownership is beset by the standing committee, a form of committee that might be slower. It is a pity that this cannot be pursued further with the available data.

Three ways of making decisions

So far, the answer to the question, 'how do the processes that ensue from the problems and interests thrown up by a decision differ one from the other?', has been in terms of their progress through time. They appear to move unsteadily from phase to phase, lasting anything from a few months to a few years. They can be delayed for many reasons, most commonly and obviously by pauses whilst information is sought, and by resistance to the course being followed. It is less obvious that having more forms of meetings and committees does *not* protract matters, on average, since they can as often speed things up as slow things down.

This is a general idea of how a subject or decision progresses over time from its advent to its outcome, from its formation to the choice of what shall, or shall not, be done. However, this description of movement over time does not characterize *different kinds of movement*. What kinds of movement, what kinds of process, may there be?

The Bradford studies data suggest three ways of making decisions. Fortunately three is an easily comprehensible number, for a fundamental problem in all research is how many kinds of anything make sense? Categories are useful when they clarify complicated material by grouping large numbers of cases into many fewer and much simpler types. Athough the 16 categories construed by Stein (1981b) from 63 questionnaires, and the seven process categories proposed by Mintzberg, et al (1976) from 25 decisions, made some advance in this direction, much more remained to be done since each categorization was based on no more than three or four cases per category and was itself still complicated. Three types, each based on 40 to 50 cases, is a further step, though surely not a final step. Finality in research is a dream if not a myth, and there must come a day when a different three, or a number other than three, is found to be better. Until that day, these three ways may serve to give a grasp on the essential nature of processes of strategic decision-making.

They are not ways of working out answers to cognitive problems. Problem-solving is about setting out alternative solutions and comparing them. These three ways of making decisions are about how a topic passes through the many hands in an organization to the point where a choice is authorized. Each describes a type of organizational, or social, process at the level of top management or administration. Whilst each is a sketch rather than a drawing complete in every detail, the outlines are clearly there.

They are outlines of *sporadic processes, fluid processes*, and *constricted processes*. The three types are derived from analysis of 136 processes on which data in the required form was complete. In addition to the characteristics of process already discussed, namely process time, disruption by delays, the impedance which causes the delays, and formal and informal interaction, seven other variables were used in the analysis.

They are shown in table 4.1. The first four, under the heading of 'scrutiny', all concern information. 'Expertise' is the number of

Table 4.1 Dimensions of process

Twelve process variables	Loadings of 10 variables on two dimensions of process (n = 136)	
	Discontinuity	*Dispersion*
Scrutiny (information sources)		
Expertise	0.35	−0.24
Confidence disparity	0.51	0.03
Externality	—	—
Effort	0.00	0.28
Interaction		
Formal	−0.35	0.29
Informal	0.24	0.05
Negotiation scope	0.08	0.38
Flow		
Disruption	0.36	0.04
Impedance	0.54	−0.05
Duration		
Gestation time	—	—
Process time	0.33	−0.16
Authority		
Level in hierarchy	−0.01	0.91

internal and external sources, from staff experts to consultants or other organizations in the same field, from which information comes; 'disparity' is the variability in the quality of that information, as indicated by the differing confidence that management had in its sources; 'externality' is the extent to which information from external sources contributed to the reduction of uncertainty; and 'effort' is how information was acquired, from merely having it on hand in people's personal experience and knowledge, to having it accessible in records, to research to collect it, to creating it by meetings or other means that synthesized it from disparate sources. In addition to formal and informal interaction (meetings versus more casual contacts), the 'interaction' heading includes a feature of the content of the interaction, 'negotiation scope', represented by a scale of seven ordered categories running from the decision not being open to negotiation at all, for example when the chief executive forces a conclusion and leaves little room for negotiation among the others interested, to so much negotiation that a decision is made when discussion is still inconclusive and dissent persists. There follow the 'disruption' of the process by delays, and the impediments encountered; and gestation time and process time, as defined earlier. Finally there is the 'authority level' within or above the organization where the process ends in an authorized decision, following which implementation can legitimately proceed. The lowest level at which such a decision was authorized was the semi-autonomous division, the highest was at national or international headquarters, and in between were the chief executive and board levels or equivalent. All these measures are detailed in the Appendix.

It had been apparent from personal familiarity with the case histories that some decisions were made in a more fluent way than others, but analysis beyond this general intuition was required to sort through the large number of cases each described by 12 process characteristics to see whether a pattern could be discerned. Hierarchical cluster analysis was used to work out a three-fold clustering or grouping of cases (by progressively minimizing the error sum of squares within clusters), in which the cases in each group have more similarities than they have with those in the other groups (Cray, et al. 1985), and, most vitally, each is a *meaningful* type (Anderberg 1973, p. 183; Everitt 1974, p. 59). Each denotes something substantial about processes, and together the three are a balanced representation, for the cases divide evenly between them into clusters of 53, 42, and 41 processes. About a third of all strategic decisions are made in each way.

Sporadic processes

The first of the three ways in which a strategic decision may be made is through a *sporadic* type of process. A summary of the characteristics of this and the other two types appears in figure 4.3. By comparison with decisions reached by fluid or constricted processes, a decision made in a sporadic way is likely to have run into more disrupting delays, due to all kinds of impediments, from having to await a report to meeting resistance. The information that came in

Figure 4.3. THREE WAYS OF MAKING DECISIONS (names of variables in italics)

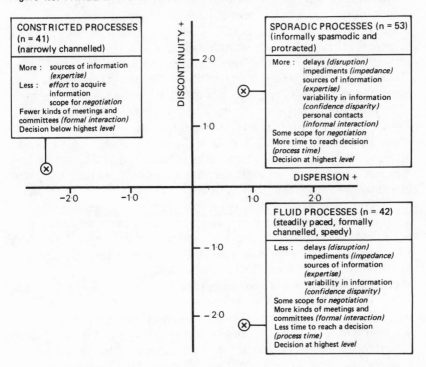

will have been of more uneven quality, for in some of it there was confidence and in some of it there was little or none, and it will have come from a wider range of sources. There will have been some scope for negotiation during a great deal of informal contact and on-and-off discussion. It will have taken longer to get to a decision, and this eventually will have been made at the highest level. That is, in terms of the variables summarized in figure 4.3, the process will probably have shown higher impedance, higher disruption, more sources of expertise, between which there are greater differences in the confidence placed in their information and views, more informal interaction, some negotiation, longer process time, and final authorization at a higher level.

This means that in a full third of the occasions when top managers or administrators enter upon a decision, they are likely to have begun on a twisting trail that will not end for a year or two, or even longer. As they make their way along it they will come up against all sorts of obstacles that delay direct movement towards a conclusion. They may have to turn aside whilst staff experts prepare fresh estimates or reassess capacity, they may have to pause until the time is judged right to move on, or have to take time to negotiate among themselves and with outsiders such as banks or customers. They will probably find that not all the information they get can be relied upon, so they and their staff will have to sift out that which they feel they have confidence in, and that which is better ignored. They will be drawn into bursts of activity in corridors and offices, in between the delays, when the matter is on everyone's mind and answers to questions are demanded there and then, until the excitement dies down as other things become even more pressing and demand attention. *In brief, a sporadic type of decision-making process is one that is informally spasmodic and protracted.*

For example, it was a sporadic process that brought the management of a nationalized industry to the decision to buy a one-third share in a firm that was a large purchaser of its products. This decision was an attempt to ensure future sales in a situation where either other interested parties might take complete control of the firm, or the firm might go out of business. Two multinational oil corporations, a multinational chemical corporation, and another very large nationalized industry were all involved, as well as the prospective subsidiary itself and the local government for its area. The prospective subsidiary wanted assured funds for expansion, and all the other interests wanted to expand or at least to protect the firm's demand for their own products. The local government, on the other hand, resisted expansion on ecological grounds.

The decision-making process in this nationalized industry moved in fits and starts. Spasms of work by departmental staff to produce forecasts of future output and costs, and to give estimates of the investment the subsidiary might make in new plant if it received an injection of fresh capital, and similar spasms of hectic toing and froing amongst senior managers, were broken by pauses whilst the reactions of the other powerful interests to reports and proposals were awaited. The financial grounds for injecting new capital by means of a takeover were very much in doubt. Time passed while successive reports and proposals were tossed backwards and forwards between the organizations concerned, and renegotiated to suit their differing interests, until after 18 months an agreement was reached. The Board of the nationalized industry made a commitment to take a one-third share in its customer firm, along with one of the oil corporations and the other state-owned industry, each of which also took one-third. A difficult uneven process came to an end.

Another prime example of a sporadic process was the hotly contested Toxicem decision, the story of which began this book. As the reader may recall, allies were sought, and opposing positions disputed until after three years the process was forced to a finish.

Fluid processes

Fluid processes as their name suggests are in most ways quite the opposite of sporadic processes. Although they, too, leave scope for negotiation, there is not nearly so much informal activity along the corridors of decision in the executive suite or administrative block, for more is handled in the relatively formal settings of meetings. More of the discussion is channelled through pre-arranged project groups, working parties, sub-committees, committees, boards and the like, and there is less hubbub in between. Impediments and delays are less likely. Fewer sources of expertise are called upon, and there is a comparatively uniform degree of confidence in their information and views. Though the decision is likely to be taken at a similarly high level, it will be reached much more quickly, in months rather than years. In terms of the variables summarized in figure 4.3, a fluid process therefore is probably comparatively less disrupted, less impeded, has fewer sources of expertise with confidence more evenly placed in each, passes through more kinds of committees, sees some negotiation, and in a shorter time reaches an outcome at a high level of authorization.

This means that almost a third of strategic decisions at the top flow along fairly fluently to quite a quick decision. In this type of process, managers and administrators attend a greater number of committees and kindred bodies, but far from getting in the way, these formally-arranged proceedings seem to facilitate a rapid conclusion, as the earlier discussion of committees suggested. While any one meeting may be frustratingly fruitless, the arranging of meetings makes sure that things move along, if not during the meetings then in between them, in anticipation of them. In these processes, there are fewer occasions when it is necessary to wait for the timing to be right, or for reports to be compiled, or for opposition to be reconciled. It is possible to move ahead comparatively steadily with at least a clear degree of confidence in the information gleaned, even if the level of confidence is less than desirable, and despite there being some scope for negotiation over the possible decision. *In brief, a fluid type of decision-making process is one that is steadily paced, formally channelled and speedy.*

The stories of two fluidly processed decisions have already been told in this chapter. The first was an example of a short process, the other an example of an average length process (the tendency of fluid processes to be shorter does not mean that none of them are of average duration, but that they tend to be average or below, rather than above average). The first is the decision in a metropolitan municipality to venture into the realms of chance by launching a lottery to augment the normal funds from local taxpayers and the national government. In not much more than a month, following the return of the leader of the council from a holiday during which he had become enthused by the idea, the proposal for a lottery was manoeuvred through a local government committee structure that was not prepared for it. With the main opposition party lukewarm and probably inattentive, outright resistance coming only from within a minority third party, and with officials failing to find any causes for procedural delays, the proposal went through the Management Board of senior officials, the Finance Committee of the municipal council, the full council, and into the hands of a specially created Lottery Sub-Committee in no time, including having gained the necessary permit from the authorities regulating gaming. It seems significant that the influential individual who brought the idea back from the seaside was both leader of the controlling party in the full council, and chairman of the vital Finance Committee.

This was a fluid process conducted properly and openly via formal meetings and committees, yet so smooth and fast as to be over probably before many politicians and officials had fully grasped the implications of what was happening.

The other fluid process was that of the savings bank whose management took the decision to upgrade it to the status of a cheque-issuing bank by applying for membership of the big banks' 'clearing house'. Essentially, the process of reaching the decision was very simple. It revolved around the deliberations of a special Working Committee of senior managers set up to consider the matter. This met constantly, steadily collating information with which to assess the costs of admission to the clearing house and of competing in the wider and tougher market that would be opened up, and sounding out competitor banks and the Bank of England on the chances of admission. In about a year the main Board had accepted the committee's recommendation to make this radical move, which if successful would transform the business. Here again this was a smooth committee-focused process ending at the highest level.

The contrast between fluid processes and sporadic processes shares something with that frequently made between 'rational' and 'political' decision-making, the rational flowing more evenly and the political more turbulently (Miles 1980, p. 181). Likewise the types of processes put forward by Mintzberg, et al. (1976) range from comparatively uninterrupted 'search' and 'design' kinds to those that are more 'blocked' and 'political'. We would resist any implication that sporadic processes are not guided by rationalities, a point that we will return to – but this having been said, the sporadic-fluid distinction fits a broad difference in the nature of decision-making that has often been intuitively assumed and alluded to.

Constricted processes

At first sight, the third type of process, *constricted*, seems sharply different from the fluid type and more akin to the sporadic. A constricted process can share some of the delays of a sporadic process, more so than a fluid at any rate, and also like the sporadics it draws on numerous sources for information and views, and is not so committee-focused. However, a second look at the summary in figure 4.3 shows that it is as different from the sporadic type as it is from the fluid. It allows less scope for negotiation about the decision, and that decision is made at a level below the highest point – though still high in the hierarchy, of course, since it is a strategic decision. Thus it is a process less fluid than the fluids and less sporadic than the sporadics.

The unique character of a constricted process is that it tends to be more held in, more restrained, than either of the other two types. Although it draws on the information and views of quite a few departmental and external experts, what is needed is readily available and requires no great effort to obtain it. No special investigations are undertaken outside the organization itself, and internally there are no undue difficulties in reconciling and synthesizing disparate material. The process is neither so informally active as sporadic processes tend to be, nor so formally active within meetings and committees as fluid processes tend to be. It ends with a decision that does not have to be made by a higher headquarters or board, but can probably be made by the chief executive without higher recourse. In the wording of the variables in italics in figure 4.3, it probably brings in expertise that can provide information and views with no great effort, it does not give much scope for negotiation nor figure much on the agendas of formal committees and the like, and it can be made at a chief executive or similar level.

This means that almost another third of strategic decisions are likely to be arrived at in a way that does not stir up so much activity as the other types of processes do. The pertinent facts and figures are already in being or can be easily put together, and to get hold of them it is only necessary to pick up the phone and ask whoever has them at his or her fingertips, or could make a routine calculation. There is not much in this to negotiate about, and the matter does not generate much coming and going between offices, nor is there any reason to set up a special project team or working party or sub-committee. It does not concern all the committees, anyway, but can go through with just the approval of a local board, or whatever. Many of those in mangement are not closely involved, and the process moves in well-worn channels under the control of the chief executive, who takes the final decision. In brief, *a constricted type of decision-making process is one that is narrowly channelled.*

A decision to modernize an insurance company was made in this way. On the surface it was merely a commitment to updating and centralizing the data processing for the main line of business, vehicle insurance, but as with a number of the other cases its significance for those concerned was in a wider context. The company had been taken over by a larger firm, and, despite assurances, its top managers recognized that there was a risk of its business being absorbed into that of the parent and the company being obliterated as a working organization. They realized that the best defence was for the parent company's management to see the subsidiary as a good profit-earner which should not be disturbed. The company was already in a leading position in its sector of the market, so that the range of insurance offered and the sales approach were felt to be as good as possible. Any move to ensure continued profitability and, equally important, to sustain an image as a vigorous up-to-the-minute enterprise had therefore to be in the direction of improving administration and organization.

The decision process circled around the chief executive within whose purview it legitimately came, never far out of his hands. There was no committee work, not even a special task force or group to work out details. Approval from the board of directors sitting as a board was not needed, though individual directors knew what was in the wind. The motor insurance department, the claims department, and other departments where appropriate, produced analyses of the existing system and what would be required of any new system. Externally, IBM were quick to offer their sales and advisory services, the insurance industry trade association was contacted about experience elsewhere, and some of the larger brokers who handled business for the company confided what competitors were doing. In just a few months, with no real delays, it was decided that a reorganization of the administration based on centralized microfilm records ought both to raise earnings by improving the premium-to-expenses ratio, and improve efficiency in the field by speeding up the calculations of premiums and cover sent out to sales agents. This, it was felt, would go as far as anything else could do to ensure company autonomy.

A constricted process may always be a possibility when there is a good base of information to start with, or where at least one can be assembled without too much effort. A corporate plan, for example, does not have to start from scratch but can begin where the previous one left off. It can proceed from the principal estimates on which the

previous plan was constructed, projecting them forwards. Departments can simply be asked to update their forecasts, which they are
well used to doing.

How the types differ

The core differences and similarities between the three types of
process can be expressed in just two words, their *discontinuity* and
their *dispersion*. Sporadic processes are inclined to be more *discontinuous*, fluid processes more *con*tinuous. Whilst both are similarly
dispersed throughout management, this is where constricted processes differ from them, for constricted processes, as their name
states, are the very opposite to dispersed.

Discontinuity and dispersion are the two dimensions in figure 4.3
against which the typical characteristics of each kind of process are
summarized. On the vertical dimension, processes towards the
discontinuous extreme at the top of the figure are relatively uneven
and broken, whereas those towards the continuous extreme at the
bottom are relatively even and unbroken. On the lateral dimension,
dispersion, processes towards the right of the figure spread relatively
widely through the management structure of an organization,
whereas those towards the left run within smaller confines.

The dimensions emerged from discriminant analysis aimed at
throwing into relief the essence of what makes one type of process
different from another (see also Appendix E). Whilst each type has a
profile of probable characteristics, what exactly is it about these
characteristics that makes the profiles different? The analysis yielded
the loadings of the process variables on the two dimensions as given
in table 4.1 (loadings indicate which variables contribute most
and least to the differentiation of the cases along the dimensions).
No loadings are given for two variables that failed to discriminate
significantly, confidence externality and gestation time. There can be
confidence in external expertise, or lack of confidence, in any type of
process just as much as another, and all types of process are equally
likely or unlikely to be preceded by a gestation period.

The features that most distinctively pick out one type of process
from another are indicated by the variables with the highest
loadings. Briefly, disruption, impedance, expertise, confidence dis-

parity, lack of formal interaction (negative loading), informal interaction, and length of process time, separate the discontinuous from the continuous types – in other words, the sporadic from the fluid. Lack of expertise (negative loading), effort, formal interaction, scope for negotiation, and decisions at the highest level, separate the dispersed from the non-dispersed types – in other words, the sporadic and fluid types (each of which is moderately dispersed) from the constricted. It is from these loadings, supplemented with case knowledge, that the profile summaries of sporadics, fluids, and constricteds in figure 4.3 are formed.

Distilling out the essence of what makes one type of process different from another makes it unnecessary to list variables as in the preceding paragraph. It condenses the main differences. These underlying variables can then be left behind, and the types simply distinguished just by how discontinuous each is, and how dispersed.

This is what figure 4.3 does. It positions the profile description of each type against discontinuity and dispersion in a way that indicates approximately where the type stands in relation to the others. An X shows the group mean (centroid) of each cluster of like cases in terms of standardized scores from +2 to −2 on each dimension.

The X around which the sporadic type processes cluster is high on discontinuity, and also out on the right towards dispersion (cluster means of 1.49 and 0.88 respectively). So the essence of the difference between sporadic type processes and any others, is that they are the most discontinuous, as has become very clear, and that they disperse through the managerial hierarchy to involve people far and wide. They are *informally spasmodic and protracted*, as said earlier, *more discontinuous than the fluid type, and more dispersed than the constricted type*.

The X for fluid type processes, as to be expected, is low on discontinuity, but the same as the sporadic type on dispersion (cluster means of −2.06 and 0.87 respectively). So the essence of the distinctive character of fluid processes is their continuity, whilst they share with sporadic processes the involving of many people throughout the hierarchy. *They are steadily paced, formally channelled, and speedy, more continuous than the sporadic type and more dispersed than the constricted type*.

The X for constricted type processes instantly picks out their essential nature. Whilst they are merely middling in terms of discontinuity, they are far to the left on dispersion – that is, they are non-dispersed (cluster means of 0.19 and −2.03 respectively). They do *not* permeate all through the organization. *They are narrowly channelled, less dispersed than either the sporadic type or the constricted type.*

This much about the three ways of making decisions had already become apparent. The dimensional analysis confirms and restates it. The analysis shows which cases of decisions are most typical of each type by the positioning of the cases on discontinuity and dispersion, so there can be confidence that the descriptions earlier of the decisions to buy a joint one-third share in the customer firm of a nationalized industry, to launch a municipal lottery, to raise the status and extend the functions of a bank, and to update the administration of an insurance company, are as true to the types of process they illustrate as possible. For the summaries in figure 4.3 are stereotypes, statements of the full character of type to which no one case fits exactly in every respect. Each type is actually a cluster of processes which shade away from those most like it to those least like it. Some sporadics are more sporadic than others, some fluids are more fluid than others, some constricteds are more constricted than others.

Fundamentals of process

This analysis, which defines discontinuity and dispersion and enables the types to be positioned on them, does more than that. It also suggests something fundamental about the ways in which decisions are made. It suggests that these two dimensions, discontinuity and dispersion, are fundamental elements of process. Once it is recognized how far a decision-making process was discontinuous, and once it is recognized how far it was dispersed, then these two concepts alone have revealed a great deal about how the decision was made. A lot has been said about decision-making when it can be recognized and described as an uneven and widespread process (here called sporadic), or even and widespread (fluid), or closely channelled (constricted). These two concepts of what is going on, its discontinuity and its dispersion, penetrate the basic character of process and can describe quite simply the stuff of which it is made.

The question why

So the making of decisions by top managers and administrators can be portrayed on two fundamental dimensions. These draw the contrasts between three types of process, the sporadic, the fluid, and the constricted. The question now must be why the three types occur.

This chapter and the two previous chapters have maintained that the process of making a decision arises from the problems and interests inherent in its subject matter. The *complexity* of these problems – including their consequentiality and multiple involvements, in particular, has been examined; and so has the *politicality* of the interests – their influence and the pressure exerted on a decision. Do the three types of process indeed arise from differences in problems and interests? Why when a decision is reached is it reached in one way rather than in another?

Part II of the book turns to this major question. It asks what explains process. What are the reasons for a sporadic type or a fluid type or a constricted type? Could it be enough to know that a decision is about a new product or about a reorganization, or about a plan or a budget, to understand which kind of decision-making takes place? That is, does the *topic* of decision explain process? Or is this just a handy but superficial label, and to understand what happens it is indeed necessary to delve beneath the topic label into *the problems and the interests* in the matter? Or could it be that the answer does not lie in the substance of the decision at all but in the *organization* where the decision process takes place? Perhaps decisions in some kinds of organizations are always made in a certain way, and those in other organizations are always made in other ways? If so, can the ownership or purpose of an organization explain how its management or administration takes decisions?

Part II
Explanations of
Decision-Making
Processes

5

Topics and Decision-Making

Decision or organization

Three types of decision processes were suggested in the previous chapter; the first characteristically sporadic; the second characteristically fluid; the third characteristically constricted. What reasons can be found to explain their differences? Although the differences between the three are not in practice clear-cut, for they are darker patches in a field of grey rather than black or white, each decision process inclines towards one or the other. Why should it? This chapter and the next two chapters try to put together an explanation.

A decision-making process does not materialize out of thin air, though to anyone not in the right circles or not there at its inception it may appear to do so. Perhaps there has been a feeling in the board room for a long time that things are not going as well as they might, as, for example, there was in one particular case of a fluid process in a leading financial institution, which led to a decision to change the organization's structure.

Business had expanded hugely over the years and whilst this undeniably represented a sustained success in selling what the organization had to offer, it put a load on the framework of the organization itself that it was not designed to bear. A gradually increasing unease about this prompted an examination of the structure of the organization, and led to a decision to insert a regional level into the hierarchy between local branch managers and the top. It represented a radical change in the view of how management should and would work.

This reorganization arose from internal management difficulties.

By contrast, another fluid process in a road transport company that led to a decision to go into the selling of Italian truck bodies, arose from a mixture of problems with their existing sales and a market opportunity. Alongside its original road haulage work, the company already sold trucks, importing the truck chassis and engines and then subconstracting the fitting of bodywork. This subcontracting was expensive and unreliable, and the buyers of trucks were often kept waiting. When the possibility of obtaining bodies which the firm's own workforce could fit was looked into, it was also realized that there was a market niche for a certain range of Italian-made truck bodies. Hence, having added the sales of trucks to its traditional road haulage service, the company now went further by deciding to add vehicle body fitting to its range of activities.

In such ways decision-making processes begin, and continue, as top managers and administrators take action according to an internal or external pressure or event. What they do about it becomes a sporadic, or a fluid, or a constricted type of process. This poses the question whether the type of process is due to the substance of the decision itself, or to the framework of the organization in which it is being made? *Which is of more significance, the matter for decision or the organization? Which better explains the decision-making process?*

On the one hand, the *matter for decision* itself must affect the route to a conclusion because the route is made by its passage and may not be visible beforehand. It is the doubts and the divisions over a reorganization, or the opportunism and the attitudes over a new service or product, that sway each move made and so shape the route taken. Because there are doubts, investigations and reports may be called for, and because there are divisions of opinion, a sub-committee may be set up to sort them out. Because there is an opportunity and attitudes are expansionist, no time may be wasted in making a quick decision with a minimum of consideration.

On the other hand, the decision may travel the route that it does because it is occurring in an *organization* where there are customary routes to follow. Perhaps because the organization is large and publicly-owned there are proper procedures which have to be conformed to. All proposals with financial implications must be seen by the Finance Committee before they are seen by the Board, and the Board will never accept a proposal without full documentation. So proposals go to the Finance Committee first, followed by a period spent completing documentation, followed by Board consideration.

That part of the route is already laid out.

This chapter now examines the relationship between process and the topic that describes the matter for decision; chapter 6 examines the relationship between process and the problems and interests inherent in that matter; and chapter 7 examines the relationship between process and organization.

Different topics, different processes

The quest for explanation begins with topics, the labels attached by those involved to the matter for decision, calling it the new product or service decision, the rebuilding or re-equipping decision, the divisionalized structure decision, or the corporate plan decision. For it springs to mind immediately that with such a range of different topics, decisions on one topic may be made in a different way to decisions on another.

Process profiles for decision topics

The classifying of topics into ten categories was described in chapter 2. In order of frequency of occurrence they were topics on technology (equipment and buildings), reorganization, controls (plans, budgets, data processing), domain (market or field of operation), services, products, personnel, boundaries (takeovers and mergers), inputs (of money or materials), and location (site of headquarters or plant).

Bar charts which profile the types of process for each category of topic appear in figure 5.1. They show the number of processes of a sporadic, fluid or constricted type for each topic label. For example, there were ten decisions on product topics among the 136 cases included in figure 5.1, six of which went through sporadically, none fluidly, and four constrictedly.

The topic categories are brought together in the figure in four groups, from left to right the *non-fluid*, the *non-constricted*, the *non-sporadic*, and the *non-discriminatory*. The fourth non-discriminatory grouping is those categories of topic which it appears can be processed in any of the three ways, whereas the first, second, and third groupings each bias against one type of process.

Figure 5.1. PROCESS DIFFERENCES BETWEEN TOPICS

n = 136 (Data missing on 14 processes)
S = Sporadic Processes
F = Fluid Processes
C = Constricted Processes

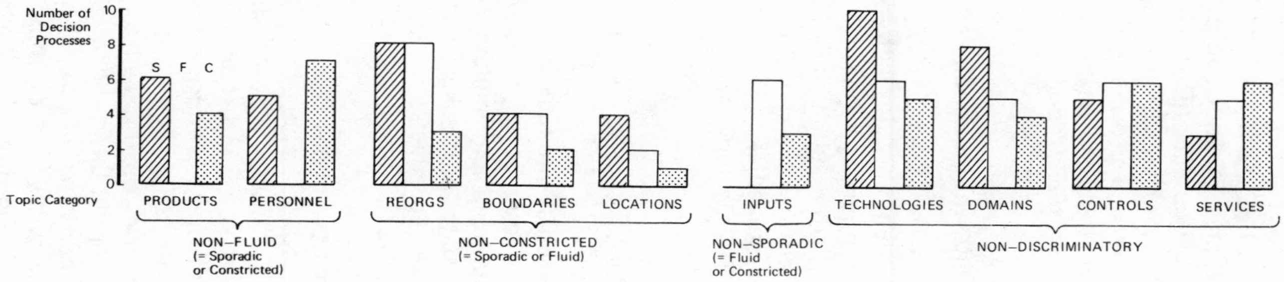

The non-fluid group of product and personnel decision topics shows not a single instance of a fluid process. It would seem that they cannot be got through in this evenly-paced, formally-channelled manner. They must undergo either the more intense oscillating activity of a sporadic process, or be held 'closer to the chest' of a top executive within the more routine channels of a constricted process. The sporadic processes are the more liable to encounter delays and impediments, but constricted processes also can do so, so that in terms of the dimensions which summarize and express the main differences between the types of process, discontinuity and dispersion, product and personnel decisions can be described as discontinuous. Their route to a conclusion tends to be uneven and interrupted.

It is significant that all the non-constricted topics in the second group are concerned in one way or another with the form of the organization itself, a point that will be returned to later. Reorganizations concern internal restructuring, boundaries concern takeovers and mergers, and locations concern where to place the whole or a part of the organization. These sorts of topics are unlikely to be handled in a constricted way (only 14 per cent are constricted in figure 5.1). The making of decisions about them cannot be held within tight bounds, but moves in a wider arena. So far as decisions about the organization itself are concerned, whether over rearranging its parts, combining it with another, or moving it somewhere else, there are insufficient 'hard' data and too many viewpoints for the process to stay within narrow channels. The process spreads throughout the organization, drawing in everyone and everything – in the managerial echelons anyway – before it is done with. In a single word, it is dispersed, for both sporadic and fluid types of process are high on dispersion, the second of the two dimensions that differentiate the types.

The non-sporadic third grouping includes only inputs decisions. More than any other kind of decision, they are likely to be processed fluidly in a speedy uninterrupted formally defined fashion, or to be among the smoother constricted processes. In a word, they are highly continuous. What they do not do is arouse the spasmodic activity of sporadic processing.

Too much should not be made of differences between decision topics since, despite the large total number of cases, when these are split into ten categories of topic the number in each category is relatively small. Bearing this in mind, the non-fluid, non-constricted, and non-sporadic groupings imply that product and personnel decisions are liable to be sporadic or constricted, never fluid, reorganization, boundary, and location decisions seem liable to be sporadic or fluid, never constricted; and inputs decisions seem liable to be fluid or constricted, never sporadic. In terms of discontinuity and dispersion, the first group of topics tend towards discontinuous processes, the second to dispersed processes, the third to continuous processes.

Processing the most strategic of the strategic

A clue as to what it is that might make one type of process more likely than another can be found in the distinction in chapter 2 between the more strategic and the less strategic decisions. Analysis there suggested that the most strategic of the strategic were location, reorganization, and product topics, whereas inputs topics were least strategic. Locations, reorganizations, and products are all in the non-fluid and non-constricted groupings; whereas inputs constitute the non-sporadic grouping. The contrast is sharpened by focusing on sporadic processes only. Not one inputs decision was made in sporadic fashion (and merely three services decisions, services being the other least strategic category referred to in chapter 2), whereas taking the non-fluid and non-constricted groupings together, almost half the decisions, that is almost half the product, personnel, reorganization, boundary, and location decisions, were made sporadically. The more strategic the decision, the more likely is a sporadic process.

This means that because of their extra strategic qualities, decisions to venture a new product, or to reorganize and merge departments, or to shift the corporation lock, stock and barrel to the other end of the country, for example, are very prone to spasmodically active, protracted processes. They are not likely to run smooth and fast, and are most likely to be drawn out and intricate affairs, because of the complexity of the information and views taken into account, and the obstacles which crop up.

However, there is more that can be said about the typical processing of each topic, and the possible reasons why – both problem complexity and interest politicality – than is conveyed by an overall view of the groupings in figure 5.1. The groupings serve to give perspective, but within and between them the differences from one topic to the next are sufficiently great as to require that each is looked at separately. How, then, is each sort of decision made? In more detail, how is a product topic dealt with, a personnel question, a reorganization, a takeover bid, and so on? And why?

The topics are discussed in sequence group by group, beginning with the non-fluid product and personnel topics.

Processes which do not run smoothly: product and personnel decisions

Product decisions

Highly strategic new product decisions are not the sort of topic that would be expected to have much chance of being fluidly processed. The consequences of deciding to launch a new product tend to be far too serious and to reverberate through the organization. Success will carry the organization forward, failure will hold it back. Reputations will be made or unmade – the Toxicem decision to produce electricity was a vivid instance of this. The effects, good or bad, will be felt for years afterwards. Parameters will be set for subsequent decisions about markets and supplies and investment, and the organization's overall strategy, witting or unwitting, will have taken another step.

The complexity of a product decision is accentuated by diversity in the make-up of the decision-set of involved interests. A count of the numbers of different categories of interest units involved in decision-making processes at one point or another, from the 14 categories of internal departments and external organizations-in-contact described earlier (table 2.6, chapter 2), shows products decisions to be far above average. As they are at the heart of what a manufacturing firm is all about, and their consequences are so diffuse, everyone pushes in or is pulled in. The big three specialisms, production, sales, and accounting, all make their estimates and give their opinions. The work and views of the research and development department are the foundation for any new product, and most

Table 5.1 Influence of interest units on different topics for decision
(n = 1,021 ratings of interest unit influences)

Interest units** ranked from most to least mean influence overall (as in table 3.1)	Topic catcogory									
	Products	Personnels	Reorganiz-ations	Boundaries	Locations	Inputs	Tech-nologies	Domains	Controls	Services
(1) Liaison and claims departments	3.0	3.3*	3.7*	5.0*	—	—	4.0+	2.5	3.7*	4.3*
(2) Sales, marketing	3.8*	1.0	3.1*	5.0*	5.0*	2.7	3.4*	4.0*	3.9*	2.4
(3) Customers, clients	3.6*	—	—	—	3.0	2.4	3.5*	3.6*	3.0	2.8
(4) Production and equivalent	2.8	3.1*	3.0	3.3*	3.9*	3.6*	3.9*	2.6	3.0	2.6
(5) Self-sufficient divisions etc.	2.0	1.5	3.0	2.3	2.9	2.0	3.2*	3.0	3.3*	3.7*
(6) Research and/or design departments	4.1*	2.0	1.7	1.5	—	—	2.8	—	2.7	—
(7) Accounting, quality control, inspection	2.4	2.3	3.1*	2.9	3.3*	2.6	2.9	2.6	3.3*	1.7
(8) Auditors, trade associations, shareholders	3.0	3.3*	2.8	2.6	3.4*	3.7*	2.4	2.4	3.2	2.6
(9) Maintenance, personnel, etc.	1.2	3.0	3.3*	—	3.3*	1.0	2.8	2.8	2.0	3.3*
(10) Supplier firms	2.6	1.5	2.8	3.6*	2.5	2.8	2.9	2.6	2.6	2.1
(11) Government departments and agencies	3.0	2.7	3.0	3.0	3.5*	2.0	2.1	4.0*	2.3	2.7
(12) Purchasing	2.4	—	—	—	3.0	3.0	3.0	—	2.0	—
(13) Competitors	2.8	4.0+	1.9	2.7	—	4.0+	2.0	3.0	2.0	3.0
(14) Trades unions	1.3	3.2*	2.6	3.0	2.0	—	1.0	—	2.0	3.0
Means of all ratings	3.0	2.9	3.1	3.1	3.4	3.0	3.0	3.0	3.1	3.0

**External interest units underlined

* indicates means higher than the overall mean for the table of 3.05.

+ indicates high means from only one or two cases in the cell.

other departments come in somewhere along the way. Major customers, suppliers, and competitors are consulted or considered, together with government, usually in discussions with the Department of Industry over a grant towards expansion of premises.

This is broadly reflected in the first column of mean influence scores in table 5.1 which shows every one of the 14 categories of interest unit exerting some influence. The table breaks down the overall influence ratings in table 3.1, chapter 3, to show how much influence was exerted, on average, upon each separate topic. (Some caution must be observed in interpreting it, for dividing even as many as 1,021 ratings of influence, the total in all cases taken together, between 14 categories of interest units and ten topic categories makes small numbers in some cells, though the average for the table is over eight interest unit ratings per cell). This visible face of power, as it was called earlier, is also shown for product decisions in graph form in figure 5.2a. It shows that though the internal heavyweights, sales, production and accounting, are influential as usual, they are outdone on decisions on *new* products by research and/or design departments. R & D carry a great deal of weight in determining feasibility or otherwise. However, they are supreme on this topic alone. Nowhere else do they have much say (see table 5.1, row six). Even on products, they are only just ahead of sales which are almost as influential, as would be anticipated, together with their external counterparts, the customers. Externally also, competitors obviously have to be assessed carefully, and government exerts influence through subsidies and regulations. Trades unions are of little consequence despite the implications of such decisions for their members.

The graph shows the political base of product decisions in the crucial expertise, that of researching, marketing, producing, and financing, and it also shows how externally orientated such a decision inevitably is.

With so many different interests both involved and influential, there are frequently contending objectives. If a proposed product carries high risks, as did the 'Old Joe Bitter' proposal, described in chapter 3, which was pushed by the larger corporation owning the brewery but resisted by the brewery's own management who saw it as threatening sales of their existing lines, the process of reaching a decision is likely to be intense and conflictful (Hage 1980, p. 121).

Figure 5.2.A. DECISION—SET GRAPH : Product Topics

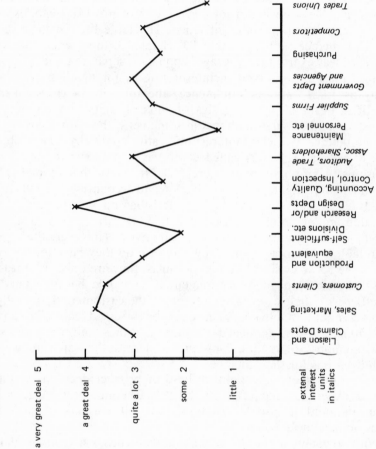

INFLUENCE

a very great deal 5

a great deal 4

quite a lot 3

some 2

little 1

Liaison and
Claims Depts

Sales, Marketing

Customers, Clients

Production and
equivalent

Self-sufficient
Divisions etc.

Research and/or
Design Depts

Accounting, Quality
Control, Inspection

Auditors, Trade
Assoc, Shareholders

Maintenance
Personnel etc

Supplier Firms

Government Depts
and Agencies

Purchasing

Competitors

Trades Unions

external
interest
units
in italics

INTEREST UNITS (left to right from most to least mean influence overall)

Figure 5.2.B. DECISION—SET GRAPH : Boundaries Topics

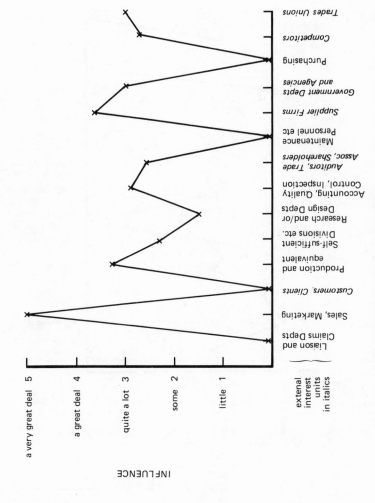

INFLUENCE

a very great deal 5

a great deal 4

quite a lot 3

some 2

little 1

extenal
interest
units
in italics

Liaison and
Claims Depts

Sales, Marketing

Customers, Clients

Production and
equivalent

Self-sufficient
Divisions etc.

Research and/or
Design Depts

Accounting, Quality
Control, Inspection

Auditors, Trade
Assoc, Shareholders

Maintenance
Personnel etc

Supplier Firms

Government Depts
and Agencies

Purchasing

Competitors

Trades Unions

INTEREST UNITS (left to right from most to least mean influence overall)

Figure 5.2.C. DECISION—SET GRAPH : Domain Topics

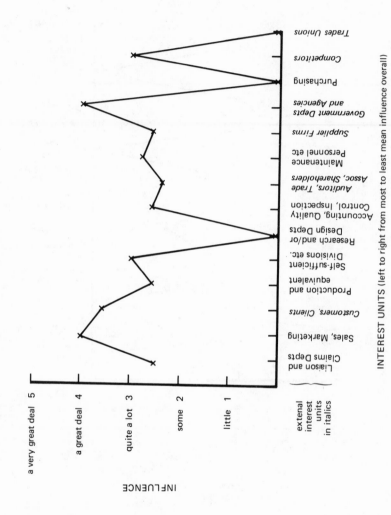

INFLUENCE

a very great deal 5

a great deal 4

quite a lot 3

some 2

little 1

extenal
interest
units
in italics

Liaison and
Claims Depts

Sales, Marketing

Customers, Clients

Production and
equivalent

Self-sufficient
Divisions etc.

Research and/or
Design Depts

Accounting, Quality
Control, Inspection

Auditors, Trade
Assoc, Shareholders

Maintenance
Personnel etc

Supplier Firms

Government Depts
and Agencies

Purchasing

Competitors

Trades Unions

INTEREST UNITS (left to right from most to least mean influence overall)

Activity is excited both among allies and between opponents, outside the orderly proceedings of formally arranged meetings and committees, and more around the office desk, over the telephone, and during lunch.

All this takes time, and new products decisions tend to take longest of all. Table 5.2 compares the process times of topic categories. The mean times do not signify very much by themselves since the variation within each category is wide. It is the ranges which are revealing. Whilst a decision on any topic *can* be reached in just a few months, the low ends of the ranges being much the same, the chances of going beyond 12 months differ sharply. No inputs decision took more than 12 months, but new products decisions often did, with two or three years not at all abnormal.

A picture emerges of new product decisions as usually both complex and political. It was already plain that they are likely to follow the sporadic type of process. Here the link between complexity, politicality, and process begins to be seen. For instance, the new automobile exhaust systems of an engineering components manufacturer, the new dump truck of an earth-moving equipment manufacturer, the risky new chemical of a chemicals manufacturer, were all highly complex and political decisions, and they were all made through sporadic processes.

Table 5.2   The duration of decision-making on different topics
(n = 150 decision processes)

Topic category *(from longest to shortest mean process time)*	*n*	*Process time in months* *Mean*	*Standard deviation*	*Range*
Products	12	22	16	2–44
Technologies	23	20	16	2–48
Locations	8	13	11	3–36
Reorganizations	22	13	11	1–36
Services	16	12	11	1–36
Personnels	12	11	6	2–19
Domains	18	10	8	1–30
Controls	19	10	8	1–24
Boundaries	11	8	7	2–18
Inputs	9	6	4	2–12

So was a decision on glass-reinforced cement with sporadic movement step by step, in time with technical development, over about four years. It was a notable case of public-sector invention leading to private-sector innovation. The eventual product enabled cement to be used in buildings and other structures such as bridges, piping and road signs in a greater variety of shapes, which therefore meant a bigger world market for both glass and cement. This had been an elusive dream, worldwide, but no one could discover how to bring glass and cement compatibly together into a single more flexible material. The eventual breakthrough was made in the research establishment of a British government agency. A privately-owned glass company then bought the rights to commercial exploitation.

Thereafter its decision-making swayed to and fro between laboratory development and associated market and cost estimates, working party investigations, and waves of discussion *ad nauseam* over internal and external doubts. Delay followed delay. It was repeatedly impeded internally by technical obstacles and ensuing anxieties, and also by the reservations of production management as to whether, even if supposedly perfected, the new material could be adequately produced. Externally, it was impeded by the publicly-vented fears of the government agency (where it had originated) that premature use could be a public danger, and by similar worries at the Department of the Environment. These latter fears could have set up worldwide suspicions of the new construction material and ruined the potential market. In the internal debate, anxieties were heightened by the huge investment that would be needed long before there could be anything to show for it, and by the effects on the company's reputation and its existing product lines if the go-ahead was given and the product either failed to be bought or, if bought, failed physically when in use. The prize, of course, was a world 'first', and the decision-making process moved towards final Board approval under the influence of a leading director with a reputation of having been right before. He backed a new form of project management team, heading an unprecedented semi-autonomous section of the organization brought together for the purpose. Its outcome can be seen today in any country where modern style buildings and 'street furniture' are made possible by the new material.

Few new products are quite so momentous, of course. This was an instance where the markets of two closely linked industries, glass and construction, were expanded, worldwide. Most new products are strategic just for the organization itself, and only indirectly affect others if they penetrate the market. Most are the successors of earlier new products in organizations where such introductions happen quite often, for few business firms have never tried new ventures and many take a pride in keeping up a flow of them. Though the product may be new, the making of a new product decision is not at all strange.

In these cases the decision does not have such lasting conse-quences, for the new product is one in a stream of new products and sooner or later it is likely to be displaced by others. It involves many fewer external interests, perhaps none directly, so comparatively speaking it is only mildly political. This is the kind of product decision that is likely to follow a constricted process (as figure 5.1 shows product decisions can do) because it is familiar and not unduly political. It stays within the usual channels with limited scope for negotiation and limited activity either in or out of committees.

The decision in a friction products manufacturer to devise a new compound with which to make vehicle brake linings was just such a case. It was launched on the French market, and represented a strategic switching of effort to Continental Europe, away from the static British market. Though success would lead to a wider use, failure would not have risked the whole firm, and new products decisions were a well known year-in, year-out occurrence. It was described as an 'objective' research-based decision, with a good deal of market research and development and testing. It moved easily between just the main departments, sales, R & D, production, and finance, in a well-practised way, most discussion being at the testing stage, until production was finally authorized by the Managing Director a couple of years after the topic first arose.

Personnel decisions

Many decisions in the personnel category, too, are made in a constricted fashion (figure 5.1). Into this category, for example, comes the white-collar national productivity agreement in a leading insurance company which attracted the attention of the Department of Employment, and a decision by a finance company to resist the unionization of its employees which precipitated a bitter drawn-out dispute that caught the headlines. More mundane was the decision in a nationalized industry to attempt an all-embracing employment policy related to job evaluation, which would standardize the terms of employment nationally in all its plants. Similarly mundane was a decision in an entertainments organization to arrange more free time for musicians in its symphony orchestra. This opened the way to rotating the staffing of the orchestra rather than obliging the same musicians always to work together.

As was noted when discussing union influence, there was not a single case of pay as such, as distinct from decisions indirectly affecting pay. Whether this was because pay was negotiated at a national level beyond the organizations studied, or because executives did not see pay decisions as strategic, could not be determined.

However, trades unions do figure rather more often, and certainly more influentially, in decision-making on personnel topics. Although these decisions are much less consequential than new products decisions, and are regarded as more medium-term within shorter horizons, they are, not surprisingly, more contentious. Hence, while they are not particularly serious in their consequences if the decision goes through, since the introduction of job evaluation, for instance, will neither make nor break the organization, should the decision-making process itself or subsequent implementation provoke all-out conflict this could become serious. Many internal and external interests are not concerned at all, including purchasing and sales departments and their counterparts the suppliers and customers, so the process can be narrowly channelled, that is constricted, but the possibility of union opposition may be a major factor. The two distinctive features of the making of personnel-type decisions are that trade unions have more influence over them than they do over any other topic (a mean of 3.2 in the second column of table 5.1); and that their impedance is highest of any (mean 7.3 against the mean for all cases of 5.1: see figure 4.2, chapter 4) which indicates that they often run into obstacles and resistance.

Employee objections must therefore be anticipated, and these are likely to hold up the decision-making process even if there is no union involved. When unions are involved, they make themselves felt, despite their weak position elsewhere, and the process is less likely to be constricted and more likely to become sporadic. The decision is too political for the process ever to be fluid. Moreover, it is hardly ever preceded by much of a gestation period, the prior months or years of covert premeditation that transpire before some decision processes get under way. Personnel decisions do not seem to hold the preparatory 'look before you leap' caution that often occurs with some other topics, for the considerations are comparatively clear, and in all likelihood management attempts to make a start and move them along as far as it can before rumours spread or hostility builds up.

When most of the decisions on or linked to job evaluation schemes were being made, governments were attempting forms of national incomes policy, and managements also had to keep an eye both on government policy and on what others were doing, as indicated by the influence of government departments, trade associations, and competitors (table 5.1).

Processes which are not confined: reorganization, boundary and location decisions

The second group of topics in figure 5.1, the non-constricted group, are about the organization itself rather than about what it is doing. Relatively few such decisions are taken in a constricted manner, because they are rare, they are novel, and they do not fit within accustomed channels. They are taken in ways which are either sporadic or fluid, a tendency towards opposites in discontinuity and continuity. Which way they go depends on whether they are sufficiently weighty and controversial to set up a whirl of activity or, despite their unusual significance, are sufficiently tractable to pass through fluidly.

They are much more indefinable than, say, new products decisions. As has been described, these can be familiar despite their importance; and their implementation is visible in production volume and sales orders. Not so with changes in organization, boundaries, or location, especially organization and location. Whilst a boundary change such as the acquisition of another organization or a merger can be seen to have taken place, and its effects on performance are probably traceable in the comparison between subsequent financial results and those of the former separate units, reorganizations and locations, probably the most strategic topics of all, are more ambiguous. Typical reorganizations among the Bradford cases were the financial institution reshaping its national structure on a regional basis, another one establishing its worldwide overseas branches as subsidiaries, the municipal authority merging departments, and a public-sector manufacturer reforming itself on divisional lines. Typical location topics were the public-sector decision to build a plant in Sweden rather than in Britain, a decision in a public utility to close showrooms in certain locations, and a decision in one of the financial institutions just mentioned not to move its headquarters from one end of England to another, but to stay put and build giant ultra-modern premises on its existing site.

The effects of these are not so plain as the effects of products decisions, and often the only thing people feel sure of is that whatever the effects may be they will be living with those effects for a long time. Of all topics, reorganizations and locations were felt to have the most indefinite consequences which would endure as long as anyone cared to foresee, on average 12 years and 10 years respectively (table 2.5, chapter 2), though such periods denote infinity rather than meaningful horizons. More than most, these decisions are a step into the unknown.

Reorganization decisions

Probably because of their unforeseeable consequences, the making of decisions on reorganizations can linger on for up to three years (table 5.2), and there is often considerable hesitancy about beginning the process at all. The majority are preceded by a gestation period which usually extends into years before anyone takes a definite step towards deciding what, if anything, to do. Perhaps this is to be expected with a topic that is the most unprecedented and novel of all (reorganizations take first place on rarity in table 2.4, chapter 2), and brings diffuse consequential changes (table 2.5). No wonder managers are cautious or, if not cautious, do not know what view to take and so do nothing towards a decision.

Not only do reorganizations tend to be complex in these terms but they tend to be political as well. Many interests will be affected by them, and exactly who will see themselves being affected cannot be foreseen. People are liable to feel threatened by mooted changes whose consequences are unpredictable. Resistance may arise in unexpected quarters, and there may be unexpected influences. There is no obvious power based in expertise, such as a sales department possesses for a market decision or a research department for a new product decision, for even if anyone supposes themselves to be an expert on organization, others are not likely to share that supposition. So all sorts of interests exert strong influences (third column, table 5.1) and give rise to high pressure contentious decision-making. 'Major structural changes, or even the possibilities of them, have political consequences' (Miles 1980, p. 183). Outsiders, including even suppliers, have to be reckoned with, and in state-owned organizations government often intrudes.

The most highly complex and political reorganization topics incline to the sporadic type of process. They are the more serious (with a higher mean seriousness score) and somewhat more contentious, and they show a higher proportion of external influence. In the case of an effort to reorganize a university's decision-making, this intervention came from the national union to which the bulk of faculty members in Britain belong, the Association of University Teachers (AUT), supported by the less direct influence of the views of the Department of Education. Since the university's origin, in the nineteenth century, its procedures for making decisions on the hiring, promotion, and firing of its academic staff had grown up in different parts of its organization in an unco-ordinated way. For years there had been complaints about arbitrary or unfair decisions ensuing from haphazard 'Victorian' processes. This growing problem lay at the heart of the organization, since to a university, especially a British one in which all academics had tenure, staffing decisions are arguably the most important that it makes.

Eventually the AUT forced the question into the open by writing officially to the university. Still nothing was done: academics shrank from taking action and declared that the question was an administrative matter, whilst senior administrators felt they lacked the authority to do anything. Continuing pressure from the AUT caused the problem to be brought before the university's ultimate governing body, its Council, on which outside interests were represented. By this time, according to a senior official, if nothing effective were done '. . . the whole b_____ place would fall apart staff-wise'. At this point the university's customary way of going about things, 'decision by committee', took over. A working party was formed, chaired by an experienced former pro-vice-chancellor (vice-president equivalent). Its membership had to span the interests of nine faculties and numerous departmental and other sub-units. Vociferous individuals representing a range of view-points were selected.

Tortuous and tortured meetings followed, accompanied by wide-spread argument in staff common rooms inside the university and pubs outside it. An impasse was reached.

Academic committee procedures having failed, the unpre-cedented step was taken of asking the university's central adminis-tration, headed by its Registrar, to take the initiative. Once given authority, they acted swiftly, and in only two weeks submitted four alternative committee structures for making staffing decisions. Further long debates followed in a number of committees and working parties, and lawyers were brought in to consider the university's constitution. A test case was submitted to a working party to see whether and how a central body would be able to cope with difficult decisions on individuals. Its outcome was the removal of a member of staff from a department. However, this manoeuvre created more problems than it solved, for it became apparent that any such body would be taking on powers hitherto reserved for the Senate, and this raised constitutional and ethical problems, and problems of power – as to who controlled Senate and who Senate controlled.

Despite the plethora of doubts, a decision was eventually reached after more than two contentious years, and in the face of continuing opposition, it set up a central staffing committee with the aim of bringing greater uniformity into the previous motley array of bodies that had taken staffing decisions. A unique, weighty and politically controversial topic had thus passed through a long, impeded, highly interactive, sporadic process in which there had been no firm evidence to rely on.

Being a reorganization, it was not a decision whose implementa-tion could be evaluated by any financial or other 'hard' criteria. It was an attempt to achieve the indefinable. When last heard of, it appeared to have failed. Unwilling to relinquish their several prerogatives, the faculties, the Finance Committee, the Senate, and the Council all frustrated the purpose of the new body. It was said to be ineffective, staffing problems being dealt with much as they always had been. The formal structure had changed: the power structure had not.

By contrast, a decision in a far larger state-owned business to reorganize on a function rather than division basis proved amenable enough to go through quickly and fluidly, as reorganizations also can do (figure 5.1). The corporation had resulted from the nominal merging of previous separated businesses, but no great changes had followed what was being called a 'phoney merger'. The government of the day intended to see that economies were achieved, however, and appointed a new chairman with a mission to get action. In just a few months he had set up a senior team to investigate organizational problems, got a proposal to change the structure, and pushed it through the main board of directors, despite some heated feelings. Here strong external influence giving backing to authority at the top of the hierarchy forced a rapid decision: by contrast, in the university case diffuse power blocked movement.

Boundary decisions

These, too, can be made in either sporadic or fluid fashion. The processes by which they are made are in the hands of a super-elite within the elite, who strive to contend with the inevitable, and usually powerful, external interests.

In general, deciding yes or no to boundary changes such as mergers and takeovers is not a protracted affair, even when it is sporadic, since other firms or, in the case of the merger of colleges, other colleges, are awaiting or pressing for a conclusion. Such decisions tend not to go through committees, since they are not within the purview of those such as production committees or middle-executive meetings which deal with more recurrent matters, and there is no time to set up special working parties or whatever. They go only to the main board or its equivalent and perhaps to a finance sub-committee of that. They are more a matter for brisk discussion at director level, or equivalent, on telephones and in offices. By the time they reach that stage they tend to be seen as a foregone conclusion anyway, an example of what we have called 'quasi-decision making' when everyone goes through the motions but has a pretty clear idea of what will be decided, usually because the preferences of powerful insiders or outsiders are apparent.

Boundaries decisions are more political than complex. Although deciding whether to make a takeover bid is susceptible to cool financial calculations, and may not be too consequential for the buyer organization itself despite the potentially severe consequences for the intended subsidiary, the negotiations can be intensely political. Internally, they involve the heads of the in-house heavyweights: sales, production, and accounting, all of which are very influential (as the graph in figure 5.2b shows), and externally they are influenced by competitors, suppliers, government, and even unions, depending upon the nature of the case.

The greater this external influence, and the more the decision is shaped by information from external sources, the more likely the process is sporadic. Considerable external influence was exerted in many of the examples given so far: the amalgamating of colleges to form a polytechnic: the buying of a one-third share in a subsidiary in collaboration with other national public- and private-sector corporations; and the taking over of another firm which was large relative to its new owner. The first of these decisions was influenced by the other colleges, by staff unions, and by the city government; the second, in a state-owned manuacturer, was influenced by the other corporations; the third, in a brewery, was influenced by the government department which had previously controlled the firm to be taken over, and by the bank which held the purse strings.

On the other hand, the more 'run-of-the-mill' buying of a subsidiary, the sort of thing that is an everyday occurrence in the business world, is comparatively straightforward and is made in fluid fashion, with much less external pressure. This was also true of a decision *not* to bid for another firm, when the management of a textile company after assessing the firm's value and capacity and meeting its board drew back from the brink.

Thus boundaries decisions focus on an elite juggling with external powers. If the matter is a straightforward acquisiton it can be processed fluidly; if, however, its implications are more fundamental, and if there are strong external influences, the process will be more sporadic.

Location decisions

The third organizational type of topic in the non-constricted group is decisions on locations. These decisions are infrequent, only eight in 150, and also rare in the sense of novel or unprecedented, for obviously the question where to place part of the organization or whether to uproot its main premises does not arise often in the same form. Many senior managers will never have witnessed such a decision during their career. When they do happen, these most strategic of strategic decisions are highly complex and political in nature. Table 2.5 (chapter 2) ranks location decisions as the most consequential of all, for they bring big changes with serious, widespread, and long-term consequences. They are also among the most political of all, attracting the highest overall influence (they have the highest overall mean rating at the foot of table 5.1) from a set of influential interests including all principal internal departments plus shareholders and customers and, frequently, government (table 5.1, fifth column). They are, of course, not only strategic for an organization but important to the individual managers who might as a result face moving hearth and home.

These weighty, pressured decisions are normally taken by sporadic processes that in the small number of cases recorded lasted up to three years (table 5.2). The decision (described earlier) in a state-owned manufacturer to build in Sweden rather than Britain is an example. But two cases *were* processed *fluidly*. Both were *negative* decisions. They were decisions not to do something, to maintain the status quo. Further, both were about the organization's main premises, determining not to uproot it but to continue on the existing site. One was the case mentioned already in a leading financial institution; the other was also in the financial world, in an insurance company which similarly determined that it might be cheaper and certainly less disruptive to stay in a rather out-of-the-way town rather than move into a distant metropolitan financial centre.

It is tantalizing to wonder why the only two negative location decisions, both in private commercial organizations in the financial sphere, should each have followed a fluid type of process, appearing to be deviants from what seems the norm for locations decisions – the sporadic type. Despite arousing a fair amount of interpersonal interaction and drawing a good deal of influence, these conclusions to stay put were arrived at remarkably smoothly with a minimum of interruptions and quite quickly (in about a year in the one instance and three months in the other). Although there are only these two cases to judge by, it looks as if there were crucial common factors. First, in both there was very little outside influence. These were decisions taken by a top few on their own terms without giving overmuch weight to the external interests that so often have to be balanced. The management of the insurance company did make its decision in response to pressure from a parent company which owned theirs, but there was just this one accepted and well-understood interest which had opened the question. Second, and

probably crucially, neither decision was contentious. Internal consensus was readily achieved. Given a choice, people – even top
people – do not willingly tear up their roots, and so do not rush into a
decision about their organization that will have a dislocating effect
upon themselves.

Processes which move easily: inputs decisions

Inputs decisions

Alone among the different topics, inputs decisions never go through
a sporadic process (figure 5.1). They above all are the fluid
prototype, even more so than the two 'stay put' locations decisions.
They are least strategic, being both broadly the least consequential
category of topic and the least novel. Having said that in general,
there are sharp differences between decisions on physical and
financial inputs. Of nine inputs cases, three concern sources of
components or materials, and five concern raising money (and one is
a change by a municipal authority in the method of collecting
taxation). Whilst those on materials are quite commonplace in
nature, those on raising money are unusual, even unique. Influence
also differs, here at last the purchasing departments having some
say, as would be expected in decisions on physical inputs, and
suppliers and competitors also being influential. Equally obviously,
it is the accounting departments, auditors, and shareholders that
influence the financial decisions. However, these are the normal
influences from a narrow range of interests: neither kind of inputs
decision is very political.

Inputs decisions, therefore, present no real difficulties. This is not
to say that they are trivial. The huge share issue by a leading
international insurance company has been instanced already to avoid
giving that impression. On the whole, though, inputs decisions are
manageable, and there is nothing to get in the way of smooth
processing. On average, they of all topics show the least impediments and delays, least toing and froing and discussion, and least
time taken to reach a conclusion (six months on average, as given in
table 5.2). Whilst the decision-making proper is frequently preceded
by a gestation period, this tends to be because those concerned are

waiting for the appropriate time, rather than because there is uneasiness about stepping into the unknown, as is the case with reorganizations decisions.

It is the financial decision-making that is thoroughly fluid. All five cases fall into the fluid cluster of processes, even though each differs from the others in the matter decided upon. Three have been mentioned before: the insurance company share issue, the municipal lottery, and the expansion of functions by a bank. The other two were a first-ever sale of shares by a family-owned brewery, to a consortium of investors, in order to increase capital, and a decision in an industrial research and development organization to approach the Department of Industry for capital.

The more commonplace decisions on physical inputs can be handled in a constricted way; they pass through customary channels without arousing much interest.

Processes which vary most: technology, domain, controls, and services decisions

The decisions in the final group of topics in figure 5.1 are those which can be taken in any of the three ways, sporadic, fluid, and constricted, depending on just how far each has complex or political features.

Technology decisions

The first category, decisions on equipment or buildings, the technology topics, in some ways resemble new products decisions, and are often linked with them. They tend to draw in numerous interests, internal and external, and so be subjected to influences from all directions (table 5.1, seventh column), and they too can take up to several years (table 5.2). In manufacturing businesses the departments and outside organizations implicated in decisions to buy new equipment or extend buildings, or indeed to close a plant down, are necessarily much the same as are implicated in products decisions. So deciding on equipment or buildings is a busy, information-packed process. But, on the whole, it is not unduly complex or political. While the more serious cases go through sporadic processes, the more manageable or familiar majority go through fluid or constricted processes.

Domain decisions

It would be a reasonable assumption that in the domains topic category are all the spectacular marketing decisions, dynamically arrived at, which launch the big advertising and selling campaigns that catch the public eye. But they are not. Conspicuous though the *implementation* of these kinds of decisions is to the general public, and critical though they can be, few are seen by management as rising to a strategic level. They put over to others what the organization *does*: it is the decisions on what the organization *is to do* that are really strategic. Only two of the 18 cases in the category are directly about sales campaigns. One was a decision in the entertainments organization to overhaul its jaded advertising and project a new image by switching to fresh advertising consultants with a more modern style, and the other was in one of the financial institutions where it was decided to switch the marketing effort away from the higher classes where the market was 'saturated' towards lower social classes. Otherwise, most of the eye-catching sales campaigns probably result from decisions below top management level, within the sales or marketing department itself, and are not the concern of the top echelon as a whole, except, perhaps, for formal approval of a report recommending them.

Strategic decisions pertinent to the operating domains or markets of organizations are much more varied. They include a decision in a primarily northern England brewery to venture into the London market for the first time, a decision in another brewery to extend from its traditional 'public house' market to the 'family eating-out' market by opening restaurants with full menus, as well as bars (there is now a national chain), a decision in a transport company to expand by taking concessions to sell Fiat trucks, the decision already described in a group of companies to standardize their names to project a common image, and other diverse cases.

These decisions are not rushed through because of market exigencies. The time they take is similar to that of other topics (table 5.2). Nor is the influence exerted on them anything out of the ordinary. The graph in figure 5.2c shows that influence in their decision-sets of interests follows conventional function-based lines, as would be expected. Sales departments and their external opposites, the customers, are highly influential, as, of course, are competitors. Research and/or design departments, purchasing departments, and unions, have little or nothing to do with such decisions. A curiosity is the high influence score for government, but this is a misleading artefact of merely two cases, one of which was the reduction of interest rates, in effect a sweeping price change, by a dominant financial institution, which was heavily influenced by the Treasury and Department of Environment whose influence ratings account for the high figure on the graph.

But it appears to be the political aspect that swings domain decision-making towards the sporadic form. The more heavily pressured, or influenced, and contentious domain decisions incline to sporadic processes.

Controls decisions

The third topic in the group, controls decisions, which divides almost exactly equally between the three forms of process, turns out to be the *prototype for incrementalism* (Lindblom 1959; Braybrook and Lindblom 1963). It includes the business plans of manufacturing firms that set sales, production and profit targets on an annual or rolling basis, and their equivalents such as an annual programme of events in an entertainments business and student enrolment targets in a polytechnic; it includes budgets and equivalent allocations of funds; and data-processing type decisions on the information systems underlying plans and budgets. Of the 17 cases in figure 5.1, five are plans, five are budgets, and seven are on data-processing systems.

Taking this topic category as a whole, controls decisions are not particularly novel, but they are regarded as serious and they are subject to pressure from all quarters (table 5.1). Yet they lead to *less change* than do most other sorts of strategic decision (ninth place out of ten on radicality in table 2.5). Here is incrementalism at its most pronounced. Serious decisions influenced by many interests yet making comparatively little change.

The extreme cases are plans. These are judged more serious for the organization than either budgets or data-processing decisions and they are subjected to greater pressure, yet they achieve no more change, indeed less than that evidenced by data-processing decisions. On the five-point rating of radicality, the five planning decisions were given 2, 2, 2, 3, and 4, compared to a mean for 150 cases of 3.2 (SD1.2), indicating little change except for the one case rated 4 which was the entertainments programme. So corporate plans do not often innovate. Rather they are projections of the status quo. Serious they may seem to be to the many interests which become involved and influence them, but planned changes are incremental at the margin, and larger changes are not usually enshrined in plans. This means that decision-making on plans is unlikely to be sporadic, and like inputs, the plans decisions show no case of a sporadic process. They are neither sufficiently pressured nor sufficiently contentious, for though the forecasts which go into the making of a plan must take into account the external world of customers and competitors and governments, the plans as such are essentially internal affairs between the heads of functions, or between them and any owner company.

Budgets, too are comparatively low-change decisions, and by no means as strategic as sometimes believed. However, if they do become contentious, which they can do, it is then that they are likely to be processed sporadically, as was a National Health Service district budget, for example. In arriving at this budget, preparatory calculations were made in accordance with recognized – but unwritten – procedures, and then the budget was negotiated over a period of months in exchanges between medical, nursing, buildings and maintenance, and other sections, with several interruptions for reassessments, even though the actual margin for deciding anything of consequence was small, since committed ongoing expenditures on salaries, drugs, local taxes, etc., made up the bulk of the budget.

But whilst budget decisions can occasion the exercise of power, and the figures in them may well denote the balance of power (Pfeffer 1981, p. 232), by comparison with other kinds of strategic decision they are not especially momentous. They are more about the locked-in distribution of power between interests than about the direction in which the organization is to go. The strivings of interests to influence the course to be taken by the organization are seen more in the sporadic processes characteristic of new product or reorganization or location decisions. Budgets are more symbolic of power than they are decisions.

In the light of this it is less surprising that decisions on the data-processing control systems which make budgets, and also plans, possible, are usually seen as bringing the greater visible changes. They vary in complexity and politicality, and accordingly may be processed in any of the three main ways. A decision in a bank to centralize data-processing, which had wide implications for work and staffing, was taken in sporadic fashion; a decision in a polytechnic merely to extend a system already introduced was taken in fluid fashion; and the decision to centralize data-processing for motor insurance in an insurance company (described in chapter 4) was a constricted process.

Services decisions

Finally on figure 5.1 come services decisions. Among them are decisions on student residences in a university; on accommodation for the aged in a municipality; on courses in a polytechnic; on radiography in the health service; on supplying a vast new coalfield in an electricity utility; and on a new credit scheme in a finance company. They appear at the opposite end of figure 5.1 to products decisions: the differences with products are so great that combining the two in an 'outputs' category was found to be meaningless. Separating them complicates matters, of course, since it mixes the kind of organization with the kind of decision. Services decisions are made in service organizations and products decisions in manufacturing organizations, so that here organizational and decisional effects are not separated, and organizational effects which are the subject of chapter 7 have already been introduced.

Whilst decisions on products in manufacturing organizations tend to be complex and political, those on services in commercial firms and public-service organizations are much less so. Although novel, they are neither very consequential nor highly pressured.

Unlike manufacturing, where new products though vitally strategic are often familiar challenges, changes in services tend to be of relatively less consequence – though their consequences often endure far into the future – and yet they are novel. And from a political angle, services attract a less diverse decision-set and are influenced by fewer interests (table 5.1 final column). There are probably neither research departments, which are the leading influence on new products, nor functionally-defined purchasing departments, to become involved, and equivalents to the classic manufacturing heavyweights, sales, production, and accounting, are less influential. This is nowhere near offset by the more influential part played by maintenance and personnel interests which advise on the adequacy of facilities (such as buildings) and staffing. 'White-collar' unions are often influential, however, to an extent that 'blue-collar' unions in manufacturing are not; and 'liaison and claims' departments are prominent. These last-mentioned have resource-allocating or co-ordinating functions which give them an 'adjudica-tion' interest in common, as discussed in chapter 3. One of the other examples of adjudication interests given there was of a Priorities Committee which influenced the decision on the radiography service in a district of the National Health Service, and others would be the Buildings and Finance Committees which brought considerable pressure to bear on the decision on student residences in a university.

The process of arriving at a decision on a service is, then, inclined to be less disrupted and shorter than that for a product decision. In general, it is far more likely to be fluid in nature, despite (or perhaps because of) passing through more committees, as fluid processes are prone to do, or to be constricted. It is, in summary, a comparatively tame affair.

The reasons why

Thus there is diversity among decisions on different topics in the likelihood of following, or not following, one type of process rather than another. On the one hand, there are some, namely product, personnel, reorganization, boundary, location, and inputs decisions, which tend *not* to follow one particular type. On the other hand, the more highly strategic new product decisions which set the future course for a manufacturing business, and structural decisions includ-ing reorganizations, mergers and major takeovers, and relocations, which affect the steering of an organization along its course, often *do* follow the sporadic type. They are more material to the fate of an organization than are the preparing of plans or budgets which though taken seriously, change little, and unless controversial, are processed in a fluid or constricted way. Decisions on new or modified services in service organizations are processed similarly, for they do not have the same import as do new products in manufacturing. Technology and domain decisions can go any of three ways, perhaps with some slight propensity to the sporadic.

Simplified summaries of the characteristics of decisions on each topic are given in table 5.3. Their diversity means that a topic label is not an instant selector of one single type of decision-making process. To know that what is taking place is about the new dump truck (in a construction equipment manufacturer); the student numbers quotas (in a polytechnic); or the integrated pipe network (in a public water utility), does not automatically tell how the decision is being handled (or was handled, or will be handled). In fact, there is no topic which is handled in one single way. New products decisions do not go through the same type of process every time, nor do personnel decisions, nor do reorganization decisions, nor do any of the others. There are no sporadic topics, fluid topics, or constricted topics.

Table 5.3   Summary characterizations of decision-making on different topics

Topic category	Summary of characteristic decision-making processes
Products	If both weighty and novel, and therefore highly complex and political, then processed in sporadic fashion stretching over several years. If familiar, a new product where new products are a practised occurrence, then may be processed in constricted fashion. But not fluid.
Personnels	Not so consequential as products and comparatively short term, implicating only a limited set of interests, and therefore likely to be processed in constricted fashion. Not fluid. However, unions are influential, and if the process is impeded by employee or union resistance, it becomes sporadic in character.
Reorganiz-ations	An unprecedented step into the unknown with indefinable widespread consequences. Approached with caution, hesitantly. If the ground is prepared in

prior years, so that people are aware of what may be coming, then the decision may be manageable enough to go through fluidly with the backing of the highest authority. But if numerous internal and external interests are implicated, with influence from unexpected quarters, then a high-pressure contentious decision processed in protracted sporadic fashion. Not constricted since it does not fit customary channels.

Boundaries   Mergers or major acquisitions of other organizations are more political than complex. Decision-making is in the hands of an elite within the elite who contend with influential external interests during a predominantly sporadic, though comparatively brief, process. The decision is usually a foregone conclusion. Straightforward decisions on takeovers of more normal proportions can be processed in fluid fashion.

Locations   Like a reorganization, an unprecedented step into the unknown. Infrequent, exceptionally weighty and strategic, highly pressured by influence from numerous internal and some external interests, and so processed in sporadic fashion. If negative, that is leaving the status quo undisturbed and not, for instance, moving location, then the process is cut short before it becomes contentious and so is fluid.

Inputs   Non-political and not so consequential, and therefore not evoking sporadic processes. If a financial input, then tractable, and with little to impede reaching a decision, rapidly processed in fluid fashion. If a physical input, then commonplace and so passed readily along well-worn constricted channels.

Technologies Similar to products decisions in the kinds of internal and external interests implicated, but neither so complex nor so political. Broadly speaking, decided in busy information-packed processes, sporadic if the matter is fairly complex and political, fluid if it is less so, and constricted if it is more familiar.

Domains

A varied range of matters for decision, whose processing has no conspicuous 'marketing' features. They are made with no special dynamism, are no faster than any other topics, and are not the object of any out of the ordinary influence. If more political, become sporadic in process.

Controls

Decisions on plans and budgets are prototypes of incrementalism. Plans, especially, although regarded as serious and being influenced from all quarters, make merely marginal changes. They rarely innovate, and determining a plan is not a sporadic process, but either fluid or constricted. Budgets are similar, but they can become politically contentious and hence be processed in sporadic fashion. Decisions on the data-processing systems which support plans and budgets can follow any of the three types depending upon the matter in hand.

Services

A complete contrast with products decisions. Less complex, for though usually quite novel, they are not very consequential, and less political, since many fewer interests become involved (though white collar unions can be prominent). They therefore follow much less disrupted and shorter processes, which, unlike those for products, can be fluid.

More's the pity, of course. If there were, the topic label would be the key to understanding decision-making. As soon as the kind of thing coming up on the collective 'agenda' was known, everyone in management and administration would be able to anticipate the general character of what was likely to happen. Whenever someone wondered whether or not to raise an issue, they would have a good idea what they would be letting themselves in for if they did. If researchers found out what a decision was said to be about, they could confidently predict its manner of processing.

Not so. A casual claim that 'things always go through in much the same way here' is unlikely to be borne out. An assertion that 'we always tackle new product questions this way' cannot be taken as instant illumination but must be treated with due scepticism. Some things might always be the same, such as that the production department always submits capacity estimates, and the Finance Committee always has to approve, but much else will vary even from one product decision to another.

For, after all, the topic is merely a label. And a label is a superficial description, not a reason. It is just the first handle with which to grasp what is going on. As a handle, it does have its uses, of course, and the summaries in table 5.3 are a practical reference list which can be turned to for insight as soon as the topic is known.

But the reasoning in the summaries as to why each type of process tends to occur is not because of its label, but because of the substance behind the label. In this chapter, recourse has been made frequently to the features of the matter under decision, to find a reason for this or that happening during the making of the decision. In short, explanations have been found in the *complexity of the problems* and the *politicality of the interests*, and not just in the topic label.

It is time that the links between these, the problems and the interests behind the topic label, and the types of processes by which decisions are made, were looked at more closely. This is the subject of the next chapter.

6

Problems, Interests, and Decision-Making

Dual explanation: problems and interests

Why do top managers and administrators find themselves embroiled in a sporadic process over one decision, swept along in a fluid process over the next decision, and channelled into a constricted process for the next? Discussions in the previous chapter of the differences between decisions on different topics repeatedly looked for reasons in the problems and the interests raised. This implicit answer to the question why processes differ guided the design of the Bradford studies and the form of this book. It is expressed diagrammatically in figure 6.1, which shows the model it assumes.

Decision problems

The first and most obvious part of this answer to why processes differ, is because the problems thrown up by one topic differ in complexity from those thrown up by another, and so each process evolves in a form fitted to the problems on hand. In figure 6.1 this is represented by the arrow from decision problems (complexity) to decision-making processes (these being of the three types, sporadic, fluid, and constricted, distinguished each from the others by their degrees of discontinuity and dispersion, as described in chapter 4).

It is plain, for example, that during a decision on even the largest share issue alternatives can be weighed up in the precise language of capitalization and financial ratios. Only the financially expert Finance Department and the Finance Sub-Committee of the Board become closely involved, and externally stockbrokers and banks.

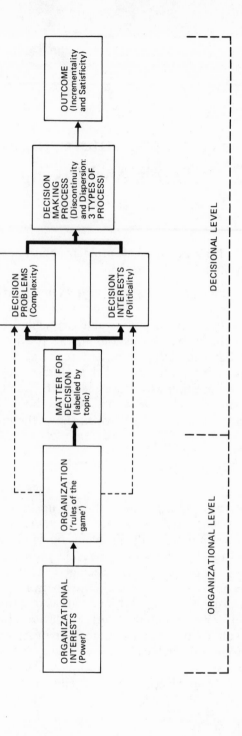

Figure 6.1. MODEL OF DECISION MAKING

Other departments, such as production or sales, or personnel or research in a manufacturing business, are not directly implicated. The question can be dealt with in what has been called a computative manner since there is general agreement on which figures and computations are relevant and what they mean (Thompson and Tuden 1964), even if the choice to be made is a delicate one. So in a giant multinational insurance company, a huge share issue could be decided upon straightforwardly in a fluid type of process.

In contrast, what to do about a possible reorganization is not at all clear. The obstacles that may arise to this or that course of action are not so readily anticipated. Everyone whose work and prospects may be directly affected is deeply concerned, and so are many whose interests are not so immediate but who see a decision as a precedent for themselves in the longer term.

Yet they find it difficult to adduce any evidence for their points of view, at any rate in the form of the data with numbers on and cost estimates attached which is conventionally demanded. The process continues in sporadic fashion until ended by a decision that is more inspiration than computation (Thompson and Tuden 1964). An example of this was the way it was decided to merge departments in a municipality.

So the set of problems in the making of one decision is more complex than the problems in another, and a different type of process results. From this point of view, managers and administrators are taken to be striving to solve the problems as best they can. Although they fall short of the 'rational deductive ideal' of 'synoptic' integration of information (Braybrooke and Lindblom 1963) and end up with 'satisficing' rather than optimizing outcomes (Simon 1960) because of their limited capacity to cope with information, the reasoning shaping the process is essentially problem-directed.

Decision interests

Yet the reasoning is not wholly problem-directed. The arrow in figure 6.1 from decision interests (politicality) to decision-making process, represents the complementary argument that the reasoning shaping process is interest-directed. Processes differ to accommodate different interests. According to this argument, processes differ because the decision-set of interests drawn in by one topic differs in politicality from that drawn in by another. From this perspective, whilst a major share issue in a company directly implicates only a limited set of interests among financial and legal directors and experts, a possible reorganization can encounter a welter of diverse interests among the numerous departments, divisions or subsidiaries, and levels of the hierarchy affected, and the influences they exert make it a very different affair.

Thus, as managers deal with the greater or lesser politicality of the decision-set implicated in a topic, influencing its interests and being influenced by them, they build up a decision-making process for reasons different to the solving of problems, yet just as much inherent in the decision-making. Sources are approached not only for information but to ensure that a decision is compatible with their interests. Committees meet not only to pool what the members know but also to allow their interests to be voiced. Reports are prepared not only to inform and recommend but also to advance an interested viewpoint. This is because the objectives of interests are answers already there awaiting a question to arise which they will then conveniently fit. 'An organization is a collection of choices looking for problems' (Cohen, et al. 1972, p. 2), so that process and outcome may be partially 'uncoupled' (Cohen, et al. 1972; March and Olsen 1976), for the outcome may follow not so much from the apparent logic of the process but from prior interests. There is 'quasi-resolution of conflicts' (Cyert and March 1963) between interests which are reconciled superficially and temporarily but not fundamentally in the 'bureaucratic politics' (Allison 1969) that are endemic.

The substance of the decision therefore offers a '*dual explanation*' for decision-making processes (Astley, et al. 1982). A process takes shape *both* to encompass the complexity of the problems raised by matters on hand *and* to accommodate the politicality of the implicated interests. This dual explanation is the subject of this chapter.

The two-sided nature of what flows from the problems raised and the interests implicated permeates thinking about decision-making (e.g. Miles 1980, p. 181; McMillan 1980). On one side, a *complex* topic which is high risk (Hage 1980), uncertain (Thompson and Tuden 1964), and unstructured (McMillan 1980), is thought likely to be processed with comparatively more search for information and more discussion (Hage 1980), more disjointed moves (Lindblom 1959), more trial and error (McMillan 1980), and more guesses in the dark or 'inspiration' (Thompson and Tuden 1964). On the other side, a *political* topic, which implicates diverse influential interests (Hage 1980; Pfeffer 1981; Cohen et al., 1972), is thought likely to be processed with comparatively more negotiation and conflict (Hage 1980), more disorder (Pfeffer 1981), more disconnection of one move from another (Cohen, et al. 1972), and to take longer (Mintzberg, et al. 1974). In brief, high complexity and high politicality as believed repsectively to produce convoluted and confused decision-making processes, and their opposites, low complexity and low politicality, are believed to produce computable and controlled processes (e.g. Thompson and Tuden 1964; McMillan 1980).

Organization

However, this dual explanation by problems and interests may not account for everything that happens. Figure 6.1 is a reminder that the process happens in the context of an organization, a context which shapes the process by determining the nature of the decision from which the problems and interests arise, and which may have a constant separable effect upon process irrespective of the particular decision matter. It determines the nature of the decision because it is the framework or 'rules of the game' for decision-making, and fixes which topics are allowable and which are not. Its norms or 'rules' govern what is mentionable or unmentionable ('I wouldn't bring that up again, if I were you'), what interests matter ('There are more important things right now than bothering our heads about what they think'), and how things should be done ('Anything like this always has to go to the Finance Committee sooner or later', or 'We have pushed our case just about as far as they'll stand on this one'). At bottom, these 'rules' govern the terms on which, and purposes for which, an organization exists and strategic decisions are made.

An organization is set up by and sustained (or destroyed) by a 'dominant coalition' of powerful stakeholders (Cyert and March 1963), including primarily its owners, but also main suppliers, main users of its products or services, and managerial and other employees. These organizational interests determine its basic purposes and are therefore the ultimate cause of what decision matters come to the surface and how they are processed, as figure 6.1 presumes.

Investigation of the effects of organization upon decision-making processes as far as these have been detected in the Bradford studies must await the next chapter. The evidence for the postulated dual explanation by problems and interests must first be examined in this chapter.

Support for a dual explanation

In chapter 2 some ingredients making up the *complexity of decision problems* were described, beginning with rarity, how far the same kind of question has or has not come up for decision before. It appears that extremely rare cases, quite unprecedented, can on occasion be whipped through to a decision exceptionally quickly. At first this is surprising, since it would ordinarily be assumed that something without precedent would be moved along cautiously and carefully, taking a long time to arrive at a decision. Often that is what happens, but there are situations when the case is so rare as to either fall outside the usual procedures and bypass them, or pass through them unusually speedily because the customary queries and delaying tactics do not apply. The obvious case in mind is that of the municipal lottery, pushed through minimal committee processes in a few weeks by powerful backers because the practices evolved over a century or more to deal with every detail of financing by taxation did not readily apply to this novel proposal.

Extreme rarity can not only cut process time, it can also centralize a decision which is less weighty than many, but which has nowhere else to go but to the top. It is rare enough that no way of handling such a question lower down has been evolved. That is how the case of a high status but recalcitrant ex-department head was processed in one public-service institution, for example. His obstruction of the central administration set up an unsettling precedent for others in the organization, jeopardizing control. Since there was no other way of dealing with the problem – it did not fit the preserves of any of the committees and their procedures, not the Planning Committee nor the Finance Committee, nor the Services Committee, nor any other committee – it went straight to the top with no intervening consideration. The chief executive and his immediate associates handled it informally and decided to isolate the problem individual. An intensely difficult matter, it nevertheless evoked a simple process. Hence there may well be something in the complaints heard from those at the apex that all sorts of oddballs which they do not want to handle keep on landing in their lap! It is not necessarily the most serious decisions which are the most centralized (seriousness of consequences and level of authorization are not correlated) but the unusual.

These instances of the 'streamlining' effects of extreme rarity must not be allowed to mislead. On the whole, complexity, which may include the unusual nature of the matter, is likely to disturb and prolong decision-making processes. The most weighty decisions are likely to be complex, and they do tend to run into difficulties along the way and to stir things up. The more serious the decision, the more prone it is to encounter impediments and delays, perhaps caused by those who oppose the favoured alternative, or perhaps just from having to await reports or external events such as legislation (r seriousness of consequences . impedance = 0.3; and r seriousness . disruption = 0.2, both beyond 99 per cent confidence level). It therefore often arouses periodic flurries of activity in the executive suite (r seriousness . informal interaction = 0.3, 99 per cent confidence), involving people from numerous departments and sections, and customers or suppliers, or government or whoever externally (r informal interaction . involvements = 0.2, 99 per cent confidence).

As might be anticipated, the processes followed by *the more political decisions* are similar to those followed by more complex decisions. They, too, create a stir along the managerial or administrative corridors, especially when subjected to the greatest pressure from influential interests (r pressure . informal interaction = 0.3, 99 per cent confidence, pressure being a summation of all the influences exerted). Pressure from outside, such as from rivals, or indeed collaborators, in a takeover bid, or from a directly interested department of government, pushes the processes to the highest possible level, such as a controlling board or owning group where the eventual decision is made. It becomes too important to be dealt with lower down, even when this means still at a very senior level (r intervention . level of authorization = 0.3, 99 per cent confidence, intervention being the percentage of total influence exerted by external interests). When objectives differ as well, then the tempo quickens and the process is more open to negotiation over the solution (r contention . informal interaction = 0.3; r contention negotiation = 0.2, 99 per cent confidence).

Hence there are grounds here for the assertion that decisions follow the routes that they do as a result of their complexity and their politicality, both together, in the way that figure 6.1 assumes. Every decision shows some degree of both, and both are stimulants to process. Greater complexity and greater politicality ginger up activity and involvement, lesser complexity and lesser politicality allow a more quiescent process.

Yet the evidence so far for this dual explanation is insubstantial. It creates an impression, but the impression is given by correlations that, whilst firm and significant, are not large. There is more going on than is apparent from a series of separate correlations. Further, three types of process, sporadic, fluid, and constricted, cannot be due just to more or to less complexity and politicality. At minimum there must be three variants of the dual explanation to account for the three variants of process, if the explanation is to be sustained. What is needed is a more holistic analysis to examine the reasons why each type of process happens.

Three modes of decision-making

Why then are processes sporadic? Is it because the making of a decision comes up against problems of a particular kind of complexity, and interests of a particular kind of politicality? Similarly, why are processes fluid, or constricted? Can they likewise be explained by other complexities and politicalities?

If so, this would mean that the response to the substance of the decision on hand drives the process down one type of route rather than another. Whether this happens could be inferred from differences between types of process in the complexities and politicalities that lead to them.

In order to express economically the essential differences between the types in the complexities and politicalities leading to them, the same discriminant analysis was used as in chapter 4, where each type was distinguished from the others by its discontinuity and/or dispersion. This time it was used to show how each type was distinguished by the complexity and politicality of the decision processed.

In table 6.1 are eight variables of complexity and politicality on which the three types of process differed most sharply. They are:

Table 6.1   Dimensions of matters for decision

Eight complexity and politicality variables	*Loadings of eight variables on two dimensions of decisions* (n = 111)	
	Dimension 1	*Dimension 2*
Complexity of problems		
Rarity	0.37	0.02
Seriousness of consequences	–0.18	0.24
Diffusion of consequences	0.32	–0.11
Precursiveness	0.57	–0.34
Diversity of involvement	0.11	0.67
Politicality of interests		
Intervention (external influence)	0.48	0.32
Imbalance (uneven influence)	–0.77	–0.21
Contention of objectives	0.01	0.79

rarity; seriousness and diffusion of consequences; precursiveness; and diversity of involvement – all aspects of complexity; and intervention or external influence; imbalance or uneven influence; and contention – all aspects of politicality.

The table gives the loadings of each variable on two dimensions defined via discriminant analyses of 111 of the cases clustered in the three process types on which complete data were available on these eight variables (loadings being the correlations of scores of the cases on the variables with the composite scores of the cases on the dimensions, as stated before). Defining these dimensions of decisions is but an intermediate step to enable differences of these kinds between the three types of process to be described. It can be seen from the highest loadings that decision dimension 1 is principally about rarity, precursiveness, external influence and balanced influence (a negative loading of *im*balance): that is, it distinguishes the rarer, precursive, externally and evenly influenced decisions from the less rare, less precursive, internally and unevenly influenced decisions. Decision dimension 2 is principally about precursiveness, diversity of involvement, and contention: that is, it distinguishes the less precursive (a negative loading), more diverse, more contentious decisions from the more precursive, less diverse, and less contentious decisions.

The important feature of these decision dimensions is that variables of *both* complexity and politicality load on *each*. One dimension is not all to do with complexity, the other with politicality. The dual contribution of both complexity and politicality reappears. Both play a similar part, for all decisions contain problems and implicate interests.

But as has been said, this is only an intermediate step. It serves the aim of finding and describing the essential differences between the types of process in the decisions from which they ensue. What the decision dimensions do is enable these differences to be clearly defined, via the further step of calculating, in proportion to the loadings of the eight variables on the dimensions (table 6.1), the mean loading of all the cases of each process type taken together on each dimension. This gives each type of process two loadings, one on each decision dimension, that between them sum up the kind of decision it is that tends to lead to that type of process.

From this, three kinds of subject matter for decision can be inferred, each leading to one of the three types of process. Simply stated – whilst recognizing that what happens in practice is never quite so simple as a summary statement implies – if each type of process most often ensues from a particular kind of matter for decision, then there can be said to be *three modes of decision-making embracing both the matter for decision and the ensuing type of process*.

The three kinds of subject matter, each a combination of complexity and politicality, are named in accordance with their characters, *vortex, tractable*, and *familiar*. Together with the associated types of processes they constitute *vortex-sporadic, tractable-fluid*, and *familiar-constricted* modes of decison-making.

Vortex-sporadic decision-making

A vortex decision is a weighty controversial matter from which eddies run throughout the higher echelons to suck everyone and everything into swirls of activity. The likelihood of a sporadic type of process arising as efforts are made to cope with such a decision is evidenced by the loadings of the cluster of sporadic cases as a whole on the two dimensions in table 6.1, which are merely 0.12 on decision dimension 1, but 0.72 on dimension 2. Leaving aside

Figure 6.2 THREE MODES IN DECISION MAKING

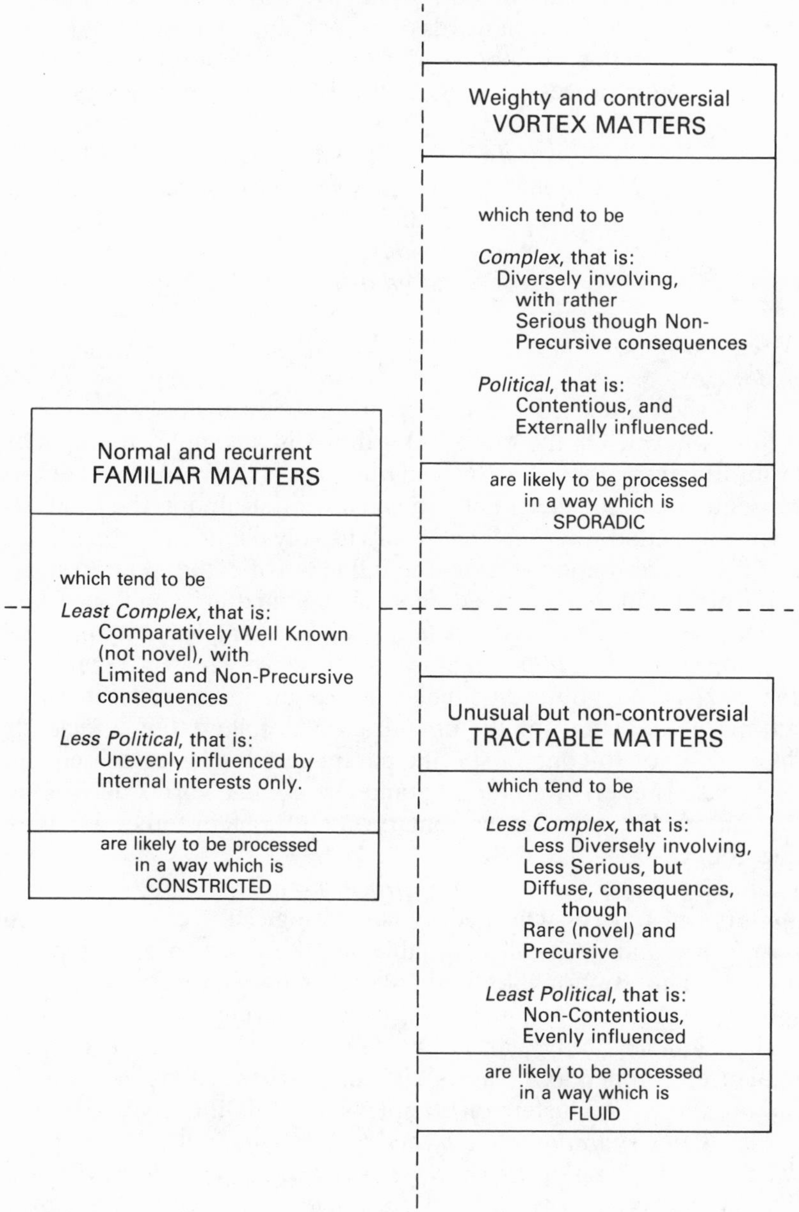

Weighty and controversial
VORTEX MATTERS

which tend to be

Complex, that is:
 Diversely involving,
  with rather
 Serious though Non-
 Precursive consequences

Political, that is:
 Contentious, and
 Externally influenced.

are likely to be processed
in a way which is
SPORADIC

Normal and recurrent
FAMILIAR MATTERS

which tend to be

Least Complex, that is:
 Comparatively Well Known
 (not novel), with
 Limited and Non-Precursive
 consequences

Less Political, that is:
 Unevenly influenced by
 Internal interests only.

are likely to be processed
in a way which is
CONSTRICTED

Unusual but non-controversial
TRACTABLE MATTERS

which tend to be

Less Complex, that is:
 Less Diversely involving,
 Less Serious, but
 Diffuse, consequences,
  though
 Rare (novel) and
 Precursive

Least Political, that is:
 Non-Contentious,
 Evenly influenced

are likely to be processed
in a way which is
FLUID

dimension 1, therefore, in terms of the five variables most loaded on dimension 2 this means in words corresponding to those in figure 6.2 (a figure drawn to correspond with the process typology in figure 4.3) that a sporadic process is likely to arise from a matter that is:

diversely involving, with rather
serious though *non-precursive*, consequences:
and
contentious, with
external influences.

We call such a combination of complex and political features a vortex matter.

Thus such a decision is inclined to be both highly complex and highly political. On the one hand it draws in a complex multiplicity of information and views, on a matter that is likely to have serious consequences. On the other, objectives differ among the interests involved, so that what shall be done is usually politically contentious, and it is made the more so by the influence of external interests.

It might not be expected that such a matter would be *non-precursive*, yet that is so. A more highly complex and political decision is probably non-precursive for those very reasons; that is, its complexity and politicality make it one on its own, strategic in setting the direction for the organization to follow, but sufficiently distinctive not to contain specific parameters for lesser subsequent decisions. They will find their parameters not in a vortex decision of this nature but in more customary bounds set by other kinds of decision.

The inference that *sporadic processes are triggered by vortex* matters can be cross-checked by comparing the average scores on complexity and politicality variables of the cases in each type of process. This confirms, as it should, that on average the cases of sporadic processes are more diversely involving, more serious (a slight tendency only), more contentious, and more externally influenced (Appendix F shows differences between mean scores of the three process clusters on complexity and politicality variables).

The *vortex-sporadic mode of decision-making* is therefore one in which the managerial approach to a complex and political vortex-like matter is to turn to a wide range of sources for reports, estimates, advice, and recommendations. All the sources are not involved all at once, of course, but on and off, throughout the process. Usually it is a process which occupies top executives or administrators, again on and off, for years rather than months. It is prolonged by all sorts of impediments, from delayed reports to outright opposition. It takes time, too, to assess a diversity of information, especially when some of it may be dubious or trivial, or both (the latter is more likely to come from external sources than from the organization's own staff). The politics of the question also take time and attention, meeting and talking to colleagues and subordinates or to representatives from outside interests such as customer firms or banks, for the matter allows plenty of room for negotiation over the eventual decision. In short, the managerial approach moves the matter towards a decision via a sporadic type of process, as efforts are made to put together 'facts and figures' on the problems raised, and to reconcile the whole gamut of interests implicated.

The previous chapter showed that decisions on new products and on re-organizations, as two instances, were often reached by sporadic type processes, and this is not surprising since both are the sort of topic that would be liable to be a vortex. A new product calls on nearly every specialist department in a business, as well as requiring contacts with main customers and suppliers, with one or more government departments over, perhaps, export problems or subsidies for expansion, and so on. Unless it is a routine product face-lift, it is a serious commitment for the business. There are likely to be those who favour taking the risk, and those who hang back, so that together with the powerful outside interests that have to be accommodated, there are a series of contending influential interests. The same is true for a reorganization decision, though more because of uncertainty over its ramifications than the commercial risk, and because many departments may be affected indirectly as well as directly. With reorganization, there is also the likelihood of external intervention from a corporate headquarters or, in the public sector, from government.

In retrospect, it can now be seen that the two examples of the sporadic type of process given in chapter 4 were responses to vortex decisions. The story was told of how a decision was arrived at in a division of a nationalized industry to take over a one-third share in a firm which bought its products, in collaboration with national and international corporations that bought the other two-thirds. This involved many diverse interests, including major external influences, in a typical vortex of problems and interests. The other example was the do-it-yourself electricity question at Toxicem, with which this book began, which became more and more a vortex of enmeshed problems and interests as it turned into a career struggle.

Vortex matters fulfil many prior speculations in what has been written about decisions. Though no one actual case may have all possible features, vortex matters do tend to have the shifting pluralistic interest groups and conflicts of the 'political power' model of decision-making (Pfeffer 1981, p. 31; and Miles 1980, p. 181) in which there is disagreement about what is wanted (outcomes), and about how to get there (causation) even if aims were agreed (Thompson and Tuden 1964, p. 198). 'Innovative or unstructured decisions are likely to highlight differences of interest' (Walsh, et al. 1981, p. 149). However, it should be remembered that a vortex in such a 'garbage-can' in which interests with ready-made solutions await suitable problems being thrown in (Cohen, et al. 1972; March and Olsen 1976) is not only political. It is also liable to be complex. The problem is heavy with consequences, and involves a complexity of people and departments – whose interests and influence engender the politicality, of course.

The chances of such a decision generating a broadly sporadic type of process were foreseen in the hypothesis that a high-risk decision would follow a network pattern of movement which did not fit the formal steps in the hierarchy (Hage 1980, p. 119). High risk, it was suggested, would prolong the process by increasing the discussion over information, whilst more numerous interests would increase negotiation (Hage 1980, p. 121). In fact, Pfeffer (1981, p. 31) has surmized that the processing of what was called a 'political power' decision is 'disorderly, characterized by push and pull of interests'.

Many published cases fall into the vortex-sporadic mode, among them those the politics of which excite the eye of the reader and must have quickened the pulse rates of those involved at the time. Pettigrew's (1973) account of the politics of a long-drawn-out choice of a new electronic data-processing system in a British retail firm would probably have been a vortex case, though it is debatable whether it was altogether strategic. Though it involved the Board of directors and external interests, in the shape of computer suppliers and a consultant, and it committed substantial funds, it was essentially just a choice of brand. But externally involving and internally contentious it was, with contention both between the staffs of the systems and programming departments, and within the Board, as to which data-processing system to buy.

The choice of a new Dean for a school of an American university was certainly a highly political vortex, as told by March and Olsen (1976, chapters 6 and 15; and summarized by Butler, et al. 1979/80). Clearly this was not strategic for the university as a whole, but it was strategic at the level of the school or department. The faculty saw the choice as either sustaining or changing the strategy consciously followed by the school since its foundation by its first Dean, whose resignation caused the crisis over a successor. There was internal contention between the supporters of candidates, external advisers were drawn in, and eventually hierarchy stepped across the politicking when the Vice-Chancellor recommended an internal candidate, a nice example of the tendency pointed out by Cyert and March (1963) for search for solutions to be 'simple minded', and end in the choice of the simpler alternative which leaves things not much different from where they were before.

Both decisions appear to have been handled in a sporadic way. In the case of the computer purchase there were discontinuities while the board hesitated over information in which it lacked confidence, while reports were prepared, while suppliers were approached, and while internal resistance made itself felt. The story suggests more informal person-to-person interaction than committee proceedings or working parties and the like. So, too, the choice of a university Dean, the matter being repetitively reconsidered in erratic bouts of activity and inactivity.

Tractable-fluid decision-making

The second kind of subject matter, a tractable decision, is one which is unusual but less awkward and more malleable than a vortex decision. This is a question of degree, or course, and is not intended to imply that every decisions of this sort is completely controllable and pliable in all respects.

The chances of a fluid type of process arising from a decision with features that can be broadly labelled as tractable are shown by the loadings of the cluster of fluid cases as a whole on decision dimensions 1 and 2 in table 6.1. They are respectively 0.67 and

−0.61, indicating that fluid types of process have a great deal to do
with *both* dimensions, positively with the variables most loaded on
dimension 1, and negatively with those most loaded on dimension 2.
Putting this in words approximating the summary in figure 6.2, a
fluid process is likely to arise from a matter that has:

> *consequences* that are not too *serious*, though *diffuse*,
> and
> *involvement* that is not too *diverse*, but is
> *rare* (novel) and
> *precursive*:
> and is
> *non-contentious*,
> *evenly influenced*.

It is *this combination of features, less complex than a vortex decision
and the least political of strategic decisions, that we call a tractable
matter*, opposite in many respects to a vortex one as the opposite
loading (negative not positive) on the second dimension emphasizes.

Although its consequences are widely felt (diffuse) they are not all
that serious and the decision is less deserving of being called
strategic. Fewer departments and others are involved, so there is not
such a complexity of information and views. From a political point of
view, objectives are compatible, and there is little or no contention.
There is an even spread of influence across the interests involved, no
one or two departments or outside interests having such a grip on the
matter that it becomes a highly political affair revolving around
them.

A tractable decision may well be a rare one, however, in the sense
that nothing quite like it has happened before. It is not novelty as
such that makes a matter highly complex and political, but its
consequences and the quality of information and the influence
exerted. Something novel can be the more tractable since it does not
come up against entrenched positions and fixed precedents. A novel
extension of the range of services, for example, perhaps in a bank or
insurance company, can be quite unprecedented in taking the
business into a fresh field, yet the demands which it makes on
management are nothing like so complex and political as those made
by a new product decision in a manufacturing firm.

A tractable decision may also be a precursive one, setting

parameters within which decisions yet to come must fall. Just as it is surprising at first to find that vortex decisions are not usually precursive, so it is surprising that tractable decisions *are* usually precursive. They are more liable to contain parameters that delimit subsequent decisions. While they do not bulk as large strategically as most vortex decisions, since their effects are not so general, nevertheless they do set particular bounds on subsequent middle-level decisions. For example, a decision to extend financial services sets parameters as to how far staff are authorized to go in giving credit or offering advice. Similarly, decisions on inputs of components or materials, among the most often fluidly processed, set parameters for decisions on production methods.

In the same way as the vortex-sporadic link is corroborated by differences in the average complexity and politicality of the cases of each process type, so the inference that *fluid processes are triggered by tractable matters* is also corroborated. On average, the cases of fluid processes involve fewer and less diverse interests and are less contentious than vortex decisions, and they are unlikely to be dominated by the influence of one or two powerful interests. On average they are also relatively rare.

The tractable-fluid mode of decision-making is therefore where a less complex and political matter, one which is comparatively malleable in that it is neither overly consequential nor contentious, allows management to approach it smoothly. It is comparatively unflurried. Fewer specialists from the organization's own departments are involved, and fewer outside interests have to be consulted than is common with vortex decisions. On the whole, the information they furnish is more reliable. The managerial and staff personnel involved are co-ordinated by bringing them together in project teams or working parties, or similar small groups, which report either direct or via senior executives to standing committees and boards, through which the matter proceeds steadily in the normal manner without any notable delays to a decision in months rather than years. In a word, it arrives at a conclusion via a fluid process.

The part played by committees and meetings of every sort – standing committees, general and specialist committees, sub-committees, working parties, and so on – in the fluid processing of tractable decisions, points once more to the functions and capabilities of such bodies which have already been discussed in chapter 4. Committees are part of the accustomed procedures in organizations, having evolved over the years to meet the requirements of the particular management. They are therefore administrative mechanisms fitted for and capable of containing the normal levels of complexity and politicality borne by the tractable decisions which pass through the most forms of meetings and committees. That implies, however, that arranged meetings and committees are incapable of digesting complex information from many sources, as every chairman or woman realizes when they rescue a meeting from confusion by requesting those concerned to think things through again and come back to the next meeting with a clearer proposal. It implies, too, that they are not fitted for the more highly politically charged 'intractable' decisions. Much of the influence-loaded interaction during sporadic processes takes place informally outside arranged meetings. Committees cannot easily handle extremes of view, as everyone knows who has tried to ease things along by negotiating a solution *before* the meeting takes place, or has let a question drop during a meeting on the tacit understanding that those concerned will try and sort it out *afterwards*.

It was shown in the previous chapter that decisions on boundaries and inputs are among those topics most frequently processed fluidly. Boundary decisions about takeover bids can be exceptionally tricky, of course, but they are tractable inasmuch as only a few executives may be involved, what were called a super elite, partly because only those with financial or marketing expertise are required, and partly because there is often little time to spare. Whether it is 'yes' or 'no', the decision goes through quickly.

Inputs decisions on finance, including share issues or approaches to other institutions for capital, are the most fluid of all. They, too, do not involve everyone, and the objectives are clear and usually undisputed. The municipal lottery decision, mentioned more than once, was a prime example. As already described, this unique decision to circumvent the traditional raising of funds from local taxpayers and open up a source completely novel to British municipalities went smoothly through the committee structure to a rapid conclusion. It was not too serious in its consequences, for should it fail, the municipality might suffer some loss of repute but no loss of monetary or other resources, internally it did not involve many departments, and externally only a lottery promotion firm; and it aroused little outright contention in objectives, despite doubts on moral grounds.

In general, it is these inputs decisions which best exemplify the tractable-fluid mode of decision-making. Whilst they may be substantial, such as a large share issue, or crucial to factory production, such as a change concerning raw materials, they are not so serious in their consequences as to threaten survival should they be mistaken, and there are many whose interests are not directly implicated by them, such as sales or personnel departments, customers or trades unions who therefore do not become involved.

It is tempting to see tractable-fluid decision-making as equivalent to the 'synoptic model' of decision-making, the nearest there is to this ideal. The ideal assumes that the necessary information will be garnered from all appropriate experts who will contribute disinterestedly in an orderly sequence of steps which culminates rationally in an obviously best outcome (Miles 1980, p. 181; Pfeffer 1981, p. 31; Braybrooke and Lindblom 1963). Tractable-fluid decision-making does appear to come nearer to this than vortex-sporadic decision-making, since the latter is comparatively more political in substance and disturbed in process. Yet it is dangerous to jump to conclusions, and force empirically-derived concepts to fit *a priori* ideas. There is a similarity, but it would be premature to say that the two are the same. The Bradford studies data do not suggest that a sporadic process necessarily fails to assemble sufficient information, rather that it comes from a complexity of sources. Nor do the data suggest that such a process involves inappropriate interests, rather that there are many of them. So it would be unwise to conclude that tractable-fluid equals synoptic and vortex-sporadic equals the opposite, since that implies that tractable-fluid decision-making is rational and vortex-sporadic is non-rational. We have remarked before that there are rationalities at work in all decision-making.

Familiar-constricted decision-making

Familiar decisions, the third kind, concern the more recognizable and limited matters. They have neither the seriousness and contending influences of vortex matters, nor the rarity of tractable matters, since something much the same has occurred before. It is from this latter feature that familiar matters derive their name. The probability that they will give rise to constricted type processes appears in their negative loadings of −0.90 on decision dimension 1 and −0.21 on dimension 2 (table 6.1). These dimensions, it will be recalled, summarize the differences between the cases clustered in each type of process in terms of variables of decision substance, that is of problems and interests: so that the heavy (negative) loading of the constricted type on dimension 1 means that it is distinguished from the two other types, not only by a characteristic form of process, but by that process being associated with the decision features indicated by the dimension. That is, fluid processes tend to occur when matters are familiar (the opposite to rare), have limited consequences (the opposite to diffuse), may be non-precursive, are internal concerns only (little external influence), but are unevenly influenced (the opposite to the negative of imbalance, an unfortunate intricacy that proved impossible to avoid), these being the variables most loaded on dimension 1.

Corresponding to the wording in figure 6.2, this means that a constricted process is most likely to be engendered when the matter under decision is:

> comparatively *well known* (not novel), with
> *limited consequences*
> and
> *unevenly influenced* by
> *internal interests* only.

This is the profile of a familiar matter, less political than a vortex decision and the least complex of strategic decisions, a matter that follows a constricted rather than a sporadic or fluid route because it has been dealt with before, and the way in which it will be handled is widely understood and accepted. Moreover, its consequences do not concern everyone, and in particular they do not implicate external interests, so that as well as being the least complex it is not a very political decision. As and when strong influences have to be reckoned with, they will be from the organization's own internal sections and not from outsiders. The affair can be kept within bounds.

It is not possible to say anything about the precursiveness of this kind of decision because the loadings for this variable tend to cancel out. It is an ingredient that is always difficult to interpret and clearly requires more attention than was given to it in this research, though interpretations have been hazarded for vortex and tractable decisions.

Differences between the average scores of the constricted group of processes and those of the two other types, repeat the picture of a familiar decision that has been drawn, and reiterate the inference that *constricted processes are triggered by familiar matters*. On average, the constricted group of processes is associated with matters that have limited and non-enduring consequences, and are decided among internal interests only with no pronounced external influences. Internal influences, even strong ones, can be coped with and controlled.

Management can guide this sort of decision along constricted pathways which have been travelled by its predecessors. The managerial response is to go through motions that have been gone through before, moving the decision along in a well defined way without too many interests becoming directly involved since those concerned 'know the form' and allow it to go ahead as usual. The appropriate departmental experts play their parts but there is no special research effort, and only the minimum committee work, for most of what has to be done can be settled informally between individuals. The decision stays within accustomed channels around a central executive such as a managing director or chairman, there being little scope for negotiation over what it will be, and that central executive takes the decision without reference to any higher authority.

The drawing up of organization-wide corporate plans, which in business firms set sales and production levels, exemplifies this familiar-constricted pattern, as the previous chapter showed. Though plans can strategically shape the future, or at least purport to do so, everyone has been through the exercise before and knows the score. Rules, if only rules of thumb, have been evolved to reduce the complexity of the problem, which is one that is expressed in figures and does not have the leap into the unknown feel of a reorganization, for example. There is no need for everyone to be continually involved in the action, for there are known stages when ends can be kept up as the plan hardens, without injecting the interruptions and unanticipated influences of a sporadic process. It is the same with familiar personnel topics, even sweeping regrading proposals, since the relevant information on earnings and past practice is clear enough from a management point of view, and many internal units such as research or sales or accounting (except for the wages office) are not involved. The process moves narrowly within the purview of the chief executive and of personnel.

Likewise, the constricted type of process described in chapter 4, by which a decision was taken in an insurance company to up-date its data-processing system as one means of preventing its closure by a new owning group, arose from a matter that in itself was familiar. This time it was of strategic moment, but everyone knew how to appraise the administrative systems and decide whether there was room for reform. It had been done before. That was why it could be handled via a process centring on the chief executive who could collate the reports from those departments that were involved.

As this case shows, the familiar-constricted decisions fulfil the hypothesis that what has been termed a 'low risk decision' (Hage 1980) which is familiar because of its frequency of occurrence can be taken in a relatively routine maner with limited search for information, limited participation, and limited discussion (Hage 1980, p. 121, figure 4.3, 'The low risk decision'). It can be tackled more by 'computation' than by 'inspiration', for 'the problem-solution appears as common sense' (Thompson and Tuden 1964, p. 198).

Dual explanation reaffirmed

Chance or certainty

To say that there are three modes of decision-making, vortex-sporadic, tractable-fluid, and familiar-constricted, is straightforward, a short way of saying a lot, since each mode contains both process and reasons for process. The straightforwardness is an exaggeration, however, if taken literally. Were it so taken, vortex-sporadic would mean that sporadic processes are always triggered by vortex decisions and never by anything besides a vortex decision, tractable-fluid would mean that fluid processes were always triggered by tractable decisions and never by anything else, and familiar-constricted would mean that constricted processes were always and only triggered by familiar decisions. In a world of single determining causes that could be so, but we do not see the world of organizational decision-making as being like that.

Hence the three modes focus what can be seen, and highlight the fundamental explanation, but they are an exaggeration if they are mistaken as statements that one kind of matter always gives rise to one only type of process. Nothing as certain as that can be claimed. The modes are named in a way that links decision matter and process because there is a very strong chance that the one leads to the other. A very strong chance, but not a certainty.

The chance is two to one, better than is usually found in this and kindred research. It is two to one that a vortex matter reaches a decision by a sporadic process, a tractable matter by a fluid process, and a familiar matter by a constricted process. This can be said since when the scores for each case of decision-making on the variables of complexity and politicality (table 6.1) are computed into composite scores on the two decision dimensions proportionate to the loadings on these dimensions, these composite scores place 63 per cent of the cases into groups equivalent to their clustering on the process variables on which the process types are based. To put it another way, 63 per cent of predictions from decision features of which type of process is followed will be right.

Of course, 37 per cent will not be right. But it is vital that among this 37 per cent of the cases there are no other groupings. This holistic analysis by case characteristics, the method preferred here to analysis by single variables, suggests that as far as the data go, three major forms of decision-making make sense, and that there may be nothing but sense-less 'noise' otherwise. There are no hints of more forms of decision-making beyond those enunciated. It is not possible to account for everything, but in the language that the study of decision-making owes to Simon (1960) this is a worthwhile 'satisficing' result that can serve until it is surpassed.

Three-way dual explanation

To call a decision vortex, tractable, or familiar, *describes the likely nature of its subject matter*. It means that the problems and interests inherent in that subject matter have a certain *probable level of complexity and politicality*, as follows:

Vortex subject matter is complex and political.
Tractable subject matter is less complex and least political.
Familiar subject matter is least complex and less political.

These levels of complexity and politicality are interpretations of the combinations of variables in figure 6.2, as shown there.

The appearance of variables of *both* complexity and politicality in the explanations of each one of the three types of sporadic, fluid, and constricted processes is a reaffirmation of the dual explanation of process as the resultant of both. There are in effect three variants of the dual explanation, a vortex variant, a tractable variant, and a familiar variant, each indicating both complexity and politicality at the levels suggested. There is no type of process that can be explained only by reason of complexity or of politicality alone, in relation to which variables of only one appear. Both concepts are always needed, though they differ in relative import from decision to decison.

Top managers and administrators cannot attend only to problems and not to interests, nor vice versa. There is no sign of decision-making concerned only with the technicalities of the matter and not with its politicalities, nor with politicalities and not with technicalities, since interests make themselves felt about things in particular. Every variety of decision-making has both a task-centred and an influence-centred aspect, a complex and a political nature. *The substance of strategic decisions is two-sided.*

It cannot be forgotten that strategic decisions are made in organizations. The dual explanation is cast at a decisional level, as figure 6.1 shows, explaining decision process by decision matter without reckoning what might be due to the organization in which the process takes place. Early on in the chapter, investigation of possible effects of organization upon decision-making processes was postponed until the evidence for an explanation by decision matter had been examined. The investigation of organizational effects must now be attempted.

7

Organizations and Decision-Making

Organizations rule

So far, we have tended to treat strategic decision-making somewhat out of context, as though it were happening in the middle of a void, nowhere in particular. But it does happens somewhere, of course. The making of a strategic decision happens among the executives at the top of *an organization*. The explanation of why one or other type of process happens must take into account the organization in which it emerges and moves. We have already shown elsewhere how making a decision in a firm to embark on a new product differed from a decision in a university to embark on a novel form of degree (Butler, et al. 1979/80, pp. 24–7). In the firm the decision was arrived at by managerial authority after technical and financial scrutiny by specialists, while in the uiversity it was arrived at by committee authority, floundering in uncertainty.

Is there then one type of process in commercial organizations and another in non-commercial undertakings? Or one in manufacturing industry, another in the services sector? One in the private sector, another in the public sector? Do bigger organizations differ from smaller in decision-making, and are professionally staffed organizations distinctive?

Furthermore, *why* should the process of decision differ from organization to organization?

This chapter faces these questions by shifting from the decisional level of analysis to the organizational level of analysis, in accordance with the diagram in figure 6.1. Instead of comparisons of processes decision by decision, it compares the processes in one kind of organization with those in another. It discusses just why it is that organizations should shape the ways in which decisions are made and what the decisions are, finding the general answer in conceiving of organizations as 'rules' for how decision-making 'games' may be played. Five specific reasons are tested, 'commercialism' (whether business or non-business) 'producerism' (whether industrial), ownership, size, and direct public accountability within the public sector. Differences between commercial and non-commercial, manufacturing and service, private and public, and professionally-staffed organizations are investigated.

Organizational interests

The reasons for existence of organizations are to be found in the dominant organizational coalitions of interests, as the figurative diagram in figure 6.1 suggests. These are the continuing interests whose tacit acquiescence at the very least is necessary if the organization is to keep going (Cyert and March 1963), not the decision-set of interests which changes from decision to decision, depending upon what the decision is about. Every decision-set includes many of these organizational interests, various management departments being involved in every decision, but each decision involves a different selection appropriate to it, shareholders not being involved in a product decision nor customers in a finance decision, for instance. Whereas the dominant organizational coalition of interests is constant across decisions, though it changes over time, of course.

In a privately-owned company, this sustaining longer-term coalition of interests would include shareholders, management, other classes of employees and their unions, customers, suppliers of materials and suppliers of money, such as banks, departments of local and national government, and probably others too. The support of each, however minimal, is required if the organization is to survive, and between them they establish the ground rules on what it is there for. Each interest has its own aims, and among individuals each has his or her own personal aims. But at any one time the bulk of the interests recognize that the organization is there primarily to achieve viability, commercially or otherwise, and to manufacture or to render services, and that it will make a certain range of things or provide a certain range of services. Even when they disagree they disagree within what they acknowledge are the established dominant aims. If these are seriously challenged, the organization is in trouble, for instance if suppliers cut off raw materials for political reasons, or unions enforce a total shut-down, or government and consumer welfare societies become threatening (as is currently the case with cigarette maufacturers). The organization's primary purposes may have to change.

Should they do so, then the 'rules of the game' (Crozier and Friedberg 1980) for decision-making also change, since the establishing and sustaining of an organization sets these rules.

The rules of the game

For decision-making, an organization *is* the rules of the game. It is the ruling framework governing both process and outcome.

Legitimized by the prevailing – though not unchallenged – norms of society (Lukes 1975, pp. 21–5; Clegg 1975; Hickson and McCullough 1980, pp. 44–53), an organization is, in effect, a 'mobilization of bias' (in the oft-quoted phrase, Lukes 1974, p. 17) before any decision-making games begin. In other words, it is a prescription of the terms on which the games are played. Explicitly or implicitly, it is the roster of topics and the premises on which they may be considered (Hickson, et al. 1981, p. 187), and therefore of the problems which arise and the interests which are implicated, for 'Organizations regulate connections among problems, choice opportunities, solutions, and energy by administrative practice' (March and Olsen 1976, p. 31). The formal structure of an organization is a statement of which problems a decision-making game should be about, and who should play, institutionalizing the rules and dealing the opening chances.

The 'two long standing fundamentals of organization, division of labour and division of authority' (Pugh and Hickson 1976, p. 4) divide the internal interest units involved. Who does what and for whom, and who has legitimate authority over what and whom, fixes the departments and similar units which take part in decision processes, and the relationships between them. 'Rules are not simply a property of actors exercising power, but are constitutive of relations between them' (Clegg and Dunkerley 1980, p. 448).

Internal units draw into decision-making processes the external units counterpart to them, giving rise to the phenomenon of influence equivalence mentioned in chapter 3, whereby internal units such as sales and their external equivalents such as customers exert much the same degree of influence.

The chances that interests have of access to decision-making, or of exclusion from it, are also defined. Some internal units are represented on crucial committees such as a special task force or a board of directors, and their members are at home in the executive suites, whereas others must await their chance to squeeze in and be heard. Among external interests, major customers may be wined and dined and consulted at length, whereas government departments may be contacted merely as a formality. Trades unions usually do not come in at all until after the decision is reached. Thus there is a range from formal co-option of representatives on to committees and similar bodies, to mere fleeting contact (Mintzberg 1983, pp. 61–6).

The bounds of managerial authority are drawn, marking out the scope for decision-making. An organization may be completely independent or it may be, and is more likely to be, one of the great bulk of organizations that are heavily dependent upon others. It may be owned by another organization, being a division or subsidiary or branch of it. It may have contracts with others that make it dependent upon them for its needs or for disposal of its outputs. Most dependent is the organization that is wholly owned by another from which, or from its subsidiary parts, all supplies are obtained, and to which all outputs are sent. It deals only with its owner and with others subject to that same owner. So its management will make few decisions of consequence, since the more dependent an organization becomes upon others, the narrower is the range of decisions its own management is likely to be able to make (Pugh and Hickson 1976, chapter 5; Hickson and McMillan 1981, p. 193). In business, for instance, it is common for the management of a subsidiary company to be limited to a maximum figure in its financial decisions. Anything above that has to go to the group head office, as too would any proposed major changes in products or services or markets. It is the same in public services.

Within whatever this possible range of decisions in an organization may be, alternatives are limited by assumptions and decision premises that are taken for granted (Pfeffer 1981, p. 115). There is 'A more or less well articulated normative system limiting the range of preferred outcomes that are seen as "feasible". That is, an overall normative context in which the bargaining and influence takes place. We will call these the limiting norms' (Abell 1975, p. 17). So decision-making does not have a free run. It moves within the limits of what are taken to be 'acceptable' and 'reasonable' alternatives.

In so doing, it takes as given the 'non-decisions', to use another oft-quoted term (Bacharach and Baratz 1962; Lukes 1974). This term is customarily applied to the powers of elites to keep potential issues out of reach of subordinate classes, but it also applies to strategic decision-making within managerial pluralism. In this the primary purposes of organizations remain unchallenged most of the time by most interests. '. . . certain potential issues are never explicitly raised, remaining in the grey area of working assumption' (Abell 1975, p. 31). This is due both to the power of the dominant coalition to see that these continue to be 'non-decisions', a mixture of unquestioned assumptions and unthought-of possibilities, and also to the inability of the individuals involved to think of literally everything every time (Simon 1960).

The case of one of the Bradford studies organizations which was so '. . . immobilized by a balance of power tipped sharply in favour of external interests' (Hickson et al. 1978, p. 33) that the researchers dubbed it the 'paralytic organization' (Butler et al. 1977/78, p. 50) has been described in these two publications. It was a state-owned electricity utility established by Act of Parliament, with its primary purpose to sell and distribute electricity and electrical appliances. There were very few strategic decisions available for the taking, and a ring of encircling non-decisions. To begin with, the region to be supplied was specified: implicitly therefore, consumers beyond that were not to be supplied, and certainly adjacent electricity utilities would have resisted encroachment. Then all electricity was obtained from the state monopoly owning the generating stations: implicitly, alternative sources were not to be encouraged and would be resisted (the Toxicem story demonstrates this).

At the time of the research, electricity could not be promoted by advertising which directly attacked other fuels, for the large state-owned gas and coal corporations would have objected, as would the private oil corporations. Nor, implicitly, was there any question of the utility itself selling other fuels such as gas to improve its competitiveness. As for its retail stores, the selling of anything beyond a limited range of appliances would have been opposed as unfair competition by private retailers. Capital could not be raised other than through the state, and certainly not through increasing prices which were under public scrutiny. 'Excessive' profits would be condemned. Only 10 per cent of costs were under the management's own control, which showed clearly how small was the room for manoeuvre in this large, imposing, nominally autonomous organization.

Even so, the rules of the game are not static. Interests have their strategies of play (Crozier and Friedberg, 1980) and by pursuing these they bring changes. They may merely set a precedent by getting around formal procedures and informal practices, as in the case of the lottery decision, already described, which sped through a municipal authority with influential backing. Or they may exceed the rules, as in the Toxicem case which broke the bounds of proper conduct and could not be contained within established committee procedures, so that the Managing Director had to find a new way, a management vote, to handle it. Or they may go so far as to alter underlying goals and with them the rules, as in the case of a paint manufacturer where a takeover by a multinational corporation opened up a range of previous non-decisions on products, distribution, and markets. But though the rules may be broken and changed, they are not ignored. They are always there and, as it was put in chapter 1, power works within rules that power itself frames.

Outcomes and strategies

Because an organization constitutes the rules of the game for decision-making processes, there is every reason to think that the decisions in which the processes culminate will be governed by the kind of organization in which they occur. The outcomes of some processes, that is the decisions, will be smaller increments of change, some will be more sweeping; some will be satisficing, some will be nearer to maximizing. But whatever they are, they are framed by the organizational context. An outcome is what it is because it is about a firm or a hospital or an airline, or whatever. Of two decisions on investment in equipment, one to order a body-scanner and the other to order middle-range Boeing jets, there is no doubt which was taken in a district running hospitals and which in an airline running aeroplanes!

Further, the outcome is usually what it is because it fits a strategy for the organization. Few decisions stand alone as isolated happenings. They have links with decisions made beforehand and with decisions that will be made afterwards, and in many cases these links are so strong as to denote that successive decisions are part of a single strategy which appears as 'a pattern in a stream of decisions' (Mintzberg 1978; Mintzberg and Waters 1982).

In exactly half of the 30 organizations included in the Bradford studies, every one of the five decisions covered fitted into such a pattern, and that pattern fitted the circumstances of the organization and the aims that the executives said were being pursued. The strategies were clear to see. Indeed, strategies could be seen in the decisions taken in a number of the other organizations, if links between three or four out of five decisions, and not five out of five, were taken as indications of strategies. Therefore it is obvious that the great majority of strategic decisions are components of broader strategies, each another move in the same general direction.

For example, a publicly-owned water utility was pursuing a *rationalization strategy* following the amalgamation into it of previously independent water suppliers. Therefore the five decisions, over a five-year period, were; to recost completely the sewage disposal and invest in new plant; to connect previously separate water pipelines into a single network; to reach a new joint agreement with three major customers (breweries) on effluent treatment; to abandon the historical practice of local governments collecting water charges with local taxes, and instead to exploit the administrative economies of the new larger organization by charging consumers direct; and to price and budget accordingly. A second example is the *expansion strategy* of the bank, referred to in earlier chapters, which was trying to achieve the status and range of services of a major bank. Decisions were therefore taken over a six-year period to promote identity by becoming legally incorporated separately from the owning group, to automate office procedures to cope with greater workloads, to improve control by centralizing computing, to apply to join the exclusive national system of clearing balances between major banks (which had far-reaching effects on operations and services), and to open head-on competition by offering 'no-charges' accounts. Somewhat similarly, an industrial research association was increasing its independence by following a *commercializing strategy*, getting clients to pay for services rendered rather than being financed wholly by subscriptions from the companies in its industry who both controlled it and used its facilities. Over a ten-year period, decisions were taken to invest in new equipment, so as to be capable of commercially attractive services, to offer two different new services, to extend services to an overseas market, and to raise substantial capital to improve services.

Life and death decisions arise from the fundamental strategy of just *surviving as an entity*. An example of this is the insurance company, mentioned already, which was endeavouring to retain some autonomy after being taken over by a larger group. Four decisions were taken in as many years to reorganize, to cut costs, to centralize certain claims to improve efficiency, not to move company headquarters but to rebuild in an out-of-the-way town (this location physically symbolized autonomy) and to expand. A fifth decision, five years later, upgraded data-processing. In total, the decisions maintained the efficiency of the company so well that its new owners did not wish to disturb it. The strategy succeeded. By contrast that of a textile firm failed. The decisions of its management not to take over another company, which would have been an expansionist move, but instead to retrench by subsequently closing a factory and by rebuilding and re-equipping others, led not to viability but to the company being the object of a takeover bid, and to 'the last decision', also mentioned before, to resist it. The resistance was ineffective.

There is therefore, a constant factor in outcomes due to the organization in which the decision-making occurs. Many of the problems and interests which arise are due to a wider strategy. Were it not so, these problems and interests would not be considered. But when the rules of the game require that successive decisions fit a prescribed strategy, each decision is oriented in the required direction and the process of making it runs up against the problems and interests that lie there.

What then of that process itself? Is the type of process also due in some measure to the problems and interests in all decisions in an organization being affected by the kind of organization it is? Indeed, is it possible that the *mode* of decision-making, the tendency for sporadic processes to arise from vortex levels of complexity and politicality, for fluid processes to arise from tractable levels, and for constricted processes to arise from familiar levels (as found in the preceding chapter), is due in some measure to the problems and interests in all decisions in an organization being affected by the kind of organization? This question is represented in figure 6.1 by the two broken arrows from organization to decision problems and to decision interests.

So, is decision-making in some organizations vortex-sporadic, in others tractable-fluid, and in yet others familiar-constricted? Tendencies for decisions in one kind of organization to be made by one type of process and those in another by another type of process would support an inference that either vortex or tractable or familiar decisions, as the case might be, were more common in some organizations than in others.

Purposes, ownership, and decision-making

Organization stereotypes

The stereotypes of different sorts of organizations do suggest that each should colour decision-making processes with its particular hue. They are in effect hypotheses about what type of process may be anticipated.

The traditional, stereotyped, difference between *commercial* profit-seeking organizations, such as manufacturers, and *non-commercial* organizations, such as health services or universities, lies in 'business drive'. Commercialism, or the drive for commercial success, should permeate decision-making. Since business is business, and business waits for no man, fast, hustling decision-making processes would be expected. If there is such a tendency, it should show up in a high proportion of fluid decision-making processes in commercial organizations.

'Producerism' overlaps with commercialism, since manufacturing organizations can normally be assumed to be commercial, but it is not the same thing. Compared to a *service* organization, a *manufacturing* organization produces tangible goods, the quantities and qualities of whose components are more or less measurable, and this should enable controlled decision-making consonant with the tenets of 'scientific management'. It should show up in a high proporton of constricted decision-making processes moving steadily under control through the usual channels.

The sharpest sterotype is of *public-sector* organizations. Their decision-making is thought to be hamstrung by public accountability, being tied to their latent social purpose and subjected to government intervention, as compared to unfettered *private enterprise* (Aharoni and Lachman 1982; Rainey, et al. 1976). Chapter 3 has shown that the departments and agencies of the state are indeed far more often involved in the decision-making of publicly-owned organizations, though they usually exert no greater influence upon what is decided than they do in private organizations. By comparison, 'business organizations are, for the most part, less overtly political than organizations in the non-profit or public sectors such as governmental agencies, hospitals, and universities' (Pfeffer 1981, p. 77). This is because private enterprise can place unambiguous commercialism first and foremost (Rainey, et al. 1976), whereas the public organizations have the additional – and ambiguous – purpose of making socially responsible decisions. The presumption applies as much to nationalized industries as to public services, both being subject to 'regulatory delays and political review' (Pfeffer 1981, p. 77) and to contending interests. There is continual tension between objectives, for whilst governments and other public interests exert pressure in favour of what they conceive to be the common good, the managers of public organizations incline the other way towards commercialism. In Israel, at least, the answer to the question 'can the manager's mind be nationalized?' is 'no' (Aharoni and Lachman 1982), for executives in the public sector appear to have the same business objectives as those in the private sector. Governmental interest and tensions over objectives would therefore be expected to produce uneven and political decision-making in the organizations of the public sector, with a high proportion of processes being of the sporadic type.

Organization differences

Table 7.1 compares the proportions of sporadic, fluid, and constricted processes in the different kinds of organization. First the 29 organizations on which complete data are available on types of processes (data are incomplete on one) are divided into those that specifically sell their products or services on a commercial basis, versus those that do not. They divide into 21 that are commercial and eight that are non-commercial. In these, 136 of the cases of

Total = 136
decisions (data missing on
1 organization, 14 decisions)

Organization category (total = 29 organizations)	Organizations	Decisions	Types of decision-making processes					
			Sporadic Decisions	%	Fluid Decisions	%	Constricted Decisions	%
(1) PURPOSE AND OWNERSHIP								
Commercial	21	98	38	38	30	31	30	31
Non-commercial	8	38	15	39	12	32	11	29
Total		136						
Manufacturing	10	45	22	49	7	15	16	35 *
Services	19	91	31	34	35	38	25	28
Total		136						
Privately-owned	16	74	24	32	25	34	25	34 **
Publicly-(state) owned	13	62	29	47	17	27	16	26
Total		136						
(2) OWNERSHIP OR PRODUCT								
Manufacturing public	2	9	7	78	0	0	2	22
private	8	36	15	42	7	19	14	40
Total		45						
Services public	11	53	22	41	17	32	14	26
private	8	38	9	24	18	47	11	29
Total		91						
(3) 'PROFESSIONAL'								
Public 'professional'								
municipality	1	5	3	60	2	40	0	0
NHS Districts	2	10	5	50	4	40	1	10
polytechnics	2	10	4	40	2	20	4	40
universities	2	8	1	13	4	50	3	37
Private 'professional'								
Industrial research	1	4	0	0	2	50	2	50
(4) PERSONAL AUTHORITY								
Chief executive dominated	4	20	5	25	2	10	13	65 ***

*chi² = 7.2 (with one degree of freedom): beyond 95% confidence
**chi² = 2.9 (with six degrees of freedom): beyond 80% confidence
***chi² = 9.3 (with two degrees of freedom): beyond 99% confidence
1. Salient percentages are underlined.

decision-making studied were clustered into the three types of process (data are incomplete for this purpose on 14 cases), 98 being in the commercial organizations and 38 in the non-commercial. Of the 98 in commercial organizations, 38 (which is also 38 per cent) were sporadic type, 30 (31 per cent) were fluid type, and the same number, 30 (31 per cent) were constricted type. Going down the table, the 29 organizations are then successively divided into those that were manufacturing and those that provided services, those that were private and those that were public, and within these categories into varieties of 'professional' organization, and lastly into four 'chief executive dominated' organizations, so that the numbers and proportions of decision processes of each type can be successively compared along the rows and across the columns. To focus comparison, the salient percentages, to which most attention is paid in the text, are underlined in the table.

Commercial versus non-commercial organizations

It is instantly clear from the commercial/non-commercial comparison, with which the table begins, that commercialism makes no effective difference. Decision-making in the commercial organizations, such as factories, breweries, financial services, transport and utilities, is divided almost equally between the three types of process (38 per cent, 31 per cent and 31 per cent respectively), and so is decision-making in the non-commercial (public-service) organizations such as the Health Service, universities, polytechnics, and municipal administration (39 per cent, 32 per cent, 29 per cent). There is no disposition in either the commercial organizations or the non-commercial organizations for decision making to be one type rather than another. Even the specific presumption – that commercialism gets there faster – is unsupported, for process time, the commercial organizations, or if it is different, may even be longer (it averages 13 months in commercial organizations compared to eleven and a half months in the others). In short, there is no evidence at all within the scope of this research that 'business drive' shapes decision-making in any detectable businesslike manner. Commercialism makes no difference and adds nothing to the explanation of processes. It need not be allowed for when investigating other possibilities, for it will not affect them.

Manufacturing versus service organizations

The second of these other possibilities is what was called 'producerism', represented in table 7.1 by the comparison of manufacturing with service organizations. Whilst the 19 service organizations show a fairly even three-way split between the types of decision-making, the manufacturing organizations, eight factories and two breweries, are visibly inclined towards sporadic decision-making (49 per cent of their decisions being sporadic) rather than fluid (15 per cent). The presumption was that they might show a larger than average proportion, not of sporadic, but of constricted processes, assuming that these latter reflected decision-making channelled in a controllable way by modern techniques, but this is not so. Instead, their tendency towards sporadic processes implies political hurly-burly, not necessarily out of control, but swirling with activity under pressure. There is no such tendency in service organizations, with which there is a clear difference in the balance across the three types (beyond the 95 per cent confidence level: table 7.1).

This tendency towards sporadic processes in manufacturing may be attributed partly to the nature of decisions on new products, which demand complex computations of capacity and costs and include investment in new equipment, and involve important external interests such as main customers, suppliers, and government departments (34 per cent of interests are external compared to 25 per cent in services). As would therefore be expected, decisions in manufacturing, tend to take longer (14 months on average against 11 months). Whereas, in service organizations – insurance or credit businesses, polytechnics or even the Health Service, for instance – it is possible to make substantial and strategic changes in services more swiftly and with much less ado since they have much less effect on equipment and jobs.

Public versus private organizations

Public ownership too, inclines organizations to sporadic processes, as anticipated. The tendency is not so pronounced as that of manufacturing organizations (the difference across the three forms of process falls below the 95 per cent confidence level: table 7.1), but taking them all together, almost half the decision-making in 13 public services, utilities, and manufacturers is of this type (47 per cent), nearly twice the proportions in the other two types. Privately-owned organizations show no such tendency, their decision-making being evenly spread (32 per cent, 34 per cent, 34 per cent). The public sector therefore shows signs of the uneven and political decision-making of which it is suspected. To exemplify this further, the mean score for decision-making in the public organizations on the impedance scale described in chapter 4 is 5.9, above the mean of 5.1 for all cases studied, and comparing with 4.5 for the private organizations. This is not a large difference, but it does accord with associations both of impedance and of process disruption, with a crude four-point measure of *public accountability* running from companies not quoted on the stock exchange, through quoted companies, and organizations owned by their members (e.g. co-operatives) up to organizations owned by either central or local government (r impedance . public accountability $= 0.3$; r disruption . public accountability $= 0.4$; both beyond 95 per cent confidence level: for these and other correlations at an organizational level of analysis, the means of the scores of the five decision cases in each organization were used so that on all variables n $= 30$ organizations). This means that public-sector decision-making is indeed more liable to be sporadically impeded, with consequent interruptions, such as having to wait for resources (e.g. finance) or for reconsideration, or being stalled by opposition.

As sporadic processes are inclined to do, it goes to the highest levels for authorization, where the choice is finally made and implementation approved (r centrality of authorization . public accountability $= 0.5$; beyond 95 per cent confidence level, n $= 30$).

Unlike the general run of sporadic processes, decisions in the public sector pass through more committees, averaging about three as against two in the private organizations (formality of interaction, or number of kinds of committees, is strongly associated with public ownership: r formality . public accountability $= 0.5$; beyond 99 per cent confidence level, n $= 30$). This is the number of sorts of different committees and other arranged meetings, and not the number of times the decision went before each committee, which will be even greater. Since it is contrary to the general tendency for informal rather than formal interaction in sporadic processes, it stands out as the mark of public-sector administration which, comparatively speaking, makes its way by committees rather than by commands.

The making of a decision in a public-sector organization is therefore more likely to be sporadic than it would be in a private firm, especially impeded and interrupted, and likely to be centralized, with the further specific characteristic of more committees along the way.

Ownership *or* product

The tendency of both manufacturing and public-sector organizations towards a sporadic type of process poses the problem of whether both 'producerism' and public ownership have this effect, or whether one of them is just repeating the effect of the other, since among manufacturing organizations there is both private and public ownership, and among public organizations there are both manufacturers and services. Manufacturing and ownership have to be disentangled. To do this, the 30 organizations studied can be separated into:

   2 public manufacturing (construction equipment and chemicals)
   9 private manufacturing (engineering, chemicals, breweries, etc.)
  11 public services (utilities, health, education, etc.)
   8 private services (financial, transport etc.).

These categories are shown in section 2 of table 7.1, but with eight private manufacturers instead of nine as the data available on one are insufficient to enable its case of decision-making to be placed among the three types.

This fourfold categorization allows ownership and 'producerism', manufacturing/service, to be held constant successively, that is controlled for, so that the distinct effects of the other can be seen.

To examine whether manufacturing/service has an independent effect, ownership can be held constant by comparing in table 7.1:

public *manufacturing* with public *services*
and
private *manufacturing* with private *services*.

Comparing first manufacturing and services when both are publicly owned, 78 per cent of decision-making in the manufacturers is sporadic (and none fluid) against 41 per cent in the services (and 32 per cent fluid). Manufacturing appears to have nearly twice as much sporadic decision-making (and much less fluid). But the basis for comparison in public manufacturing is relatively slender, only nine cases of decision-making in two organizations. This is not surprising since the state owns relatively few manufacturing businesses, and to have even two examples among the organizations studied is therefore an unusual advantage, but to place confidence in the result of the comparison it is essential that it be repeated in the comparison of manufacturing and services when both are privately owned. In fact it is, with 42 per cent sporadic in private manufacturers, against 24 per cent in services, and once more as marked a difference in the opposite direction in the proportion of fluid decision-making, 19 per cent against 47 per cent. It is clear that there are sharp differences between manufacturers and services, manufacturers, generally speaking, being twice as prone to decision-making of the sporadic type, and services being twice as prone to decision-making of the fluid type. This fits the differences between decisions on products and on services described in the previous chapter, but it is a wider result which shows that processes on a variety of topics in a manufacturer tend to be sporadic, not just products, and likewise for fluid in service organizations.

Thus the organizational rules of the game in manufacturing do seem to give rise to greater hurly-burly. The prevalence of the sporadic type of process means that decisions are more often felt to be more serious, with the future of the enterprise at stake, and there is more contention over objectives. The division of labour creates a greater number of specialist units of the kinds whose crucial information draws them into decision-making, for example production planning or market research, and more external interests are likely to be involved. Whereas decision-making in service organizations, such as insurance or credit companies, or utilities, does not so often face this level of complexity and politicality, and consequently can proceed fluidly with less excitation.

This picture is given sharper focus by table 7.2 which shows the results of applying analysis of variance to the distribution of scores of each of four categories of organization – public and private manufacturing, and public and private services – on the entire range of variable characteristics representing problem complexity, interest politicality, and process. The ten variables shown, from openness to level in hierarchy, are those on which there were the greatest

Table 7.2 Differences between organizations in selected characteristics of decision-making processes (variables discriminating between four categories of organization on analysis of variance at beyond 95 per cent confidence)

Category of organization	Public manufacturing		Private manufacturing		Public services		Private services		An analysis of variance**	
Number of organizations	2		9		11		8			
Number of decisions	10		45		55		40			
Variables	Rank order	Mean score (SD)	Rank order	Mean score (SD)	Rank order	Mean score (SD)	Rank order	Mean score (SD)	F	Confidence level %
Complexity										
Openness	1	5.9(3.4)	2	4.4(2.8)	4	3.6(1.8)	3	3.7(2.5)	2.9	97
Involvement	1	10.2(2.3)	2	8.8(3.7)	3	8.2(3.1)	4	7.2(2.6)	3.2	98
Diversity of involvement	1	6.3(1.5)	2	6.2(2.6)	4	4.6(1.2)	3	4.5(1.4)	9.2	99
Politicality										
Intervention	1	39%(23%)	2	32%(18%)	3	26%(18%)	4	24%(17%)	3.1	97
Imbalance	1	3.8(0.4)	2	3.5(0.7)	3	3.2(0.9)	4	3.0(1.1)	4.2	99
Process										
Formal interaction	2	2.2(1.4)	4	1.8(1.2)	1	2.8(1.8)	3	1.9(1.0)	5.5	99
Informal interaction	1	5.3(0.7)	3	4.1(1.2)	2	4.3(1.3)	3	4.1(1.2)	3.0	97
Disruption	1	2.9(0.9)	3	2.3(1.2)*	2	2.5(1.0)	4	1.8(0.8)	4.6	99
Impedance	1	8.2(2.3)*	3	4.8(3.2)*	2	5.3(3.2)	4	4.2(3.3)	4.1	99
Level in hierarchy	1	5.6(1.5)	4	4.4(1.3)	2	4.9(1.2)	3	4.6(1.3)	3.1	97

*Data incomplete on one decision.
**With three degrees of freedom.

differences between the categories of organization. In absolute terms the differences between the mean scores that are listed are not large, but the general tendencies are very clear and most unlikely to be fortuitous (the lowest confidence level is 97 per cent; table 7.2).

The propensity across all their cases of decision-making for manufacturing organizations to face both greater complexity and greater politicality is plain to see in the rank orders. These place each of the four categories of organization from 1 to 4 on each variable by comparing the four mean scores. Public manufacturing and private manufacturing are invariably in first and second place. They have the least foregone (most open) conclusions, most interests and most diverse interests involved, most external influence (intervention), and are most influenced by minorities of exceptionally influential interests (imbalance). However, their sporadic processes are not generated solely by the complexity and politicality of the decisions, since they do not hold an unbroken first or second place on process. The *private* manufacturers slip down in the ordering on process variables, from second to third or fourth place. This is a hint that ownership has separate effects.

To look at it the other way around, therefore, and to examine whether ownership has an independent effect, manufacturing/service can be, in turn, held constant by comparing in table 7.1:

public manufacturing with *private* manufacturing
and
public services with *private* services.

The first comparison, between publicly-owned and privately-owned organizations when both are manufacturing, shows the publicly-owned manufacturers have about twice the proportion of sporadic decision-making (78 per cent to 42 per cent), and none fluid (against 19 per cent). The private manufacturers have more constricted decision-making (40 per cent against 22 per cent). Whilst again the small number of cases in public manufacturing should not be overlooked, the result is once more strongly reinforced by the same differences appearing among the service organizations, where the publicly-owned have nearly twice the proportion of sporadic processes as do the privately owned (41 per cent to 24 per cent), and the latter have more fluid processes (47 per cent to 32 per cent). Indeed, the highest proportion of decision-making in private services is fluid, while the highest proportion of decision-making in public services is sporadic. It is clear that there are sharp differences between organizations in the public and private sectors, roughly speaking public ownership disposing decision-making to be twice as prone to sporadic type processes, and private ownership conversely disposing it to be fluid, perhaps constricted.

Here it is the rules of the game in the publicly accountable state-owned organizations which seem to generate the sporadic processes. Public interest and public scrutiny bring government departments and agencies into the process of decision-making more often, complicating it with external interests in addition to numbers of internal units. A minority of influential interests dominate decisions that tend to be serious and contentious. In sum, the complexity and politicality of public-sector decision-making is clear. Even though it is contained by well developed committee systems, it still brings many impediments and disruptions.

This is brought into focus in table 7.2 by the invariable first places of decision-making in *public* manufacturing on both complexity and politicality, and by its first places on all process variables except formal interaction (committees), on which *public* services come first. Public ownership plainly adds to the complexity of problems and the politicality of interests, and thereby encourages highly interactive, spasmodic, committee-conducted, centrally-concluded decision-making – although, it should be said, *no slower* than in private organizations (there are no appreciable differences in the time taken to arrive at decisions in the four kinds of public/private organizations given in table 7.2, which is why process time is not included in the table).

It is apparent, therefore, that organization purpose and organization ownership both influence how decisions are arrived at. They have separate but similar effects. *Processes in both manufacturing organizations and publicly-owned organizations are more likely to be sporadic, whilst processes in both services and privately-owned organizations are more likely to be fluid.* This is plain in section 2 table 7.1 in the progressions from 78 per cent down to 24 per cent in the proportions of sporadic processes, and, inversely from 0 per cent up to 47 per cent in fluid. Given the association found between sporadic processes and what have been called vortex decisions, and between fluid processes and what have been called tractable decisions, it may be suggested that manufacturing organizations and public organizations are prone to vortex decisions, and those privately owned have more tractable decisions, (vortex and tractable features were summarized in figure 6.2).

Ownership *and* product

This means that decision-making in every organization is subject to *double effects*, from what it does, manufacturing or services, and from its ownership. As public ownership and manufacturing incline towards the vortex-sporadic mode, and private ownership and services incline towards the tractable-fluid mode, there are in every organization either congruent or non-congruent effects. In publicly-owned manufacturers, both ownership and what the organization does influence decision-making congruently in the same direction, towards the vortex-sporadic mode. In privately-owned manufacturers and publicly-owned services the effects are non-congruent, ownership working in one direction, and what the organization does working in another. In privately-owned services, there are again congruent double effects, this time influencing decision-making towards the tractable-fluid mode. This can be summarized as in table 7.3:

Table 7.3   Ownership, purpose, and mode of decision-making

Organization	Mode towards which decision-making is influenced by: Ownership	Purpose	Effect:
Public manufacturing:	vortex-sporadic	vortex-sporadic =	congruent
Private manufacturing:	tractable-fluid	vortex-sporadic =	non-congruent
Public services:	vortex-sporadic	tractable-fluid =	congruent
Private services:	tractable-fluid	tractable-fluid =	non-congruent

Therefore, publicly-owned manufacturing and private services are at the opposite extremes, with the largest proportions of decision-making that is either vortex-sporadic or tractable-fluid, respectively.

These double effects can be traced in each of the four sorts of organization.

Publicly-owned manufacturers

Nationalizing a manufacturer, which, being a manufacturer, already has a propensity to the vortex-sporadic mode of decision-making, adds a further impulse in the same direction. It makes publicly-owned manufacturers the most remarkable of all the kinds of organization covered by the Bradford studies. The two that are covered – only two, but their characteristics are in line with those of the other categories of organization discussed so far – are a maker of large construction equipment that came into public ownership because it was part of a group that was given financial support by the state and thence step-by-step was taken over, and the chemicals branch of a long-nationalized industry. Whilst the first was barely yet experiencing public ownership, the second was well integrated into the public sector. Whilst the first showed some signs of fitting the pattern with two of its decision-making cases sporadic, none fluid, and two constricted (there was data missing on the fifth case which therefore could not be classified), the second organization showed the full double effect with every one of its five cases sporadic.

Taking together the ten cases of decision-making in the two organizations, they stand out remarkably, though in the light of at least seven being sporadic, not surprisingly, on nearly every aspect of decision problems, decision interests, and process. They experience, on average, the most of nearly everything.

This has already been seen in the first column of table 7.2, where decision-making in the public manufacturers takes first place on every single variable except formal interaction. What is more, although the variables left out of the table do not discriminate effectively between the four categories of organization taken together, it should be said that on 11 of these variables, too, the public manufacturers are in first place. Together with the nine first places in table 7.2, public manufacturers are therefore first on averages on no less than twenty variables.

This means that their decision-making is extremely likely to deal with problems that are novel (rarely occurring), consequential (making the greatest changes with serious, diffuse, and enduring consequences), open (outcomes not at all foregone conclusions), and diversely involving. That is, highly complex problems. They are also likely to have the most political decision-sets of interests, with the highest proportions of external interest units, the greatest likelihood of domination by a handful which are exceptionally influential, and the greatest likelihood of clashes of objectives (contention).

No wonder, therefore, that this level of complexity and politicality – which together mean a strong tendency to vortex decisions – frequently arouses in public manufacturers the most action-packed tortuous sporadic processes with the features both of public ownership and of manufacturing. Efforts are made to tap the most extensive information sources, even though this can make things more difficult since there is usually little confidence in some of them. Contending interests are drawn in. The scope for negotiation is wide during intense interaction which runs into many impediments and disruptive delays. In accordance with the point made earlier, that decision-making under public ownership features committees, there is high formal interaction.

It often takes a long time to arrive at the decision, which is then formally made at the most centralized level.

Theirs indeed are the vortex decisions, drenched with data and influences, and the sporadic processes, alive with disjointed activity. The complicated nature of manufacturing organization, and the accountability and visibility of public ownership, both take effect.

Each was very much felt in the making of a decision in the public chemical manufacturer to buy a one-third share in a large purchaser of its products. This was described in chapter 4 as an example of a sporadic process, a response to a complex and political decision. It was complex not only over questions of how far the manufacturer would continue to produce the particular material, and the extent to which the intended partial subsidiary would consume it, but in the number and diversity of interests involved. Internally, these included several production departments, the development department, finance, personnel, and central administration. Externally, there were the oil corporation and the other nationalized concern which eventually bought the other one-third shares; a multinational chemical corporation and a second multinational oil corporation, both of which were interested in securing their sales to the company that was to be taken over; a local government interested in protecting the environment; the prospective subsidiary itself; and the national head office of the state-owned industry of which the chemical manufacturer was part. The differing priorities and pressures of these multiple interests heightened the politicality of the case.

However, as it happened, no department of national government was directly involved. This aspect of public manufacturing was more to the fore in another decision in the same chemical manufacturer, described in chapter 3, to place a new plant in Sweden. Its management was caught between the British Treasury and Department of Industry, pressing it to invest in Britain, and the Swedish Government, which welcomed the prospects for Sweden. Although the case showed the British Government's departments being unsuccessful in their efforts, it exemplifies the frequent involvement of government in one form or another in public-sector decision-making.

Private manufacturing

By comparison, private manufacturers, often regarded as the epitome of 'free enterprise', are pushed towards tractable-fluid decision-making by their ownership, but towards vortex-sporadic by their manufacturing. And not only towards vortex-sporadic, but perhaps more so towards familiar-constricted if the tenets of scientific management enable familiar decisions that hold no surprises to be made in a controlled manner, as suggested earlier.

For example, a decision was arrived at in a friction products manufacturer which potentially opened up a whole fresh export market at a time when this could have been critical for the firm. It was decided to risk making a certain new material and to launch it on the French market. Yet because dealing with proposed new products was a familiar enough occurrence, this was dealt with by a constricted process, limited to the principal departments, which progressed readily to a conclusion in a well practised way.

In general, 'free enterprise' decision-making is smoother than that of public ownership. In table 7.2 the private manufacturers are distinctly lower than the *public* manufacturers on impedance (mean 4.8 against 8.2), an indication of fewer obstacles and less resistance on the whole – there are larger numbers here to rely upon, of course, 45 decisions in nine varied firms in total. Their decision-making is obviously inclined to be less active and less centralized than in their public counterparts whether manufacturing or service (third and fourth places in table 7.2 on the other process variables as well as impedance). Their different rules of the game allow less public interest in their affairs and do appear to let them get on with things with fewer interruptions.

Yet, when all is said and done, though the way of the private manufacturers may be rather smoother, they get there no faster. The lack of meaningful differences in the average time it takes in the four kinds of organization to arrive at decisions means that public manufacturers are just as fast, or as slow, as private manufacturers, both averaging 14 months.

Private manufacturers are manufacturers, nonetheless, always more liable to sporadic processes than are services. Hence, in the same friction products manufacturer, the management took more than two years to reach a decision to invest a major sum in replacing a variety of dated plant for weighing and mixing asbestos with a single central plant. Being privately-owned, it had no contact with any arm of government during this process, except for the factory inspectorate over safety with asbestos. But being a manufacturer, and the decision being on a technological topic, many other interests were drawn in. There were the production, sales and accounting 'heavyweights', there were engineering, production engineering, work study, and research and development, sections of the group owning the firm, and another subsidiary of the group which was also interested in using the same premises as were eventually used for the new plant. Despite the process being spurred by a new production director (formerly a consultant), by new laws governing the handling of asbestos, and by forecasts of increased needs, there were successive hold-ups. These were due to the inertia of departments who, although recognizing the inadequacy of existing plant were accustomed to it, to uncertainties over a possible site, and to group headquarters who 'sat on' a report for several months. This illustrates that the complexities of making decisions in manufacturing, and the numerous interests, are just as prevalent in private as in public industry, which table 7.1 reflects with as many processes being sporadic as constricted (42 per cent against 40 per cent).

Public and private services

The public services are a heterogeneous set from an airways and utilities, to universities, polytechnics, and health services, 11 organizations and 55 cases of decision-making. The analysis above of the differences between manufacturing and service organizations has drawn attention to the comparatively more fluid decision-making of the latter, and therefore public-service organizations are, as would be anticipated, a framework for a greater proportion (32 per cent) of fluid processes than occurs in either kind of manufacturing organization (table 7.1). But they are publicly-owned, and this keeps up the proportion of sporadic processes (41 per cent), as also shown in their first and second place rankings in table 7.2 on all the process variables. In brief, they are less prone to sporadic processes than the manufacturers, but more prone than *private* services. They are between the two.

But the heterogeneity of the public services defies generalization beyond this, and requires comparisons among themselves which are made later in the chapter.

The eight *private services*, including insurance, credit and housing loans businesses, a bank, a road transport firm, a vehicle research association and an entertainments organization, are the opposites of public manufacturers. Being neither publicly-owned, nor producers of goods, they show a double effect in the opposite direction. On the whole, their decision-making faces less complex and political topics, and therefore proceeds more regularly and readily. Of decision-making in all forms of organization, it is probably the most tranquil.

This is shown by the private services having the highest proportion of decision-making that is fluid (47 per cent, table 7.1), higher than in public or private manufacturing or public services, and the lowest proportion sporadic (24 per cent). In line with this, they are lowest on the variables in table 7.2, where they are ranked in third to fourth place.

It is tempting to advise that for a *relatively* quieter life in general – and the emphasis must be on relatively and in general, for the occasional vortex decision disturbs the situation – get a job in a private service organization! That is something of a leap in inference, for the Bradford studies did not cover personal stress at all, but their results do point in this direction. It may well be a hardworking life, but the decisions can be less troublesome.

Certainly in one of the financial institutions, a market leader and a household name, the organization-wide structural shake-up referred to earlier was determined speedily and without resistance, in the tractable-fluid decision-making mode. It had become tractable, as the previous chapter shows that reorganizations can do, by being mooted for years beforehand, so that people were used to the idea, and it was almost taken for granted by the time it was positively decided upon. The prolonged gestation period had prepared everyone for it. The organization was huge with high street branches and agencies throughout the country, and as branches and clients multiplied so the strain on national headquarters increased, for there was no intervening regional echelon. The matter was often raised in conversations among the top group of managers at headquarters, and at conferences of branch managers. Whilst it was felt that to insert a regional level would diminish the standing of branch managers by lessening their personal contact with the top, it was also felt that their problems would receive quicker and more informed attention. The day came when the national General Manager personally decided it was time to move. He spoke to his immediate colleagues, compared the structures of other private-service organizations in the financial world, and recommended a regional structure to the Board of Directors. There were no special meetings of managers or directors, and the Board speedily decided in favour. It was a trouble-free private-service organization decision, fluidly reached in weeks rather than months, with minimal activity and fuss.

Generally speaking, it is easier to reach decisions, especially on a reorganization, or a change in services, in a private-service organization. There are not so many differing interests as there are in the public sphere, in universities or hospitals or municipalities, for example, nor is there the clash between different specialist functions characteristic of manufacturing.

Size of organization and decision-making

However, the organizations in the four categories whose decision-making has been compared, public and private manufacturing and public and private services, are not all the same size. The two public manufacturers are smallest with 1,800 and 2,000 employees, the private services are next largest, averaging 4,700, not much larger are the private manufacturers at 5,600, and very much largest of all are the public services which average 10,200. Although there are wide ranges within each category, because each includes one or two giant organizations with tens of thousands of employees (sizes are listed in table 1.1), there are sufficient size differences between the categories, especially between the public services and the others, to question the conclusion that purpose (manufacturing/service) and ownership are major influences upon decision-making. Perhaps size has effects which have been confused with these?

Certainly research has shown again and again that 'big is bureaucratic' (voluminous references and critical comments appear in Kimberley 1976; also Child and Kieser 1981) in country after country (Hickson and McMillan 1981) and relative to other factors (Pugh and Hickson 1976, chapter 5; Pugh and Hinings 1976, chapter 4). There is therefore every presumption that size must also affect top decision-making, by a bureaucratic formulation of the rules of the game.

It is a presumption that is substantially contradicted by the Bradford studies cases. It finds no support from a series of all ways round comparisons both controlling size and varying it. Comparing public with private services (so as to control purpose whilst varying ownership and size), private manufacturing with private services (to control ownership and size whilst varying purpose), and *within* both private manufacturing and private services separately (to control *both* purpose and ownership simultaneously whilst varying size), no differences appear in the proportions of each type of decision process which could be attributed to size. There appear to be no general tendencies, within the scope of the characteristics summed up in the three forms of process, for size systematically to shape decision-making. The rules of the game for these top management processes do not differ in larger or smaller organizations. Managerial practice is managerial practice whatever the scale of operation. And whilst the bureaucracy that comes with greater size governs the working behaviour of lower echelons, most of the stategic decision-making of those at the apex takes place above the bureaucratic structure and is not regulated by it.

Bigger means more committees

It cannot be said, however, that there are no differences of any kind due to size. There is one feature that *is* consistently size-related, cutting across more general patterns as it did with public ownership. This is formal interaction, the number of committees, and other kinds of meeting, through which the decision topic passes. The bigger the organization the greater the number of committees (r log .

size . formal interaction = 0.6: beyond 99 per cent level of confidence. n = 30 organizations). This applies also to the relative size of an organization within an owning group, there being more committees in the organizations that are larger parts of overall groups.

It is an effect separate from that of public ownership, as is shown by comparing matched pairs of organizations. Among the 30 organizations studied, there are five pairs matched on both purpose and ownership; two breweries and two insurance companies, all privately-owned, and two Health Service districts, two polytechnics and two universities, all publicly-owned. In each pair, one organization is larger than the other, so that five comparisons of mean numbers of committees in decision-making can be made in organizations of different sizes but with the same purposes and ownerships. In four of the pairs the larger organization does use more committees in decision-making, and in the two polytechnics the numbers are the same. This strongly supports the implication that larger organizations, as well as publicly-owned organizations, proliferate committees.

Smallest and largest

There is also an intriguing similarity between the smallest and the largest organizations in the level of impedance and disruption to process. If the 30 organizations are grouped according to three breaks in their size distribution into small (seven organizations with from 100 to 750 employees), medium (ten organizations from 1,000 to 2,800), large (nine from 4,000 to 9,000), and giant (four from 14,000 to 57,000), a curvilinear pattern appears in which the small and the giant at the extremes of size show less impedance and disruption than do the medium and large. The mean score on impedance is 4.5 for small, rises to 5.6 for medium and 5.5 for large, and drops to 3.5 for giant; similarly the means for disruption are 1.9, 2.4, 2.5 and 2.1. These are not dramatic differences, but they do hint at a little less troublesome decision-making at both ends of the spectrum. In the smaller worlds of the smallest organizations, which tend to be more closely controlled either by individual or corporate owners and to be more directly customer-responsive, rather fewer impediments occur, such as are due to difficulties of co-ordination or waiting for information or opposition arising – and decisions can be pushed along more easily. Managements in the giant organizations can do the same but probably for a different reason. Though their worlds are more extensive, they have greater power over them; moreover, they have the slack of spare resources as a cushion against untoward events. As a result, their decision-making at the very top of the very largest organizations proceeds with a little more detachment and fewer dislocations than occurs in big but less than giant organizations. It should be noted that three of the giants are multinational businesses and are the world leaders in their fields.

As would be expected, if speed is any advantage then the smallest organizations sometimes have an edge over the others in being marginally quicker in reaching a decision. The mean process time for the small organizations is eight months (Standard Deviation 6), as against 14 months for the medium sized group (SD11), thirteen months for the large (SD11), and fifteen months for the giants (SD13). Though variation is wide as the standard deviations show, smallest does seem to be fastest.

Decision-making in professional organizations

As has been said, the 11 public-services organizations studied are a heterogeneous set. They include five different kinds of professional organizations: a municipality, two Health Service District organizations, two polytechnics, two universities, and an industrial research association (listed in table 7.1). To call them professional organizations is a useful convention but a misnomer, since it is not the organization itself which is professional, but rather the occupations of those employed in it. Broadly, a professional organization is one in which a large proportion of the staff have undergone a lengthy training under the control of an institution, such as an accountancy society or a medical association, that is external to the employing organization, and where the hierarchical line of command of the organization is staffed by these professionals (Hall 1969, chapter 4). This is a matter of degree, varying between the form of organization, and the professional standing of the occupations. In Britain, professional status runs from doctors and lawyers through qualified engineers, and administrative occupations such as accounting, down to ancillary medical occupations such as radiographers and managerial occupations such as factory managers (as measured, for example, by the scale of professionalization in Hickson and Thomas 1969). The five kinds of professional organizations studied here all employed large numbers of professionally qualified staff, mainly engineers, accountants, and teachers in the municipality, specialist consultants, general physicians and nurses in the Health Service Districts, and academics of all kinds in the polytechnics and universities.

Tensions in professional organizations

It has long been held that there are two potentially tense relationships in professional organizations. One is the relationship between professional and bureaucrat. Professional training and an element of exclusive expertise lead the professional to expect to decide what best should be done without being interfered with by administrators who do not have the same qualifications. The protection of discretion in matters professional means that 'the professional is expected to utilize his-her judgment and will expect that only other professionals will be competent to question this judgment' (Hall 1968, p. 93). The professional employee has a dual allegiance both to the standards embodied in the pertinent professional society and to the requirements of the job in an organization, and these allegiances may clash.

Second, there are tensions in the relationships between departments staffed by professionals. The five kinds of organization were typical of professional organizations in that they rested not upon the sequential interdependence of the factory, in which work passes in sequence from one department to another, but upon a comparatively limited pooled interdependence in which departments depend upon (and contribute to) a common central pool of resources, but otherwise are largely mutually independent (Thompson 1967). There are few task links between them. Each could continue to function even if the others did not exist. In a municipality, the highway engineers have nothing to do with the teachers, and in a university the medical school has nothing to do with the business school. Hence each department or sub-unit is able to pursue goals for the organization and for itself as its members conceive of them, free from restraining links with others and even if the goals of each are mutually incompatible.

It is therefore easy to imagine professional organizations as uncontrollable conglomerations in which professionals engage constantly in sterile bickering, whilst the administrative hierarchy tries feebly to hold them together. Educational organizations in particular, give rise to the 'garbage can model of decision making' (Cohen, et al. 1972) in which multiple interests with predetermined views await the arrival of problems to which they can attach their solutions ready made to suit themselves.

Decision-making in the seven public professional organizations in table 7.1 does show one effect of this nature. Since they are all public, they all do show some instances of decision-making handled in sporadic fashion, whereas the one privately-owned professional type organization, a research association serving an industry and employing numerous scientists and engineers, shows none at all, its cases being equally divided between fluid and constricted.

Otherwise, the municipality, the Health Service Districts, the polytechnics, and the universities, taken together, prove to be something of a surprise. The vibrant image of the tension-ridden politicking professional organizations creates the presumption not that some of their decision-making will be in a relatively political mode, but that it will be overwhelmingly so, and rarely fluid because there are continual impediments, rarely constricted because top management is unable to hold it within narrow channels. Yet table 7.1 does not show this at all.

Most obviously, they have substantial proportions of fluid processes (and so does the private research organization), though the polytechnics at 20 per cent have least. Even though the numbers in each type inevitably are small when the decisions in each category of organization are divided between the types, in total there are 37 cases, and the similarities and differences between organizations are consistent.

So there is no support for the presumption that decision-making in public professional organizations is typically a stultified maelstrom. It is not. It is often smooth and orderly. Perhaps the image that has grown up has resulted from too little research that makes direct comparisons with non-professional organizations, and too much influence from evidence on professional organizations alone (for example, Greenwood, et al. 1980 on local government in Britain;

Haywood 1974, and Levitt 1976, on the British Health Service; Harding and Scott 1982 on colleges in Britain; Baldridge 1971, Axelsson and Rosenberg 1979, and Kort-Krieger and Schmidt 1982 on American, Swedish, and West German universities respectively). For here, where they are placed alongside other service organizations, the professional services do not appear as sharply different. Furthermore, it should be recalled that strains between professional and bureaucrat are greatest when the former are trained in small-scale private practice and then move into large organizations, and are less when professionals receive their formative training within organizations and are socialized into them before becoming employed by them (Hastings and Hinings 1970). Virtually all the professionals in the organizations studied were trained within organizations.

Direct public accountability

What also shows up are the differences among the public professional organizations themselves. The differences between any *one* kind and the next are small, but the steady *progression* from the highest proportion of sporadic processes in the municipality, to hardly any in the universities, is plain, as is the inverse progression, from no constricted processes in the municipality, to higher proportions in the polytechnics and universities (table 7.1). These progressions are in line with differences in the directness of public accountability in the four forms of organization. That is, as the rules of the game change so that public accountability become less direct and more tenuous, so the proportions of sporadic processes fall and those of constricted processes rise. Sporadic processes occur most in the political party-controlled, directly publicly-accountable municipality, and least in the politically independent and less directly publicly-accountable universities. The reverse applies for constricted processes.

A municipality

The municipality was a metropolitan district covering a sprawling semi-industrialized area containing small towns and many industrial villages, in total a population of 400,000, as mentioned in chapter 4. It had the usual structure of local authorities in England which 'operate through committees and departments, and with various kinds of permanent or temporary groups' (Greenwood, et al. 1980, p. 2). It presented an immensely complicated array of committees and sub-committees of elected councillors and officials, some of them responsible for a department providing one of a wide range of services from roads and refuse collection and numerous welfare services to education (everything from infant schools up to colleges), and some of them attempting to co-ordinate.

The decision to introduce a public lottery went through or around this structure fluidly with startling speed, but it was unusual. Since the organization was directly and immediately accountable to the public through its council of elected members, which swayed it to and fro according to which of the dominant parties, Conservative or Labour, held the majority of seats and controlled the committees, so political party contention often shaped decision-making. It was conspicuous in a decision upon housing.

Like all metropolitan districts, this one was responsible for planning residential construction, both private and public, and itself built the public housing which was intended for renting by lower-income tenants. National politics precipitated events when government abandoned a scheme to buy land, and offered to the municipality a comparatively large tract which had been acquired under the scheme within the municipality's territory. This land, by the village of Upperton (the name is fictitious), was taken over and provisionally scheduled for building private houses. Its size made it a major matter. To avoid local builders being pushed aside by large national firms, a consortium of builders was formed which began negotiations with the municipality. Work on roads commenced.

Then a nationwide reorganization of local government intervened and halted all negotiations. A fresh form of the metropolitan district emerged, the majority political party changed, and the question was reconsidered. From several alternative plans put forward by officials, the new membership of the Housing Committee preferred not private house building, but the whole area being devoted to public housing in smaller units at twice the density of population. The private builders' consortium disbanded.

Now resistance arose from Upperton. Its residents were against being enveloped by public housing and feared losing all trace of their village environment. Time passed as individuals and the Upperton Residents' Association protested their case to party councillors at public meetings and in the media. Elections approached, and the majority party attempted to get the matter through committee procedures and finally settled so that the decision could not be overturned if its opponents gained control. It failed in this and when, as a result of the election, political control changed once more, the question was again reopened. Eventually, a compromise was put through, by which some housing of each type was to be built. The decision had taken a good two years of intense activity in the vortex-sporadic mode, on which the direct political accountability of the organization had made a great impact.

National Health Service Districts

The two Health Service Districts were rather less directly accountable for what they did. As operating units of the huge National Health Service organization, each responsible for numbers of hospitals, for dentistry, and for diverse community medical care (family doctors, vaccination, ante- and post-natal care, physiotherapy, and so on), they were encased within its towering structure. This began in the Cabinet, with the Minister responsible, while under him was the Department of Health and Social Security (DHSS) in London. It descended layer by layer through Regional Health Authorities (RHAs) and beneath them Area Health Authorities (AHAs, a tier subsequently abolished), until it reached district level where district management teams of senior medical, nursing, and administrative officers ran the actual service. Decision-making at district level was constantly caught up with AHA, RHA, or DHSS, waiting for one or other of these levels to approve plans or decide funding, but this hierarchy also meant that the district level was buffered from governmental and political party pressures. Whilst there was some direct public accountability in the form of community health councils, which represented political parties and voluntary societies at local level, these were only opinion-sounding bodies. Direct interest by the media or Members of Parliament was less than in the metropolitan municipality. In short, public accountability was less direct and immediate.

Polytechnics

This was again the case with the two polytechnics. These came under the education departments of two local government metropolitan districts, for which they were the high points of an education service which began with infant schools and ended with the degree-level work in the district's polytechnic. They therefore had considerable local status, and though they drew most of their students from the areas where they were located, the colleges were advertised in national directories and drew a proportion of their students from all over Britain, and some from overseas.

Although there was degree-level teaching it was a small part of the whole, most teaching being for examinations set by professional or semi-professional institutions, or for college certificates. Counterbalancing local government control, therefore, was that exercised upon syllabuses, and hence on staff and students, by external examining institutions. Moreover, the polytechnics were not themselves empowered to award their own degrees. These were under the control of a university-dominated awarding body, the Council for National Academic Awards. This multiplicity of external academic controls, plus the academic authority of the polytechnic staff, restricted the elected metropolitan district councillors to a relatively distant and general involvement – even those who sat on the polytechnics' governing bodies. They established parameters by fixing the polytechnics' budgets or making buildings available, but party politics rarely touched the decision-making within the two organizations themselves.

Universities

Least directly accountable of these publicly-financed professional organizations were the two universities. These were not directly accountable to any non-academic bodies, being incorporated like all British universities by Royal Charter given by the monarch which created them as legally independent degree-awarding organizations, not in a formal sense owned by government, even though government paid for them. Their supreme Councils represented the public

interest by including nominees of the neighbouring local government, professional societies, trades unions, and the like, but none of
these represented a body with any authority over the university.
State funds came to the universities via the national University
Grants Committee, and this was composed almost entirely of
academics. The principle of academic freedom, and the academic
prestige of their faculties, sustained a unique independence for the
two organizations, as for all universities. Though when the decisions
that were studied took place the autonomy of the universities was
being eroded by inflation, which forced frequent recourse to the
UGC, and by the UGC to the Government, for funds, whereas in
former days there had been longer-term financing, nevertheless
there was still substantial freedom (later financial cuts which made
further inroads into that freedom had not yet taken place). Party
politics were remote and there were no organs of the state or of any
other body which exerted direct influence. Accountability was rather
to the educational ideals written into the Royal Charters, to students
for whom there was a competitive market, and to academic
standards which ruled the competition for prestige.

Under these basic rules of the game, decision making in the two
universities showed remarkably high proportions of fluid and
constricted processes (50 per cent and 37 per cent, table 7.1). Whilst
this is on eight cases only (full data for analysis by type were not
available on two further decisions) it fits and completes the
progression from more vortex-sporadic cases in the municipality to
more of the other modes in the educational organizations.

For example, just as in any other organization, a budget decision
can go through a university in an uneventful constricted process. It
need not be highly political. Chapter 5 has shown that whilst a
budget is a diagram of power, any one budget is unlikely to be
momentous. At most it makes marginal changes. Thus, a twelve
month budget went through the procedures of one of the two
universities, just as it might the very similar budgeting procedures of
any organization, in three months without interruption. It first
surfaced in the Development Committee, a widely representative
body composed of the Vice-Chancellor, the senior administrative
officers, the chairpersons of faculties, professors from a range of
departments, and student representatives. During several meetings
this committee decided to give some future priority to appointments

of a new faculty in arts subjects, and recommended budgeting accordingly. A general meeting of all heads of departments discussed possible trends and gaps in subject coverage. The Finance Committee then approved a budget with these views in mind, which was routinely ratified by the university's Council. Curiously, on this occasion, prior ratification by the Senate – a wholly academic body, whereas the Council included outsiders – was skipped because the procedures were running behindhand and the Senate members knew the proposals from their other committees: the routine sequence was capable of flexible adjustment.

A budget is a familiar affair, of course, and unless unusually contested may be expected to be constricted in process. But a novel decision may also go through readily enough, if it suits the interests most closely implicated and others are disinterested. In the other of the two universities, a decision was arrived at in only three months to forge a link between itself and a larger university in another city, about an hour away by road. They established a unique joint school of 'alphanumerics' (as the subject will be called here). Formal organizationally instituted links between universities are most unusual, as each guards its independence and attempts to be self-sufficient. But in this case, most of the staff in alphanumerics suddenly left the larger university and it was faced with a crisis. There were students already enrolled and no one to teach them. Its Vice-Chancellor turned to the smaller university for help, and though the response of academics to such an approach would commonly be wary, and there would be suspicion of higher work loads for no return, in this instance the status and security of the alphanumerics department would be enhanced by the link with the more prestigious institution and its faculty responded positively. The proposal for an official joint school went fluidly through the entire committee structures of both universities at departmental, Faculty, Senate, and Council levels.

If a proposal does not suit the interests of departments or faculties the story can be different. The highly political, sporadically processed, and ultimately ineffectual attempt to change the method of appointing staff to a university, which was described in chapter 5 as an instance of a reorganization topic, showed how powerful interests when openly confronted may at the time allow a change to be formally decided upon but afterwards can nullify its implementation.

However, the unavoidable inference must be that most strategic decision-making at the top in universities is not all that complex or political. It is certainly not more so than in other organizations, and may be less so. The point is made somewhat tentatively, since it contrasts abruptly with prevalent views of what happens in universities. They have had the most politicized image among professional organizations. As 'organized anarchies' (March and Olsen 1976), in which power differentiated by the level of scholastic paradigm development in the arts, social sciences, technologies and sciences (Lodahl and Gordon 1972; Beyer and Lodahl 1976; Bresser 1984) and by resources (Pfeffer and Salancik 1974) tangles the threads, they were believed to experience the most conflict (Baldridge 1971). Perhaps this is an image which should be modified.

With considerable foresight, a warning had been given against too vivid and too general a view (Mohr 1982). The garbage-can model of decision-making in organized anarchies (March and Olsen 1976) should not be applied indiscriminately to educational organizations, nor to governmental organizations, for whilst 'it appears that some governments and some colleges and universities are characterized in large measure by this decision making pattern . . . we are probably not so fortunate as to be able to say *all* governments and universities or even nearly all' (Mohr 1982, pp. 173–4).

Decision-making in universities may therefore not be what it has seemed to be. Do the academics who write about it project too much of their own experience into their interpretations of research results? Because they personally experience the incessant talk and controversy of committee room and common room, do they too readily see this as the main feature of all decision processes, especially if their experience is not right at the top?

University committees

Where is all the noise whilst decisions pass through fluid and constricted processes? The noise is simultaneously vented by, and bounded by, the rules of the game in universities which funnel decisions through committees. Of all the variety of organizations in the Bradford studies, universities were the most 'committeed'. On average, their decisions passed through more kinds of committees than did those in any other form of organization, about four different sorts, from faculty meetings and specialist sub-committees to the higher level Senates and Councils, compared to about half that number for all decisions in all other organizations (mean formal interaction for ten decision-making cases in universities = 3.7 committees, in all other organizations = 2.1). This fits with the frequency of fluid processes in universities, for those tend to go through more committees.

These numerous committees were also predominantly standing committees, more so than in other organizations which had more *ad hoc* groups and working parties (mean number of standing committees in universities' decision processes = 3.1, in all other organizations 1.4), and they were bigger, allowing more voices to be raised (mean number of members in committees in universities = 41; in all other organizations 11: as this comparison is dominated by a Senate of 147 members in one university, a median membership of 19 compared to 7 may be more representative, but the difference is still substantial). Thus universities have structures of exceptionally numerous, permanent, and large committees – more of them, more routinely, with more members.

This structure has evolved to cope with the multiplicity of internal departments and similar sub-units which, because of their mutual independence, are each in a position to advance the claims of their own unique 'product' of teaching and/or research, and to defend their interest in it. Committees legitimize political behaviour, and at the same time diffuse responsibility for decisions so that those present are freer than they would otherwise be to negotiate and compromise (Miles 1980, p. 163; Hage 1980, p. 128). The tumult in committees, and in common rooms and corridors and on telephones between committee meetings, is not only about the decision problem but about which and whose interests should or should not be represented – academics, students, or whoever (see, for example, Kort-Krieger and Schmidt 1982).

So in a comparison of decision-making in two universities and a Health Service District with that in five business firms – a piece of research associated with the main Bradford studies – it was found that 'what happens during and within the process itself' was crucial in the universities, and also in the Health Service District (Rodrigues 1980, p. 289). It seemed that in the universities a process which led to a successful decision was not the same as one that led to a successful decision in a business firm. In a firm, adequate information and adequate resources to implement a decision were the main conditions for success, but in the universities adequate participation and agreement were more important (a successful decision was one that brought not only the benefits that had been expected but unforeseen gains in addition, and did not create any further difficulties: Rodrigues 1980).

Whilst managers in business firms appeared to emphasize comparatively instrumental requirements, academics appeared to put greater store by the process of getting to a decision. To them, success was as much or more a process in which influence could be exerted by a diversity of interests and the hierarchy was not unduly influential, and there was an element of agreement, as it was a successful outcome. Success was not necessarily linked to resources being available to carry the decision through. It might not be an exaggeration to say that academics are concerned with participation on the way to a decision more than they are concerned with the feasibility of what is decided! In this sense, the deciding is more important than the decision. At the least, in an organization of relatively mutually independent departments, as a university is, their representation in the process of deciding is primary to the success of the decision, and finding the wherewithal to implement it can be secondary.

The clear implication is that the apparently cumbersome system of decision through committees is required to represent and contain interests. It could not be dispensed with. Moreover, it is not as cumbersome as might be thought. Despite the noise in and between committees, the major decisions move step by step through each committee, and from each committee to the next, in well used orderly sequences. Discussion there is, but the matters for decision most often move smoothly onwards. Seeing the system as a whole, rather than from the perspective of a jaded committee member, decisions do move through it in a way that is fluid or constricted more often than in a sporadic way.

It may come as a relief to those who administer universities that major decisions get through this system no slower than they get through other organizations, a finding to be anticipated from the absence of any association between numbers of committees and process time already reported in chapter 4 (mean process time for ten decision-making cases in universities = 13.1 months, in all other organizations = 12.3 months). This also matches the findings for the municipality, the other kind of organization conspicuous for its committee system, which it too has evolved to cope with multiple interests. Its mean number of committees per decision-making process is almost exactly the same as in the universities, yet the average time taken by its five processes to reach a conclusion was even a little less than the general average (mean = 12 months).

The 'committeed' nature of university decision-making completes an accumulating impression of where and why this medium is most used. The findings discussed in this chapter have shown committees to be most frequent in the proceedings of publicly-owned organizations, outstanding in this respect being the municipality and the two universities, and also in larger organizations. This suggests that *committees are the response to the demands for representation and for co-ordination made either by governmental interests or by multiple internal interests, or by both.* Governmental interest is greatest in the public-sector organizations, most notably in a municipality, and internal fragmentation is greatest in large organizations and in universities.

Personal dominance

Whatever the purpose of an organization may be, and irrespective of public or private ownership or of professionalization, its strategic decision-making is in the hands of a relatively small number of people at the top. Even if the organization is large and most of its employees will never see its chief executive, it is possible for the individual in that position to exert considerable influence over the small top elite. The influence of chief executives on decisions, whilst being only one among many influences, is greater on average than that of any other single influence (table 3.1, chapter 3). Given the power base of this top job, some who hold it keep an exceptionally tight grip upon what goes on, so that decision-making never moves far from their presence and they are prominent in initiating and concluding it.

This can be seen in those organizatons in which constricted processes most occur. There are four organizations, an engineering manufacturer, a credit company, a polytechnic, and a police force, in which more than half of the processes studied were of this kind, four out of five processes in the manufacturer and three each in the others. Taken together, 65 per cent of the decision-making processes in these organizations are constricted (table 7.1, bottom row). By itself this might appear to be just an oddity in a few organizations and no meaning would be attached to it. But they have a unique common feature which explains it. Leaving the police aside for the moment, the other three all had dominant, driving, chief executives. Whilst this was not substantiated by any research directed upon the individuals themselves, it was the abiding impression of the members of the research team who met and talked to the three men, and to their senior compatriots who held this view of them, and in one instance, of a member of the research team who happened by coincidence to have worked in the organization in contact with its senior managers earlier in his career. These impressions were formed years before the data were finally analyzed and the high proportions of constricted processes noticed. The three men each had forceful personalities and strong views about the direction in which the organization should go, and this made an impact upon those who met them, and upon the managers with them. Whatever took place in senior management circles revolved around these individuals. Their authority, perhaps authoritarianism, was all-pervading. It shows here in constricted processes, kept within reach of the chief executive by diminishing the interaction and negotiation between other managers and interests, and focusing activity upon himself.

That the police force should be similar, not because of any single dominant personality but because of an authority system more prescribed and precise than that of any of the other organizations studied, comes as no surprise.

A forceful system of authority, whether one-man based or otherwise thus has a constricting effect upon decision-making, in addition to the effect traceable to differences between decisions. Since the organizations in which this appears are a privately-owned manufacturer, a privately-owned service, a publicly-owned educational institution, and a publicly-controlled police force, it appears that this effect can occur in any kind of organization. In particular, forceful personalities make their mark at the top in the public sector as well as in the private.

Organizations and decision-making

Personalities aside, organizations are the structural frameworks across which the games of strategic decision-making are played, and which are changed by the play. They are from this point of view the rules of the game which define the problems that occur and the interests which are implicated. So certain types of process are more likely in some organizations and less likely in others, because organizations influence the complexity of the problems and the politicality of the interests from which the decision processes arise. Since the chances of processes being sporadic, fluid, or constricted differ from one kind of organization to the next, it can be deduced that the chances of decisions being vortex, tractable, or familiar also differ, to the extent that each type of process appears linked with a typical form of decision. The conclusion has to be that the kind of organization in which a decision is made cannot be ignored. Organizations load the chances this way or that. They vary in how far they are inclined to a vortex-sporadic, tractable-fluid, or familiar-constricted mode of decision-making.

Reasons why decision-making differs in different organizations

Five principal reasons why decision-making differs in different organizations have been examined here (it is not implied that these exhaust all possible reasons). Three are supported, and two find little or no support.

First, there is no evidence that *commercialism*, in businesses which sell their products or services, disposes decision-making to be of one type more than another. Nor is there any evidence that the *size* of an organization matters as much as might be anticipated. Bigger organizations do not have some strikingly characteristic bureaucratic mode of making *top* decisions, because strategic decision-making processes move above the realm of bureaucratic regulation. Except in one respect: their decisions pass through more sorts of committee, though there is an intervening reason for this which is not to do with size alone – the variety of interests concerned.

There is plenty of evidence that both the *purpose* and the

ownership of an organization affect its mode of decision-making. If the purpose is manufacturing and not the provision of services, then decision-making is more likely to be vortex-sporadic. If the ownership is public rather than private, the same applies.

The fifth reason is *directness of public accountability in the public sector*. In the municipality, Health Service Districts, polytechnics, and universities studied, the more direct the accountability, the more vortex-sporadic the decision-making seemed likely to be, and the less direct the accountability, the more familiar-constricted it seemed likely to be.

For one characteristic in particular, the number of sorts of committee and arranged meeting through which a decision passes, there is a specific reason that operates in several kinds of organization. Committees appear to be a means of coping with *multiple interests*. In large organizations these may be numerous internal departments. In publicly-owned organizations they may be public interests such as departments of government. In universities they are not so much external public interests as internal academic interests.

So what modes of decision-making can be anticipated in different kinds of organization? In *nationalized manufacturing* above all, ownership and what the organization does together suggest that strategic decisions are likely to be weighty, troublesome, controversial matters with many outside influences, and arriving at them is likely to be a spasmodic drawn-out affair. That is, their managements are more likely than those in any other kind of organization to live with a vortex-sporadic mode of decision-making. For the same reasons – ownership and what the organization does, the managements of *private services* are more likely to have the very different experience of tractable-fluid decision-making. In private insurance, banking, credit, transport and other services, their less controversial problems will more often be amenable to a smoothly-paced formally-channelled speedy response. Private manufacturers and public services come in between these opposites.

Decision-making in *local government* cannot be constricted within narrow channels because of its representative structure with close political party involvement. It is likely to be vortex-sporadic where complex political matters crop up, because of this direct accountability, but routine budgets and the like are tractable enough to be processed fluidly. *Districts of the National Health Service* are very similar to this. *Universities* incline to fluid, even constricted, processes, their committee procedures holding internal politicking within bounds and carrying decisions along much more evenly than might have been thought. Indeed, there is little support for the idea that 'professional' organizations just because of the high proportion of professionally qualified personnel they employ, and their loose structures, are hampered by ineffective decision making. They evolve appropriate procedures and get there just the same.

Yet it can not simply be said that all public-sector decision-making is like this, and all private-sector decision-making is like that. Nor that in factories it is this way, in insurance companies that way, and universities another way. There are no vortex-sporadic organizations, tractable-fluid organizations, or familiar-constricted organizations. The tendencies that have been described are there clearly enough, but none are overwhelming. Apart from the public manufacturers where there is a strong bias (though to say this is to rely on two organizations only and one of them especially), decisions are made in all the groupings of organizations in all three ways. Drop into an organization a matter that raises complex problems and involves a very political set of interests, and an erstwhile placid scene becomes turbulent. Drop in something familiar which can be coped with in an accustomed way, and a scene that is often turbulent becomes placid. To decision-making, the nature of the organization matters, but so does the matter for decision. The next, and final chapter, will try to answer the fundamental question, which matters most?

8

Conclusion: A Wider Perspective

Research for what?

When the Bradford studies of decision-making began, we knew that organizations could be seen as *ensembles des jeux*, sets of overlapping power games (Crozier and Friedberg 1980). Many of these games were played out in the arenas of strategic decision-making among the members of a dominant coalition of interested parties (Cyert and March 1963), though top management itself normally remained supreme and especially so early and late in the process (DIO International Research Team 1983). Decision-making processes were circuitous (Mintzberg, et al. 1976), repeating themselves over and over again as they wended their ways towards their conclusions. Reached by routes that were not susceptible to programming by routine procedures, these conclusions were unlikely to be optimum decisions. They were much more likely to be satisficing, a blend of satisfaction and sufficing that denotes a decision not wholly satisfactory to anyone nor maximizing in any respect but good enough to carry things on for the time being (Simon 1945; 1960). They were inclined to be incremental, piecemeal little by little rather than bold strokes (Braybrooke and Lindblom 1963).

This was and is 'descriptive theory', justifiably called theory because there was more than a touch of inspired conjecture to the description it gave (Mohr 1982, p. 160). Empirical evidence was and is slender. The description, though insightful, was generalized and unduly conjectural. It was not and is barely yet sufficient grounding for 'explanatory theory', the kind of theory which tries to explain something by something else, as when disease is explained by bad sanitation or bureaucratization is explained by the difficulties of controlling and co-ordinating large-scale organizations. Nor was it a 'variance theory' (Mohr 1981, p. 156) since it did not cope with differences. It told a great deal about decision-making in general, but it had barely begun to tell anything about decision-making anywhere in particular. In which organizations with what kinds of problems and interests was decision-making more this way or more that way?

Beginnings had been made with explanation, for incrementalism was thought to be a way of 'muddling through' in public administration (Lindblom 1959) but to be more 'logical' in private business (Quinn 1978; 1980), implying that the ownership of organization and all that went with it should explain differences between them. Decision-making was also thought to differ in response to the complexity of the problem faced, and problems in educational organizations like colleges and universities were thought to be most frequently complex, as well as political (Axelsson and Rosenberg 1979; March and Olsen 1976). Yet still there was no ready means of comparing the circumstances and process of one decision-making situation with another. There was 'no generally accepted "typology" based on empirical research of the kinds of decision processes organizations make' (Mintzberg 1979, p. 59).

A typology of decision-making modes has been put forward in this book which contains descriptive theory, variance theory, and explanatory theory. The descriptive theory is that it is feasible to describe the general character of a decision-making process. The variance theory is that variation can be encompassed in three main types of movement. The explanatory theory is that one decision-making process differs from another because of differing problem complexity and interest politicality, the chances of which are loaded by the kind of organization in which the process takes place.

'Descriptive theory': what decision-making is like

The crucial widening of perspective which led to the typology was gained from the narratives of 150 cases of strategic decision-making described by executives and administrators in 30 varied organizations, on which they then answered a range of detailed questions, and from following three of these cases as they happened. It affirms the assumption that the great majority of decisions of this order arise from deliberate managerial strategies (chapter 7), as moves on a course along which management is steering. While most are positive, to do this or to do that, a surprisingly substantial minority are negative in some degree, either preserving the status quo, for example, by not making a takeover bid or not moving company headquarters; or undoing something, for example, by closing shops or hospitals (chapter 2). Strategic decisions not only do things, they refrain from doing things or undo things.

Extensive differences in *process* from decision to decision appear immediately in the wider perspective. Major decisions at this level can take as little as a month or two, or as long as four years, a vast variation. The bulk take between six months and two years (chapter 4). Contrary to popular belief, public administration can be very fast in decision-making, for instance over novel decisions which can be pushed through procedures that have been evolved to fit the usual recurrent topics that occur time and again but are not framed to deal with novelties; and private enterprise can be slow if painstaking efforts are made to gather and sift information, for search costs time. So does talk along the corridors of management, exchanging information and sounding out opinion, but if personal interaction is channelled into meetings of groups or committees it need not take more time. That is, though committees obviously do consume the hours of their individual members, on average they do not prolong the process of reaching a decision. They are a labour intensive means of smoothing the path to a conclusion.

Numerous impediments crop up in the path of decision-making processes, most often delays either due to problems which impel a re-examination of the situation, or due to opposition. Moreover, whilst some processes quickly gain momentum, others are preceded by a prolonged sluggish gestation period during which it is felt – by some if not all – that a move towards a decision could be made, but no one makes it, usually because it is feared that if the matter becomes too visible too soon it will incite opposition. Timing can be vital.

The differences found can be encompassed within a typology that allows for them because it is based upon them. Accepting the thesis that all decision-making is incremental in some measure, then within this incrementalism three main types of movement can be discerned (chapter 4). Some processes are inclined to be *sporadic*, that is informally spasmodic and protracted. Decisions to launch new products are more likely than most to be made in this way, and so are decisions on where to locate an organization's headquarters or one of its plants (if in manufacturing); products because the difficulties of dealing with diverse information on an important matter and with multiple interests in it impede the process; relocations because they are usually an unprecedented step into the unknown, and that too implicates many interests. Other processes are comparatively *fluid*, that is, smoothly-paced, formally-channelled, and speedy, such as decisions on sources of finance like a major share issue which though highly significant for the future of an organization is not politically contentious. Yet others are comparatively *constricted*, that is narrowly channelled. Deciding the budget for an organization as a whole may well be a constricted process since although this is a serious affair budgets have been decided before and so the matter can proceed along recognized channels drawing on just the usual sources of information at the appropriate stages.

If processes differ, so too do the *problems* and the *interests* from which they arise. Some problems are much more complex than others (chapter 2). This may be because they are unprecedented, or at least rare, though this alone does not make a problem complex. It may be so also, or alternatively, because it is highly consequential. That is, its consequences run far and wide because they are radical and/or serious and/or extensive and/or long-lasting.

Complexity is heightened when many interests are involved. Twenty or more different internal sections or departments, and external auditors, government departments or agencies, suppliers, customers and so forth, may enter the process at one point or another. About 40 per cent of involvements are from external interests, on top of all the internal activity. Nor does this take account of the much larger number of *individuals* who come and go from both internal and external interests. Of course, there are wide differences, and in some cases involvement is relatively simple.

Simpler, too, are those problems where it is reckoned that the decision has as good as been made already, and what is happening is really just going through the motions without affecting the end result. With less at stake, even nothing at stake, there is not the uncertainty that otherwise makes things feel more complex. It is startling to discover that this '*quasi-decision making*' occurs in a third or more of all cases (chapter 2).

Contrary to the imagined world of power-filled top corridors, not all strategic decisions are highly political. Some are, some are not. The influence brought to bear by the involved interests differs enormously both from decision to decision and interest to interest (chapter 3). There are decisions which are felt to be heavily influenced by most interests, that is high-pressure decisions, and others in which few interests exert much influence, that is low-pressure decisions. But pressure is potential rather than actual politicality. Actual politicality is shown more by contending objectives, when influence is exerted in opposite directions. There can be extremely high pressure where all the influence is in the same direction, in favour of the same outcome, a situation which although fragile, since a switching of influence could completely change it, is not yet so political as a situation fraught with contention.

Whilst being only one influence among many, general management, and specifically the chief executive, have more influence on average than any other single source, and they together with their departmental or divisional colleagues mostly keep the balance of power tilted internally in their favour. They hold a constrained domination over a managerial pluralism of interests. It is a hold that nevertheless can be broken on occasion by the influence of interests outside the working organization itself. The involvement of external interests such as suppliers, or perhaps subsidiaries of the same owning corporation, or indeed group head office, increases the total numbers of interests concerned, unbalances the pattern of influence so that a few exert much more than others, and can result in external influence being the greater especially in boundary decisions such as takeovers, or domain decisions on prices or market image and the like.

Usually, however, external interests are outweighed by what have been called the 'internal heavyweights' (chapter 3), the production-type, sales, and accounting units which are involved in the great majority of decisions and are highly influential. Less often involved are research and design departments, but when they do come in on those decisions that are relevant to them they can be very influential. Purchasing, personnel, and maintenance units are comparative lightweights, as are trades unions.

Indeed, the influence of trades unions is something that differs little from case to case and time to time. It is constantly weak. Unions do not change decisions. If they achieve anything it is during the implementation of decisions long after they have been made.

Government does somewhat better, from its own point of view. Whilst most of the time the cajolings of its departments and agencies when backed merely by routine subsidies and the like are of little significance, every now and then the intervention of a major department such as the Treasury or Department of Employment in a particular decision for a particular purpose can be most influential (though not always successful, for despite this influence the decision can still go against it). Remarkably, the arms of the state are no more effective in state-owned organizations than in the private sector, and conversely, are as effective in private companies as in state-owned organizations. The difference is that they reach into public-sector organizations more often, which means that the proportion of occasions when they are materially influential is in fact lower!

'Explanatory theory': why process are one type rather than another

The enlargement of 'descriptive theory' summarized above reduces appreciably the extent to which it has to rest on conjecture (Mohr 1982, p. 160). Decision-making is no longer just a muddled, complex, political affair, but one which varies discernably in process, in complexity, and in politicality. Its outlines begin to emerge, with some impression of how often and how much it varies in each of these. As the outlines emerge, so ingredients of 'explanatory theory' begin to be evident.

For the threefold typology of sporadic, fluid, and constricted movement demands an explanation of why decision-making processes are as they are. It expresses in a manageable form the differences that call for explanation, and it poses the question why processes should differ like this. Why, as decisions arise, do managers and administrators in the top levels of organizations turn to their colleagues and to outsiders for information and advice, confer among themselves in offices and committee rooms, negotiate alternatives, pause for further investigation or because they meet opposition, reconsider, and come together on a board or council for final authorization? Why do they do these and all the other things, which make up a process spanning months or years, in a manner that becomes more one type of process rather than another? Why if a decision is reached in sporadic fashion should it have been reached that way and not in any other way? The same question can be asked of decisions reached in the other two ways.

The answer proposed is because of the problems and the interests that arise. Because the problem raised, and the interests implicated, by one decision are not the same as those encountered by the previous decision – nor will they be the same as those in the next – the process of arriving at each will differ. Each episode of decision-making combines a complexity and a politicality that is dealt with by those at the top by engaging in the activities that are here called processes.

Some decisions are both sufficiently complex in problems and political in interests to generate a vortex into which all are swept. It is the combination of high complexity and high politicality that justifies calling them vortex decisions, the weightier controversial matters from which eddies run throughout the managerial echelons to suck everyone and everything into the swirl of activity (chapter 6). This activity is most often a sporadic type process, so that the first of three modes of decision-making which explain process by a typical combination of complexity and politicality is *vortex-sporadic*. It bears out Hage's (1980, p. 121) forerunner hypotheses that 'high-risk situations' bring out the latent conflicts between interest groups, conflicts that can be managed and reduced by information search and discussion during lengthened processes.

The second mode ensues from a combination of lower complexity and least politicality in less awkward and relatively unfettered matters, which, though they are unusual and strategic, and not routine, are comparatively tractable. They can be handled in more fluid fashion. This is the *tractable-fluid mode*.

Third are those matters which are recognizable, more usual, shorter-term, and less widely influenced. Because they bring familiar problems, probably least complex of all, and familiar interests, probably no more than mildly political in nature, they can be processed in a constricted way. This is the *familiar-constricted mode*.

By no means does every case of decision-making fall into one or other of these three modes (chapter 6), but they are the only pronounced pattern found.

Decision-making processes are therefore explicable first and foremost by the complexity and politicality to which they are a response. *Both* complexity and politicality must always be taken into account, never just the one or the other, in what can for this reason be called a *dual explanation*. Since there are three identifiable combinations of complexity and politicality, that is vortex, tractable, and familiar combinations, each is a variant within the dual explanation. Thus there is a *three-way dual explanation*.

Thus movement towards a decision is best explained by the levels of complexity and of politicality in the matter for decision. Each combination is linked to a type of process that, by implication, arises from it. To know the process, first know the complexity of the problems and the politicality of the interests.

It is sometimes possible to foretell something of the likely mode of decision-making from the *topic* of decision (chapter 5). And the other way around, it is possible with some topics of decision to foretell which mode is *not* likely. Decisions about inputs of finance or materials, such as a share issue or components supplies, are relatively straightforward and have none of the vortex character which engenders a sporadic process. They are neither mystifyingly complex nor politically blocked.

Decisions on new products or on personnel questions such as job assessment or union recognition are never tractable enough for a fluid process. They are always liable to run into difficulties that are both complex and political.

Decisions on any aspect of organization, including internal reorganizations, mergers with or major acquisitions of other organizations, or the siting of a headquarters or a large plant, are hardly ever familiar enough to be held within a constricted process. Their novelty and their uncertain ramifications raise them to a level of complexity and politicality that cannot be held within the 'usual channels'.

Looking at what is likely to happen rather than at what is not likely to happen, the vortex features of most of these reorganization, boundary, and location topics, all of which contain complex and political imponderables, incline them towards sporadic processes, though they can be made in more fluid fashion particularly if they are long anticipated and are pushed through with the backing of highest authority. New product questions are also inclined to the vortex-sporadic mode, except in a firm where everyone is used to launching new products, in which case they can be familiar-constricted. In contrast, decisions on services in service organizations do not have the same impact as new products in manufacturers, being neither very complex nor very political. Although they are relatively unusual, for service organizations do not repeatedly change their range of services in the way that some manufacturers change their product range, they are less troublesome. As for plans and budgets, although drawing them up is regarded as a serious business, they too have much less impact for they change things marginally, if at all. They are statements of the balance of power more than they are flights of fancy about the future. This incrementalism allows them to be handled in ways that are mostly tractable-fluid or familiar-constricted.

However, the topic of decision is just a label for the matter in hand and, whilst it can give some indication of what the decision-making will probably be like, it does not *add* to the explanation of process given by problem complexity and interest politicality. To that explanation has to be added the rules of the game that organizations set (chapter 7).

The framework of organization in which strategic decisions originate forms the rules for decision-making. It establishes the internal divisions of work and of authority which fix the interests involved and the scope of decisions, and defines which other organizations, the suppliers, unions, governments, or whatever, are likely to become interested. It prescribes the bounds of what in normal circumstances may not be considered, as well as what may. Whilst all modes of decision-making occur in all forms of organization, the rules of the game are slanted in organizations so that in some there are likely to be more decisions which are complex and political, whilst in others fewer decisions will be complex and political, and because of these differences, different modes of decision-making are more likely or less likely to occur.

Purpose and ownership, what an organization is for and who in the last resort determines what it is for, are basic to this. Organizations that are either manufacturing in purpose, or state-owned, are inclined to decision-making in the vortex-sporadic mode. Publicly-owned manufacturers, therefore, show a congruent double effect disposing their decision-making in this direction. The public scrutiny to which they are exposed contributes to an exceptional frequency of weighty controversial decisions in sporadic processes. At the opposite extreme are private services such as insurance, banking, credit, and transport, where in less ruffled waters there is a congruent double effect of ownership and purpose which accentuates the tractable-fluid mode. In between are private manufacturers, and public services.

Procedures are developed to facilitate decision-making in the circumstances created by the rules of the game. the most noticeable example is the committee, in any of its many forms from *ad hoc* group to standing council or board. It is prevalent in the decision-making of all those sorts of organizations in which multiple and potentially contending interests are the norm, for committees serve to represent and to vent them. Three sorts of organizations stand out in this respect, first state-owned organizations of every kind from nationalized utilities to municipalities, second, larger organizations either public or private where specialist departments multiply because of their size, and third organizations in which internal units are minimally interdependent and so can most easily pursue their own ends, as in universities.

Contrary to beliefs that organizations with big proportions of professionally qualified employees, like universities, polytechnics, Health Service districts, and municipalities, resound with bickering between different professional sections, which stultifies decision-making, they do not show undue frequencies of the vortex-sporadic mode that might reflect this. Their decision-making is often tractable-fluid, indeed. Whatever bickering there is takes place along corridors and within committees in a manner that on the whole does not frustrate the major decisions. Universities are the extreme example of organizations in which numerous committees absorb the verbiage so that the matter proceeds onwards nonetheless.

Nor is there any obvious evidence for a belief that business drive markedly distinguishes decision-making in commercial organizations. Contrary, too, to the belief that decision-making in larger organizations is bureaucratically ponderous and unwieldy, there is no evidence of this in decision-making at the strategic level, as distinct from the more routined programmed decesion-making lower down, apart from a tendency in the very smallest organizations, and only in these, to reach decisions rather sooner.

But, even so, organization counts. Decision-making is swayed towards one mode rather than another in manufacturing, in services, under state as against private ownership, and if in state ownership by more direct public accountability. Yet there is no kind of organization, manufacturing, public, or any other, in which all decision-making is in one mode only. How much, then, does organization count?

Decision or organization: which matters most?

A decision may stumble along sporadically, or flow along fluidly, or circle constrictedly, because of the kind of complex and political matter it is, and because of the kind of organization it is in. Both matter. *Which matters most?*

On the one hand, it is the complexity and politicality of what is under consideration that brings top managers and administrators to search for information in the hope that it will tell them what to do or will support their argument, to consult and persuade one another, to hold meetings, to seek outside views, to do all the things that make up a decision process. That is, the process is their attempt to solve problems and to accommodate interests.

On the other hand, they only do this because they *are* top managers and administrators, and they are top managers and administrators because they are in an organization that makes them so. Its features influence the problems to be solved and the interests to be accommodated.

Is it possible to walk into an executive suite, or a central administrative building, and say to yourself: 'I know what's going on here. Broadly speaking, decision-making in all these corporations is much the same. Whatever is bothering them at the moment they will be tackling it in much the same way as all the others, and the process by which they get there will be much the same'? Or must you be more circumspect, and before you start thinking very far at all find out what it is that is bothering them, and only then begin to anticipate what may be going on?

Evidence

The evidence is simple. It suggests essentially that all three modes of decision-making, vortex-sporadic, tractable-fluid, and familiar-constricted, occur in every kind of organization studied, and that all three modes *can* occur in any one organization. There is no such thing as vortex-sporadic organizations or tractable-fluid organizations or familiar-constricted organizations, as the previous chapter said. There is too much variation from decision to decison for that.

With one exception, each of the *kinds* of organizations grouped in table 7.1 shows all three types of decision process. The exception is the two publicly-owned manufacturers, neither of which show any fluid processes. However, it can hardly be said on the basis of findings for only two organizations that there never can be a fluid process in a publicly-owned manufacturer, especially as other public organizations and other manufacturing organizations do show cases of fluid process.

Within each single organization, too, variation is the rule. The majority show at least one case of each type of process, and there is no consistency among those which show just two types that could be grounds for believing that decisions could never be made in them in the third way. Again, the publicly-owned manufacturers are an exception – for in one of them all five cases of decision-making follow the same, sporadic, kind of process. This is an exception that draws greater attention to the prevailing variation, and it is not by itself enough to throw doubt on the presumption that from decision to decision different processes are to be expected.

Different topics in the same organization

Thus decisions on different topics in the same organization follow different processes. It would be extraordinary if they did not. It is hard to imagine that in, say, a brewery, a decision on a takeover of another brewery, a decision on a financial reconstruction, and a decision to computerize, would all be made in the same way. Nor were they, for these are actual cases, the first of a sporadic process, the second fluid, the third constricted. The first was a huge takeover, relative to the size of the original brewery, a decision that was the outcome of a series of on-and-off sporadic negotations. The second was a historic change from total owner control to a substantial injection of outside capital, which despite family disagreement went through comparatively fluidly. The third was a major but familiar enough reappraisal of computer needs and systems that was made via a constricted process.

In another example, as it happens also with liquid outputs, there were all three types of processes within a publicly-owned regional water utility. A drawn-out, sporadic process reached a decision on large-scale, long-term investment in an integrated regional pipeline network. A fluid process arrived at an annual budget that was also in effect a decision on the price that consumers everywhere should be charged. A narrowly channelled constricted process coped with a decision to revoke a longstanding arrangement with local governments whereby they had collected the water charges along with their own rates, or local taxes, and to bill consumers direct, which required a big administrative reorganization and accepted risks and costs hitherto incurred by the local governments.

Same topic in different organizations

Not only do decisions on different topics in any one organization follow different processes, but the converse is also true: decisions on the same sort of topic in different organizations often follow the same type of process. For instance, a corporate plan is a plan wherever it is and whatever kind of organization it plans for. The same sorts of estimates are requested from the various sections of the organization, and the same exercises in collating them are undertaken centrally. Similar discussions arise over who has what, while similar final overall estimates pass to and fro and are scaled up or down. The same wide array of those whose positions are affected choose their time (or have it chosen for them) when they may put their point of view. So in the normal course of affairs, decisions on plans everywhere follow conventional channels. If these are broad enough to involve all parts of the organization far and wide, then a dispersed fluid process takes place, but if the matter is confined to narrower channels the process is relatively constricted.

Thus corporate plans were drawn up in *both* a Health Service District and in a private industrial firm in a similar fashion, being a first-ever strategic appraisal of future hospital and domiciliary medical services in the Health Service District and a 15-year rolling sales and production plan in the firm. Likewise, plans in *both* an entertainments organization and a publicly-owned manufacturer were drawn up in a similar constricted fashion, the one covering a symphony orchestra's programme for the season and again the other covering sales and production.

The matter for decision matters most

What answer does this suggest to the question of which matters most for process, the decision or the organization? If different decisions in the same organization are made by different types of processes, and the same sorts of decisions are made in different organizations by the same types of processes, this is further evidence that it is the complexity and politicality of what is under decision which matters rather than the organization.

It is the nature of what is under decision that creates greater or lesser complexity. Perhaps it is a rare, or even unique, decision for the organization – or perhaps it is a comparative commonplace. It may be potentially consequential, a radical change with widespread and long-range effects, or not all that consequential. Perhaps it is wide open to all possibilities, or perhaps it is already half decided. It may involve numerous sources of information, internal and external, or there again only a few sources.

In the same way, it is the nature of what is under decision that creates the politicality. It may attract influence from many quarters, or not many. It may be subject to a great deal of pressure, or to very little; be highly contentious, or not at all contentious.

Clearly, decisions at the strategic level cannot be organized into a uniform pattern of action so that in a given organization they all take place in the same way. Of course, to those who take part the same powerful faces appear, the same indiscretions have to be guarded against, the same frustrating meetings are held, the same anxieties persist, the same insider wisecracks get the same laughs. On the surface the busy managerial round may appear to flow on much the same. Yet within it, the currents of activity change from one strategic decision to the next. The processes of decision-making that wend their ways through it frequently differ. For these processes arise in ideas and events that cannot be subjected to the administrative control systems of an organization. Bits of them can be, of course. Forms are filled in, and standing committees meet regularly, and so on. But these are mere fragments within such a process. By definition these decisions are not routine, even if some recur periodically as plans and budgets do. Routines, procedures, instructions, and the like govern mostly what is done lower in the hierarchy. They govern the work that implements – or is supposed to implement – the strategic top decisions. The processes of making these strategic decisions are *in* the structure of an organization but not wholly *of* it.

The difference made by being in one kind of organization rather than another is that matters of a particular nature are either more likely or less likely to come up for decision. Highly complex and/or political decisions seem more likely to arise in some organizations, for example in industrial firms. Less complex and/or less political decisions seem more likely to arise in others, for example in commerce. There is a greater or lesser propensity for what we have termed vortex or tractable or familiar matters. The organization loads the chances, though not so heavily as to exclude completely any one mode of decision and process.

Therefore to tell, or to foretell, what manner of things are happening or may well happen, that is what the character may be of the process of actions and events that leads up to a strategic decision, it is best to bear in mind *both* decision and organization. What is the decision itself about, and how complex are the problems and how political the interests? What kind of an organization is the decision in, who owns it and for what purpose, and how big is it? But of the two it is more important to think primarily of the decision. *The matter for decision matters most.*

This means that as managers and administrators put their minds to the making of a decision, they run up against much the same problems and interests wherever they are. For instance, whatever the firm and whatever its ownership, the same sorts of questions about future sales and supplies are entailed in considering a possible new product, and the same kinds of views are expressed. Whatever the organization and whatever it does, the same sorts of difficulties are encountered in reshuffling responsibilities and departmental territories, and the same kinds of sensitivities are met. What is more, the similarities of response generate similar decision-making processes.

Managerial rationalities: and football in a garbage can

Implicit in this assertion is the theory that the rationalities of coping with the matter for decision are the foremost driving forces behind the process of pronouncing upon it. Managerial rationalities lie behind the way in which the matter is processed.

There has long been a model of managerial problem-solving, but not of the process of decision-making, and the two are not the same. The classic model of problem-solving, following a logical sequence which begins by defining the problem and continues through scanning information and assessing alternatives to choosing a solution, has been profusely criticized as unrealistic, and suggested variations upon it have proliferated. Though it continues to be a managerial aspiration as to how to tackle a problem, it was not and is not the *social process* of reaching a strategic decision. There is a sense in which this has to be looked at the other way around. 'Although often equated with decision making, problem solving is defined by its origin, whereas decision making is defined by its ending – a decision' (Starbuck 1983, p. 91). In other words, there are two different questions being asked. One asks how a problem should be, or is being, solved, the other asks how a decision comes about.

This book, within its limits, has been trying to answer the second question, since the means of getting there is important of itself: 'the outcomes are almost beside the point, and the true focus and emphasis are instead on how one gets to them' (Mohr 1982, p. 158). It would be an overstatement to say that to understand strategic decision-making is to understand organizations, for there is more to organizations than that. But to understand how these decisions come to pass is to understand more about the innermost workings of the top echelons who govern organizations.

Managers and administrators do not do what they do during decision-making without rhyme or reason – not in their own eyes at any rate. Collective reasonings underly their actions. It has been said (chapter 6) that the first of these is problem-directed reasoning. Thus the classic model of problem-solving, whilst not a model of the process of decision-making, is a rationale for some part of what transpires during each process. It is an aspiration that guides the seeking for information, the compiling of reports and the weighing of possibilities. It is a *problem-solving rationality* that underlies many of the steps taken.

If there were an acknowledged classic model of the accommodation of interests, equivalent to that of problem-solving, it would presumably postulate a logical sequence, from demarcating what is at stake for each interest, through elucidating the preferences of each, to exploring the range of acceptable and unacceptable alternatives (some models of this kind have been worked out, for example by Thibaut and Kelley 1959). It has been implied that it is with aspirations of this kind that people are approached for their views, possibilities are mulled over, and influence is exerted. Theoretically, therefore, the steps taken in decision-making are also explicable by an *interest-accommodating rationality*, whereby what is done is done in recognition of the viewpoints and degrees of influence of the implicated interests.

These dual rationalities, problem-solving and interest-accommodating, underlie the explanations of decision-making which have been put forward. They mean that for top managers and administrators not only are skills in assessing costs, capacity, and so on, important, but so are skills of judgement and political finesse. There is no top decision which does not call for both the know-how to deal with the complexity of problems and the 'know-who' to deal with the politicality of interests.

These two rationalities are necessary but not sufficient, for they arise from the further *rationality of control* that guides the management and administration of organizations themselves and therefore shapes the rules of the game. For good or for ill, organizations control the daily activities of large numbers of people, so that work gets done in a co-ordinated way. Each is a regulated social machine, despite the machine having plenty of play in it or seizing up now and again. Even the decision-making of the powerful is subject to rules.

Yet decision-making games shaped by these managerial rationalities need not be rational. The product of simultaneous rationalities is not wholly rational in terms of any one of them. The best way of tackling a problem may not allow for opposing interests, the incursion of influential interests may prohibit some otherwise suitable problem solutions, and either may offend the rules of the game. Decision-making and its outcomes are therefore to a degree non-rational, though in practice the blending of different rationalities is usually reasonable – if this is not too great a play on words – and decision-making is fundamentally about how they can be reasonably blended.

Football in a garbage can

Indeed, what happens is usually reasonable and usually humdrum. Of course, there is drama here and there from time to time as each process unfolds, but it is rarely melodrama. While what happens is strategic and worrisome to those concerned, every tale is not of action-packed excitement. The tale of the contest between Alwyn and Giles in the firm of Toxicem, with which this book began, is one of the exceptions, not the only one in the Bradford studies, but still an exception.

There may be what have been called 'organized anarchies' where decision-making reaches such a pitch that what is wanted, how it is to be done, and who is involved, are so confused and unconnected that the occurrence of a topic for decision can be likened to dropping garbage into an unsteadily whirling garbage can, to see what happens (Cohen, et al. 1972). But whilst the image of rollicking in a dented dustbin is fun, the wide differences in decision-making belie it as a general model. Some instances in the vortex-sporadic mode look a little like it, but those in the tractable-fluid and familiar-constricted modes do not look like it at all. Given the many interests that are implicated, an organization is certainly 'a collection of choices looking for problems' (Cohen, et al. 1972, p. 2), but decision-making does not lack all direction. 'Participants generally think actions do promise to solve problems; most problems are generated or remodelled to justify intended actions. Participants also see logic in problem-solving activities despite their disorganization, and participants react to actions' results' (Starbuck 1983, p. 91). From the worm's eye view of the individuals who suffer in colleges and universities (Cohen, et al. 1972; March and Olsen 1976), most decisions may appear to be in a whirling garbage can (assuming worms in garbage cans) because they see the endless talk, exaggeration and coming and going that agitate the daily round, but something nearer a bird's eye view shows that the strategic decisions transcend this (chapter 7). Some decision-making on some topics, such as reorganizations (March and Olsen 1983) may be more garbage-can-like more often, but the aspersion of 'organized anarchy' is 'unfair' (DIO International Research Team 1983) to all but a small minority of decisions in some organizations. It is more fruitful to envisage several modes of decision-making that change from decision to decision.

Nor is decision-making typically as chaotic as has been fancied when it has been likened to a soccer football game with many balls on a round sloping pitch surrounded by goals, and the players coming on and off as they please (March and Romelaer 1976, p. 276;

Weick 1976)! This football in a garbage gan, if the metaphors may be mixed, is too haphazard, too chaotic, and too individualistic.

The decision-making game is played by groups, or by individuals backed by groups, who act deliberately, even though what they do does not necessarily have the result they hoped for because so much else is happening at the same time. A more fitting image than soccer is that of American football, a kind of outdoor chess game in light-weight space suits. It is a team game of continually redefined problems and recalculated tactics which swings to and fro in bursts of action between pauses. Though the analogy fits well, a decision-making game naturally has a few embellishments beyond the normal football game. The field has an elastic boundary and is bumpy, and there are numbers of teams trying to get their hands on the ball. Some teams are much bigger and have thicker protective padding and harder helmets. Though there is a common aim to get the ball from one end of the field to the other, during the game there may be disagreement on where the ends are. Eventually one team or coalition of teams pushes its way through, holding the ball to where it says the end is. Since there are elastic boundaries, different numbers of teams, and movable ends, the mode of play changes from game to game.

Diagnosing and changing

Diagnosis and prognosis

Since the mode of play does change from one occasion to the next, what scope is there for diagnosing what is happening, or for a prognosis of what is likely to happen? While there can be no question of determining every move that is made, there can be an attempt to comprehend the general character of the process. The character of what is happening or is likely to happen can be understood by considering the *organization* where it is happening, the *topic* which it is said to be about, and the *substance of the matter* being decided.

First, the organization. The analysis in the previous chapter suggests the questions to ask. Is it manufacturing or is it a service? Is it public-sector or is it private-sector? If a public-sector service, is it immediately and directly politically accountable, or is it accountable in a comparatively indirect way? Is it large, or is it small?

Though the answers to these questions will not take a diagnosis or prognosis very far, they are a beginning. As was said earlier, they will show the direction in which the chances are loaded. At its simplest, it may be inferred that being in manufacturing industry, or in the public sector, often increases the complexity and/or politicality of the matter on hand – in a word, makes it more of a vortex – and thereby increases the chances of a sporadic process. Being in services, whether commercial such as financial institutions or non-commercial such as colleges or health, or in the private sector, allows lower complexity and/or politicality – so matters are more likely to be tractable or familiar – and thereby increases the chances of fluid or constricted processes. Among public-sector services, the greater pressures of direct accountability mean greater politicality and again, therefore, the tendency to sporadic processes. All fragmented organizatons, such as the very largest which are broken down into many sections and departments, or municipalities with multiple separate divisions, or universities divided into semi-independent faculties and departments, tend to practise decision by committee so that their many fragments can be represented, a labour-intensive but not a procrastinating method of making decisions.

However, knowing a little about the organization is only a guide to probabilities. It has been asserted that the matter for decision matters most for the *type* of process, and therefore it is to this that the greatest attention must be paid. The topic that it is ostensibly about may give a clue. Those concerned will label it, and the label will place it in a topic category. For instance, it may be spoken of as merging of departments (reorganization category), an attempt to raise more capital (financial input), an investment in new equipment (technology), a plan or a budget (control system). As some categories of topic are inclined more towards certain types of process, to know the topic gives a greater guide again to what is likely. Which categories of topic are inclined to which types of process were summarized in table 5.3. A product decision in a manufacturer, for example, is likely to be made in sporadic fashion; but if the firm frequently ventures into new products so that such decisions are familiar, it can be made in constricted fashion.

Putting two and two together, and taking a step that is an inference from figure 5.1 on topic differences and table 7.1 on organization differences, we might suggest that sporadic, fluid, or constricted processes are *most likely* as follows:

Sporadic processes on product, personnel, reorganization, boundary, location, and perhaps technology topics
in
publicly-owned organizations, especially manufacturers.
Fluid processes on inputs, reorganization, boundary, controls, and
services topics
in
private services (and universities).
Constricted processes on product, personnel, controls, and service
topics
in
private manufacturing industry (and universities).

But until there can be research with greater numbers of cases in each topic category this must remain something of a guess. Even if accurate, it is insufficient because decisions on many topics are equally prone to either of two types of process, and some to any of the three types. To sort out which decision is most likely to be processed which way, more needs to be known than the decision topic and the nature of the organization, useful though these are. The substance of what it is about must be known, and known in a balanced way.

This is because the dual explanation of process by the complexity and the politicality of the matter for decision means that only by knowing something of both these two aspects can a tolerably reliable diagnosis or prognosis be made.

The questions that must be asked about the decision topic are, first, *how complex is it?* To what extent is it without precedent, radical and far-reaching in its possible consequences, open to an uncertain range of alternative conclusions, and involving diverse interests? Second, *how political is it?* To what extent is it liable to be influenced by numerous interests, particularly from outside the organization, and to be contentious?

For example, if the answers for a reorganization topic are that it is, in relation to other decisions, outstandingly serious in its consequences, implicating diverse influential interests – which have contending aims, some of them external – then it is presumably a *vortex* decision. All these criteria need not be met, as long as most are mostly met. If the decision is of a vortex kind, then it may be hard to know how to handle, and it may fall outside the usual remit of standing committees and customary procedures. A special project team or working party selected just for this may be formed. Differing views will have to be accommodated, one way being to represent them in the membership of such a special team, but if this is not practicable (as it is not with outside interests) then contacts will have to be made and views sounded out. It will take time to draw upon a range of sources of opinion and for people to talk things over along the way, and there will be delays whilst reports are awaited, resistance is overcome, or alternatives thought out afresh. In other words, the chances are that there will be a relatively lengthy *sporadic* process over a year or two, oscillating between slack periods and bursts of activity.

If instead the answers for the same topic should be that it is, in relation to other decisions, unusual with widespread consequences, but nevertheless not so serious as many other strategic decisions nor so contentious, having evenly-balanced influences and no dominant interest to be dealt with – then it is a relatively *tractable* decision. Despite its unusual nature it will not be so difficult to handle as vortex decisions are, having less varied points of view to be reckoned with and less chance of dispute. Interruptions and delays will be less likely since there will be greater confidence in most sources of information and therefore less need to pause for reassessment. Information will be more quickly obtained, and hold-ups due to opposition are unlikely. Normal procedures will be adequate, including the customary meetings and committees. In other words, the chances are that there will be a relatively speedy *fluid* process, concluded in months rather than years.

But if the answers should be that the matter is, in relation to other decisions, fairly commonplace and well-rehearsed with limited consequences that do not directly involve outside interests – then it is presumably what has been termed a *familiar* decision. Although strategic, it is the kind of thing which people have become used to and for which procedures have evolved. It concerns a number of internal departments or sections, one or two of which will influence it strongly, but it will not require consultations outside the organization. A senior executive or official, probably the chairman or managing director or equivalent, is likely to be able to steer it through without checking with any more superior authority, and with the minimum of committee work, turning for information to the usual departments. In other words, the chances are that there will be a relatively narrowly channelled *constricted* process.

Hence the diagnosis and prognosis of process depend upon at least a modicum of knowledge about the *complexity* and *politicality* of the matter to be decided. If enough can be found out, or surmised, to suggest whether the complexity and politicality are at a vortex, tractable or familiar level, then the most likely type of route to a decision – sporadic, fluid or constricted – can be deduced. The topic alone is, by comparison, only broadly indicative.

Changing the process and its outcome

In general, managers and administrators are satisfied with, or at least uncomplainingly inured to, the methods by which decisions are attained in their organizations. Despite the everyday humourism about too much 'jaw-jaw', and the sarcasms of those whose personal time is swallowed by meetings in the most 'committeed' organizations, when asked about specific cases managers and administrators have very few criticisms to make. Looking back over what was done, they see the information on which they drew conclusions as having been sufficient, within what was practicable at the time, and the whole affair as having been tolerably expeditious. They make no distinction whatever between topics in this respect. They do not see new products decisions as having gone along well but reorganization decisions as having been handled badly, or anything of that kind. They are equally content with the handling of all topics.

There is just a slight inclination to be less content with cases in the vortex-sporadic mode, and to be most satisfied with cases in the tractable-fluid mode. It is an inclination that matches the presumption of the classic model of problem-solving, mentioned before in this chapter, that there should be an orderly uninterrupted progression to a solution. In short, top managers and administrators prefer smooth fluid decision-making where it proves possible, though they accept that often it is not and do not complain when it is not.

However, should a change in the way things are being done be desired, or a change in the probable outcome, then clearly the most effective move is to change the matter that is under consideration.

This will change the process and its outcome.

Most decision-making is preceded by a long gestation period during which there are comments about and allusions to a possible decision, but no definite step is taken towards one. It is during this period that the whole matter is least public, least defined, and most open to being construed differently. Those who see it as likely to take shape in a form that they would welcome will be wanting to put the idea on an agenda or to ask for departmental reports on it, or to take some other step that will, so to speak, start the ball rolling. Those who have doubts will want to hold back and postpone any step of this kind to give time for the matter to be put in a different light and perhaps redefined. Given time, circumstances may change, or attention may be caught by something else, or some whose interests are implicated may move out or may be reorganized out. There is a chance that it may never happen.

For the doubters, all is not lost even when the process proper of making a decision is under way. It may still be possible to reconstrue the matter in some degree. This is what Alwyn did during the process at Toxicem (see chapter 1). After an opening phase in which opinion went against him, he succeeded in putting the same question, whether or not to generate electricity, in a fresh light. He did not redefine it, but made it appear more wide open and more uncertain than before.

But what a decision is about can be redefined and relabelled. For instance, what begins as an idea for a complete new product line can be scaled down so that the topic under consideration becomes just a modification to existing product lines. Thus its consequences will become less serious and more susceptible to confident forecasts. Fewer diverse interests will be involved, for the research department will be less interested and will leave it to the development engineers, and the project will fall below the level of expenditure that requires head-office authorization so they will not intervene. Being less strange and risky, the idea will become less contentious. So a vortex matter is replaced by one that is familiar and can be moved along in a less bothersome constricted way. Similarly, a proposal for a wide reorganization can be scaled down to become a trial arrangement of a section, or a total rebuilding can become just an extension of premises. This is incrementalism in practice, dealing with simpler matters that are mere increments of change and avoiding leaps into the dark for as long as possible.

It is also possible to take decision-making out of its usual course by spotting the odd-ball. A peculiar topic outside the usual run can bypass or slip through normal procedures, as did the lottery decision in a municipality, because neither procedures nor participants are prepared for it. It can be slipped through quickly. The condition for this to be done is the backing of influential individuals who otherwise could impede its passage. By definition, peculiar topics with influential backing are not going to occur often, however, and therefore this is not a tactic that will be available frequently enough to be easily foreseen and taken advantage of.

Hypothetically, it might be possible to opt for a quiet life by avoiding or scaling down all matters that look as if they could be tricky and weighty, such as relocation and reorganization proposals, new product ideas, new personnel-grading schemes, wholesale re-equipments or rebuildings, controversial budgets, and anything else of such a genre. They might then be disposed of with less trouble in less time. But this might not be realistic. It could mean a timid avoiding of anything very complex and political. It could mean a stagnating organization in which the potentially most strategic decisions were never taken. It could mean a consistent focus upon the more familiar matters from which there is little to be learned. It could mean failing to keep up with the times.

Looking back and looking forward

Diagnosis, prognosis, and change all rest upon hypotheses about *what* decision-making is like and *why* it is like that. These hypotheses are not certainties, but attempts at better interpretations of data that are never enough, with ideas that always need improvement. Though the growing understanding is plausible, researchers have to admit that deep down they cannot be sure of what they are doing and what they are saying in a world that might be fundamentally incomprehensible. They strive to provide an understanding of it, knowing that especially in the study of decision-making '. . . there are no clear universals. . . . Although organizations appear often to satisfice rather than to maximize, some reasonably clear counter examples can be observed. Although individuals and groups in organizations often act strategically in the face of conflict of interest, they sometimes fail to do so. Although organizational actions are

often incremental, they sometimes seem to reflect heroic leaps.'
(March 1981; 235). In other words, the uncertainties of life and the
inadequacies of research are manifold. In a way, all research is bad
research.

Apart from this ever-present sense of inadequacy, we regret in
particular our failure to accomplish any systematic comparison of the
step by step sequences in decision-making processes over time.
Whilst this book contains many histories of actions and events, and
compares many of their features, it does not contain chronological
comparisons of one process with another in terms of what follows
what. Something of this sort may yet be achieved, but so far it has
eluded us. We ourselves need more time for analysis, and we may
need more data.

However, what was achieved was a form of comparison in more
all-embracing terms. Many aspects of decision-making were made
use of not to compare which step followed which, but to compare the
flow of events as a whole. The movement of decision-making
processes through time was typified as sporadic, fluid, or constricted
movement. That this could be done demonstrates the practicability
of characterizing processes in organizations. The making of a strategic
decision is a process in the tangled history of an organization élite,
and it can be characterized in the same manner as periods in the
histories of dynasties or of governments are characterized when they
are described as stable, or eventful, or turbulent, or whatever. Like
nations, organizations can be understood in the character of what
happens over a period. History is the flavour of events rather than a
list of dates.

Moreover, it was found possible to comprehend by this form of
characterization a very large number of processes, an overall total of
one hundred and fifty. This begins to give a feel for what decision-
making is like upon all sorts of topics and in many kinds of
organizations. Generalizations from a single case or from a handful
of cases can be placed in perspective. It can be firmly asserted that
there are different decision-making processes in different circumstances.

These circumstances are the combination of an organizational
setting, and a matter for decision that holds both problems and
interests. From this combination each process ensues. It has been
argued that while organizations dispose decision-making towards
more of one type of process than another, since different types of

process occur within any one organization it is the matter for decision and not the organization that has the greater import for the way in which a decision is arrived at.

The model of decision-making from which this conclusion is drawn, and on which the research was based, is the straightforward one that this book has followed. It postulates no more than what has just been said: process derives from organization, problems, and interests. Despite its simplicity, it was only reached over a number of years by trying out, and modifying or rejecting, a series of alternative formulations. As those who have preceded us in the study of decision-making also found, the making of a decision of any magnitude is a complicated affair, difficult to make sense of. Because of this difficulty, a simple model is needed to bring it to understandable proportions. The model having been arduously evolved to formulate what is widely accepted, though usually unstated, it may be able to serve as a point of critical assessment from which to begin future research.

Future research should certainly grapple with the link between processes and outcomes which the model assumes. Even though there are speculations as to just how much of a link there is, it being said that the decision in which a process concludes might not be its outcome at all but rather the resultant of tangential forces, these speculations are all the more reason why a closer look should be taken. We regret that we had to stop short of this, and concentrate upon the processes themselves. That took us long enough, without going on into the elements of what was decided and its implementation or non-implementation.

The most compelling need is for future research to have broader societal horizons. Here again, we had to stop short of this, and focus upon decision-making by British managers and administrators. We had no time for more. Yet while there has been comparative research in a variety of countries, the USA and Canada (Nutt 1984; Quinn 1980; Mintzberg, et al. 1976), in Denmark, Norway, and the USA (March and Olsen 1976), and in The Netherlands (DIO International Research Team 1983), always decisions have been compared but the possible similarities and differences between nations and cultures have not – excepting the incessant discussion of Japanese versus American practice. Although the coherence of what is known of decision-making suggests that there is an international core of common practice guided by common managerial rationalities, how far there may be variation nonetheless is not known. In any case, none of the research referred to has included African, Arabic, Asian, East European, or Latin lands.

As always, there is much to be done, and much scope for thought. The ideas in the Bradford studies, along with all other ideas, remain open to this further research, as and when the decision-making processes of those who want to do research, and of those who might finance it, permit.

Appendix A

150 decisions

Organizations	Decisions	Topic category
Public manufacturing		
Construction	1 New line of trucks	Product
equipment	2 Standard company name/image	Domain
	3 Expand capacity	Technology
	4 Production plan	Controls
	5 Re-equip	Technology
Chemicals B	1 Plant investment	Technology
	2 Divisionalization	Reorganization
	3 Plant in Sweden	Location
	4 Employment policy	Personnel
	5 Takeover share in company	Boundary
Private manufacturing		
Metal	1 Takeover bid	Boundary
components	2 Open new plant	Technology
	3 New components line	Product
	4 New components line	Product
	5 New components line	Product
Textiles	1 New manufacturing premises	Technology
	2 Not to make takeover bid	Boundary
	3 New manufacturing premises	Technology
	4 Close factory	Technology
	5 Resist takeover	Boundary
Chemicals H	1 New chemical	Product

	2 Generate own electricity	Product
	3 Land acquisition to expand	Technology
	4 Extend manufacturing plant	Technology
	5 New source of material	Inputs
Paints	1 Handle agency lines	Product
	2 Not to enter market	Domain
	3 Direct distribution	Domain
	4 Extend product range	Product
	5 New premises	Technology
Tool	1 Novel material in product	Product
components	2 Novel department	Reorganization
	3 Expand premises and plant	Technology
	4 Business plan	Controls
	5 Data-processing	Controls
Friction	1 New plant	Technology
products	2 New line	Product
	3 Employee grading	Personnel
	4 Stock control mechanization	Controls
	5 Business plan	Controls
Glass	1 Plant in Sweden	Location
	2 Novel product and material	Product
	3 New committee decision structure	Reorganization
	4 Massive plant investment	Technology
	5 Takover bids	Boundary
Brewery J	1 New division	Reorganization
	2 New market	Domain
	3 Not to launch new line	Product
	4 Labour deployment	Personnel
	5 Price structure	Domain
Brewery T	1 Takeover bid	Boundary
	2 Financial reconstruction	Inputs
	3 Computerization	Controls
	4 New market	Domain
	5 New department/laboratories	Reorganization

Public services (commercial)

Air transport	1 Larger capacity helicopters	Technology
	2 Replace divisional with functional structure	Reorganization
	3 Merge pilot forces	Reorganization

	4	Reduce flights	Service
	5	Order new generation aircraft	Technology
Electricity	1	Massive new current supply	Service
	2	Complete transmission overhaul	Technology
	3	Close selected retail showrooms	Location
	4	New retail sales line	Service
	5	Adapt transmission	Technology
Water	1	Budget	Controls
	2	Regional supply network	Technology
	3	Financial appraisal of network	Technology
	4	Joint service collaboration with customers	Domain
	5	Direct billing	Inputs

Public services (non-commercial)

Health	1	Budget	Controls
Service B	2	Close hospital	Boundary
	3	Physiotherapy service delivery	Reorganization
	4	Strategic plan	Controls
	5	Body-scanner purchase	Technology
Health	1	Geriatric closure	Technology
Service L	2	Reallocate psychiatric services	Reorganization
	3	Radiographer services increased	Service
	4	Catering programme	Personnel
	5	Pathology services centralized	Reorganization
Municipality	1	New administrative premises	Technology
	2	Housing project	Service
	3	Lottery	Inputs
	4	Merge departments	Reorganization
	5	Joint financing of service for aged	Service
Police	1	Close police stations	Location
	2	Staff appraisal	Personnel
	3	Police travel/mobility policy	Personnel
	4	Civilianization of work	Domain
	5	Traffic division	Reorganization
Polytechnic H	1	Overseas students policy	Domain
	2	Staff development policy	Personnel
	3	'Short course' resources	Service
	4	New courses	Service
	5	Data-processing	Controls

Polytechnic L	1	Amalgamation with colleges	Boundary
	2	Plan	Controls
	3	Location of 'schools'	Location
	4	Boards of studies	Reorganization
	5	Allocation of resources post-amalgamation	Controls
University L	1	Information service	Domain
	2	Student residences	Service
	3	New department	Reorganization
	4	Budget	Controls
	5	Administrative job grading	Personnel
University S	1	Staff appointment system	Reorganization
	2	Novel interdisciplinary form of degree	Service
	3	Departmental conflict	Personnel
	4	Collaborative school with other university	Reorganization
	5	Student intake	Service

Private services

Insurance B	1	Cut costs to avoid merger	Service
	2	Expansion or merger	Boundary
	3	Centralization of claims	Controls
	4	Data-processing	Controls
	5	Stay on existing site	Location
Insurance R	1	Massive share issue	Inputs
	2	Overseas subsidiaries	Reorganization
	3	Separate the reinsurance work	Reorganization
	4	Productivity agreement	Personnel
	5	Takeover bid	Boundary
Bank	1	Customer charges	Domain
	2	Data-processing	Controls
	3	Centralization of operations	Controls
	4	Changing from division to subsidiary	Reorganization
	5	Joining London clearing houses	Inputs
Credit company	1	New market	Domain
	2	Takeover bid	Boundary
	3	Resist unionization	Personnel
	4	New service	Service

	5 Not to launch new 'readycheck' facility	Service
Housing loans	1 Segment the market	Domain
	2 New 'mini-branches'	Domain
	3 Regionalize structure	Reorganization
	4 Interest rates	Domain
	5 Head office to stay on existing site	Location
Road transport	1 Sell Italian trucks	Domain
	2 Fit Italian vehicle bodies	Inputs
	3 Container repair section	Reorganization
	4 Hire instead of own vehicles	Inputs
	5 New depot for container repairs	Location
Industrial research	1 Training for industry firms	Service
	2 Type approval testing	Service
	3 Overseas market	Domain
	4 Raise capital	Inputs
	5 New test facility	Technology
Entertainment	1 Advertising strategy	Domain
	2 Management structure	Reorganization
	3 Budget	Controls
	4 Staff allocation and availability	Personnel
	5 Plan programme	Controls

Appendix B Data-collection methods

(Sample, and further details of data collection, are described in chapter 1.)

Intensive

In each of three organizations, a utility, a university, and a manufacturer, two cases of decision-making were studied intensively (Wilson 1980; 1982). The researcher spent many hours each week in each organization for between two and three years, talking with executives informally, interviewing them, and searching files and documents, to compile voluminous case histories. In each organization, one case was traced back historically and one was followed as it happened.

Interview

A seven-page schedule of 41 questions was developed during early trial interviews and from the experience of the intensive case studies. It began with a narrative account of what had happened, and then reiterated or expanded upon aspects of the case with open-ended questions. In nine of these, the informant additionally expressed the answer by a rating on a five-point scale, with the advantage that what was rated and the meaning of the rating score were known to the interviewer. A *selection* from the interview schedule is as follows:

(1) How often do decisions of this nature arise?

(2) Are they bunched or evenly spread?

(3) How and when did it start?

(4) What was the main sequence of events (and of departments, committees, working parties, etc.)?

(8) To what level did this go for authorization, even if later ratified at a higher level?

All internal units/departments and external units/organizations that were involved at any time were listed and the following three questions asked:

(12) What did each initially want?

(13) What did each do to make known what they wanted?

(14) How much influence did each have in this decision?
1. Little
2. Some
3. Quite a lot
4. A great deal
5. A very great deal

(21) Was there a feeling during discussions that the decision had already been made?

(22) If things went wrong, would it be serious for the organization?
1. Not at all
2. Slightly
3. Quite
4. Very
5. Extremely

(23) How was the correctness of the decision judged? For example, 'hard' criteria like costs, outputs, sales, tests, etc., and/or 'soft' criteria like reputation, attitudes, etc?
(24) How far ahead did people look when deciding this?

Appendix C   Data analysis: operationalization

Interview data were used to operationalize variables as follows (where answers to questions required coding, this was done by a minimum of three members of the research team working together):

Complexity of problems

Rarity The frequency with which similar matters recur, indicated by the number of times per year that such a topic occurs (as most occur much less often than yearly, this gives negative scores).

Radicality of consequences How far the decision changed things, indicated by a score on a five-point rating (1 = not at all; 2 = a little; 3 = quite a lot; 4 = substantially; 5 = radically).

Seriousness of consequences How serious it would be for the organization if things went wrong, indicated by a score on a five-point rating (1 = not at all; 2 = slightly; 3 = quite; 4 = very; 5 = extremely).

Diffusion of consequences How widespread were the decision's effects, indicated by the number of categories of criteria used to judge its correctness from 11 categories (profit, quality, output, costs, sales, return on investment, service rendered, morale, personnel benefits, image, market share).

Endurance of consequences How far ahead people looked when making the decision, to the nearest tenth of a year.

Precursiveness How far a decision was likely to set parameters for subsequent decisions (non-precursive = the alternatives considered followed parameters within an overall strategy; precursive = any or all of the alternatives had no such parameters and therefore themselves set parameters for subsequent decisions).

Number of interests involved The number of internal units/departments and external units/organizations named as having been involved.

Diversity of interests involved The variety of interest, indicated by the number of *categories* of internal and external interests involved from 14 categories of interest (see table 2.6).

Openness to alternatives How far there was a feeling that the decision had already been made (4 = no feeling of this kind; 3 = partly, yes and no; 2 = yes, clear to *some* interest groups; 1 = yes, obvious to *all* interest groups).

Politicality of interests

Pressure of influence How great a weight of influence was exerted, indicated by the mean for all interest units of ratings by informants of the influence of each interest involved (1 = little; 2 = some; 3 = quite a lot; 4 = a great deal; 5 = a very great deal).

Intervention How far external influence was exerted, indicated by the percentage of the sum of influence ratings for all interest units that was due to external units.

Imbalance How far the total pressure was uneven across interest units, indicated by the range of the influence ratings between them (narrow range = balanced influence, wide range = imbalance).

Contention of objectives How far the interest units that exerted influence did so in opposite directions, indicated by the *range* of scores on a five-point scale of opposition to, or support for, the eventual decision (−2 = strong opposition; −1 = qualified opposition; 0 = neutral; + 1 qualified support; + 2 = strong support).

Process

Duration-process time How long it took to arrive at the approved choice (or process outcome), indicated by the number of months from first deliberate consideration of a topic to an authorized decision.

Duration-gestation time How long it took for a topic to emerge, indicated by the number of months from first recognition of a potential topic to the commencement of process time.

Disruption How far the process was interrupted by delays, indicated by the highest score for the process on a four point scale (1 = no delays; 2 = intermittent; 3 = continual; 4 = prolonged).

Impedance How far the process encountered impediments, indicated by the highest score for the process on a ten-point scale (the nine points listed in figure 4.2, plus a zero score for no identifiable impediments).

Formal interaction How many *kinds* of pre-arranged meeting were included in the process, indicated by the number of general committees/boards/councils, etc., specialized committees, e.g. finance or sales, and special purpose working parties/project teams.

Informal interaction How much discussion, toing and froing, or arguments took place, indicated by the highest score for the process on a six-point scale (1 = none; 2 = little; 3 = some; 4 = quite a lot; 5 = a great deal; 6 = a very great deal).

Negotiation scope How far there was room for negotiation and dissent, indicated by a score on a seven-point scale (1 = decision not open to negotiation; 2 = negotiation only in final stages; 3 = negotiation possible on choices but one man chooses the course of action (for example, the chief executive); 4 = collective decision; 5 = negotiation including dissenting parties, but subsequent consensus; 6 = negotiation resulting in limited consensus to the exclusion of dissenters; 7 = decision reached with dissent remaining such as in voting).

Information sources – expertise How many sources of data were drawn upon, indicated by the number of internal or external units providing information or views.

Information sources – externality How far information from external sources contributed to the reduction of uncertainty, indicated by the percentage of the sum of confidence-ratings for all sources that was due to external sources.

Information sources – confidence disparity How much variation there was in the quality of information, indicated by the *range* of ratings of sources on a five-point scale of confidence in the information provided. (1 = little; 2 = some; 3 = quite a lot; 4 = a great deal; 5 = a very great deal).

Information sources – effort How readily information was accessible, indicated by a score on a four-point scale (1 = information *available* from personal knowledge or opinions; 2 = information *obtained* readily from records; 3 = information *researched* by scanning, for example by market survey; 4 = information *synthesized* by integrating disparate information from diverse sources, e.g., via a meeting to collate information or a report.

Authority – level in hierarchy How high in the hierarchy did the process culminate, indicated by a score for the level at which implementation was authorized and could then commence (1 = below divisional level or equivalent; 2 = divisional level or equivalent; 3 = chief executive; 4 = chief executive and ratified by board; 5 = board or equivalent top governing body; 6 = board and ratified at higher external level; 7 = outside and above the organization).

Appendix D Distributions of scores on variables*

Variables	Mean	Standard deviation	Range min.	max.
Complexity of problems				
Rarity	−0.9	2.1	−12.0	0.0
Radicality of consequences	3.2	1.3	1.0	5.0
Seriousness of consequences	3.4	1.1	1.0	5.0
Diffusion of consequences	2.2	1.3	0.0	6.0
Endurance of consequences	8.1	6.4	0.1	20.0
Precursiveness	—	—	0.0	1.0
Number of interests involved	6.8	3.2	2.0	20.0
Diversity of interests involved	5.2	2.0	2.0	12.0
Openness to alternatives	3.0	1.1	1.0	4.0
Politicality of interests				
Pressure of influence	3.1	0.7	1.6	4.5
Intervention (external influence)	28%	18%	0%	90%
Imbalance (uneven influence)	3.3	0.9	4.0	1.0
Contention of objectives	2.6	1.2	0.0	4.0
Process				
Duration-process time (months)	12.4	10.6	1.0	48.0
Duration-gestation time (months)	17.4	36.0	0.0	288.0
Disruption	2.3	1.1	1.0	4.0
Impedance	5.1	3.3	1.0	10.0
Formal interaction (committees)	2.3	1.5	0.0	11.0
Informal interaction	4.2	1.2	1.0	6.0
Negotiation scope	4.2	1.4	1.0	7.0

Information sources – expertise	4.8	2.3	1.0	13.0
Information sources – externality	28%	20%	0%	100%
Information sources – confidence disparity	1.9	1.1	0.0	4.0
Information sources – effort	2.8	0.9	1.0	4.0
Authority-level in hierarchy	4.7	1.3	2.0	7.0

*n = 150 on 15 variables. On 9 variables data were incomplete as follows: on openness on 26 cases, information sources – externality on 10 cases, rarity 5, radicality 4, precursiveness 2, gestation time 2, impedance 2, endurance 1, disruption 1.

Appendix E Discriminant analysis between process types on process variables

Differences between process clusters	F value (10, 124 degrees of freedom)
Sporadic and constricted	21.94*
Sporadic and fluid	27.50*
Constricted and fluid	26.04*

*over 99% confidence

Appendix F Mean scores of each process type on eight complexity and politicality variables
(see chapter 6)

Variables	Sporadic	Fluid	Constricted	F ratio	Significance	
					Degrees of freedom	Confidence level beyond
Complexity of problems						
Rarity	−0.9	−0.4	−1.6	3.3	2,131	96%
Seriousness of consequences	3.7	3.1	3.1	4.28	2,133	98%
Diffusion of consequences	2.2	2.2	1.9	0.7	2,133	Not significant
Precursive/non-precursive	28%/72%	50%/50%	10%/90%	—	—	—
Diversity of interests involved	5.5	4.4	4.9	5.1	2,133	99%
Politicality of interests						
Intervention (external influence)	34%	26%	22%	—	—	—
Imbalance (uneven influence)	3.3	2.9	3.2	5.5	2.133	99%
Contention of objectives	3.0	2.2	2.4	6.0	2.133	99%

Bibliography

Abell, Peter (1975) 'Organizations as bargaining and influence systems: measuring intraorganizational power and influence' in *Organizations as Bargaining and Influence Systems*. P. Abell (ed.), 10–40. London: Heinemann, and New York: Halstead Press/Wiley.

Aharoni, Yair and Ran Lachman (1982) 'Can the manager's mind be nationalized?' *Organization Studies*, 3/1: 33–46.

Aldrich, Howard and David A. Whetton (1981) 'Organization-sets, action-sets, and networks: making the most of simplicity', in *Handbook of organizational design, vol. 1*. Paul C. Nystrom and William H. Starbuck (eds), 385–408. Oxford: Oxford University Press.

Allison, Graham T. (1969) 'Conceptual models and the Cuban missile crisis'. *American Political Science Review*, LXIII/3: 689–718.

Allison, Graham T. (1971) *Essence of decision*. Boston: Little, Brown.

Anderberg, Michael R. (1973) *Cluster Analysis for Applications*. New York: Academic Press.

Astley, W. Graham, Runo Axelsson, Richard J. Butler, David J. Hickson and David C. Wilson (1982) 'Complexity and cleavage: dual explanations of strategic decision making'. *Journal of Management Studies*, 19/4: 357–75.

Axelsson, Runo and Lennart Rosenberg (1979) 'Decision-making and organizational turbulence'. *Acta Sociologica*, 22/1: 45–62.

Bacharach, Samuel B. and Edward J. Lawler (1980) *Power and Politics in Organisations*. San Francisco and London: Jossey-Bass.

Bachrach, Peter and Morton S. Baratz (1962) 'The two faces of power'. *American Political Science Review*, 56: 947–52.

Baldrige, J. (1971) *Power and Conflict in the University*. New York: Wiley.

Bass, Bernard M. (1983) *Organizational Decision-making*. New York: Irwin.

Bauer, Michel and Eli Cohen (1983) 'The iron law of "private governments" in the French industrial system'. Paper presented at the *6th EGOS Colloquium*, Florence.

Benson, J. Kenneth (1975) 'The interorganizational network as a political economy'. *Administrative Science Quarterly*, 20:229–49.

Benton, T. (1981) 'Objective interests and the sociology of power'. *Sociology*, 15/2: 161–84.

Beyer, Janice M. and Thomas M. Lodahl (1976) 'A comparative study of patterns of influence in United States and English universities'. *Administrative Science Quarterly*, 21/1: 104–29.

Braybrooke, David and Charles Lindblom (1963) *A strategy of decision.* New York: Free Press.

Bresser, Rudi K. (1984) 'Structural dimensions of university departments and their context: the case of West Germany'. *Organization Studies*, 5/2: 119–46.

Brown, W. (ed.) (1980) 'The changing contours of British industrial relations'. Working paper, *Industrial Relations Research Unit*, Warwick University, England.

Butler, Richard J., W. Graham Astley, David J. Hickson, Geoffrey R. Mallory and David C. Wilson (1979/80) 'Strategic decision making: concepts of content and process'. *International Studies of Management and Organization* ix/4: 5–36.

Butler, Richard J., David J. Hickson, David C. Wilson and Runo Axelsson (1977/78) 'Organizational power, politicking and paralysis'. *Organization and Administrative Sciences*, 8/4: 45–60.

Child, John and Alfred Kieser (1981) 'Development of organizations over time' in *Handbook of Organizational Design, Volume I: adapting organizations to their environments.* Paul C. Nystrom and William H. Starbuck (eds) 28–64. Oxford: Oxford University Press.

Clegg, Stewart (1975) *Power, Rule and Domination*, London and Boston: Routledge & Kegan Paul.

Clegg, Stewart and David Dunkerley (1980) *Organization, Class and Control.* London and Boston: Routledge & Kegan Paul.

Cohen, Michael D., James G. March and Johan P. Olsen (1972) 'A garbage can model of organizational choice'. *Administrative Science Quarterly*, 17: 1–25.

Cray, David, Richard J. Butler, David J. Hickson, Geoffrey R. Mallory and David C. Wilson (1983) 'Proactive and reactive decision making'. Presented at Conference on Policy and Structure, Carleton School of Business, Ottawa.

Cray, David, Geoffrey R. Mallory, Richard J. Butler, David J. Hickson and David C. Wilson (1985) 'Sporadic, fluid and constricted processes: three empirical types of strategic decision making in organizations' (forthcoming).

Crozier, Michel (1964) *The Bureaucratic Phenomenon.* London: Tavistock.

Crozier, Michel (1976) 'Comparing structures and comparing games' in *European Contributions to Organization Theory'*. Geert Hofstede and M. Sami Kassem (eds), 193–207. Amsterdam: Van Gorcum.

Crozier, Michel and Erhard Friedberg (1980) *Actors and Systems*. Chicago: University of Chicago Press (published in French in 1977 by Editions du Seuil).

Cyert, Richard M., H. A. Simon, and D. B. Trow (1956) 'Observation of a Business Decision'. *Journal of Business*, 29: 237–248.

Cyert, Richard M. and James G. March (1963) *A Behavioral Theory of the Firm*. Englewood Cliffs: Prentice-Hall.

Dahl, R. A. (1961) *Who Governs? Democracy and Power in an American City*. New Haven: Yale University Press.

DIO International Research Team (1983) 'A contingency model of participative decision making: an analysis of 56 decisions in three Dutch organizations'. *Journal of Occupational Psychology*, 56/1: 1–18.

Donaldson, Gordon and Jay W. Lorsch (1983) *Decision Making at the Top*. New York: Basic Books.

Drenth, P. J. D., P. L. Koopman, V. Rus, M. Odar, F. Heller and A. Brown (1979) 'Participative decision making: a comparative study'. *Industrial Relations*, 18/3: 295–309.

Dunkerley, David, Tony Spybey and Michael Thrasher (1981) 'Inter-organization networks: a case study of industrial location'. *Organization Studies*, 2/3: 229–48.

Edwards, C. (1978) 'Measuring union power: a comparison of two methods applied to the study of local union power in the coal industry'. *British Journal of Industrial Relations*, xvi/1.

Etzioni, Amitai (1967) 'Mixed-scanning: a "third" approach to decision making'. *Public Administration Review*, 27:385–92.

Evan, William M. (1971) 'The organization-set: toward a theory of inter-organizational relations'. J. D. Thompson (ed.) *Approaches to organizational design*. Pittsburgh: Pittsburgh University Press.

Everitt, Brian (1974) *Cluster Analysis*. London: Heinemann.

French, John R. P. and Bertram Raven (1959) 'The bases of social power' in *Studies in Social Power*. D. Cartwright (ed.) 150–67. Ann Arbor: University of Michigan Press.

Grandori, Anna (1984) 'A prescriptive contingency view of organizational decision making'. *Administrative Science Quarterly*, 29/2: 192–209.

Greenwood, Royston, Kieron Walsh, C. R. Hinings and Stewart Ranson (1980) *Patterns of Management in Local Government*. Oxford: Martin Robertson.

Hage, Jerald (1980) *Theories of Organizations: form, process and transformation*. New York: Wiley.

Hall, Richard H. (1968) 'Professionalization and bureaucratization'. *American Sociological Review*, 33/1: 92–104.

Hall, Richard H., (1969) *Occupations and the Social Structure*. Englewood Cliffs: Prentice Hall.

Harding, Peter and Gordon Scott (1982) 'Management structures in colleges of further education'. *Educational Management and Administration*, 10: 45–55.

Hastings, A. and C. R. Hinings (1970) 'Role relations and value adaptation: a study of the professional accountant in industry'. *Sociology*, 4/3: 354–66.

Haywood, S. C. (1974) *Managing the Health Service*. London: Allen and Unwin.

Heller, F. A., P. J. D. Drenth, P. Koopman and V. Rus (1977) 'A longitudinal study in participative decision-making'. *Human Relations*, 30/7: 567–87.

Hickson, David J., W. Graham Astley, Richard J. Butler and David C. Wilson (1981) 'Organization as power', in *Research in Organizational Behavior, vol. 3*. L. L. Cummings and B. . Staw (eds), 151–96. Greenwich, Connecticut: JAI Press.

Hickson, David J., Richard J. Butler, Runo Axelsson and David Wilson (1978) 'Decisive coalitions', in *Managerial Control and Organizational Democracy*. B. King, S. Streufert and F. E. Fiedler (eds) 31–42. New York: Wiley.

Hickson, David J., Richard J. Butler, David Cray, Geoffrey R. Mallory and David C. Wilson (1985) 'Comparing one hundred and fifty decision processes', in *Organizational Strategy and Change*. J. M. Pennings (ed.). San Francisco: Jossey-Bass.

Hickson, David J., C. R. Hinings, C. A. Lee, R. E. Schneck and J. M. Pennings (1971) 'A strategic contingencies theory of intraorganizational power'. *Administrative Science Quarterly*, 16/2: 216–29.

Hickson, David J. and Arthur F. McCullough (1980) 'Power in organizations' in *Control and Ideology in Organizations*, G. Salaman and K. Thompson (eds) 27–55. Milton Keynes, England: Open University Press.

Hickson, David J. and Charles J. McMillan (eds) (1981) *Organization and Nation: the Aston programme IV*. Farnborough, Gower Publishing.

Hickson, D. J. and M. W. Thomas (1969) 'Professionalization in Britain: a preliminary measurement'. *Sociology*, 3/1: 37–53.

Hinings, C. R., D. J. Hickson, J. M. Pennings and R. E. Schneck (1974) 'Structural conditions of intraorganizational power'. *Administrative Science Quarterly*, 19/1: 22–44.

Hofstede, Geert (1980) 'Angola coffee – or the confrontation of an organization with changing values in its environment'. *Organization Studies*, 1/1: 21–40.

Jacobs, D. (1974) 'Dependency and vulnerability: an exchange approach to the control of organizations'. *Administrative Science Quarterly*, 19/1: 45–59.

Kaplan, Abraham (1964) 'Power in perspective' in *Power and Conflict in Organizations*. R. L. Kahn and E. Boulding (eds), 11–32. London: Tavistock.

Karpik, Lucien (1972) 'Les politiques et les logiques d'action de la grande enterprise industrielle'. *Sociologie du Travail*. 1:82–105.

Katz, Daniel and Robert L. Kahn (1966) *The social psychology of organizations*. New York: Wiley.

Kenny, Graham K., Richard J. Butler, David Cray, David J. Hickson, Geoffrey R. Mallory and David C. Wilson (1985) 'Strategic decision making: influence patterns in public and private sector organizations'. (in draft)

Kimberly, John (1976) 'Organizational size and the structuralist perspective: a review, critique, and proposal'. *Administrative Science Quarterly*, 21/4: 571–97.

Kirsch, W. and M. Kutschker (1982) 'Marketing and buying decisions in industrial markets, 'in *Studies in Decision Making*. Martin Irle (ed.) in collaboration with Lawrence B. Katz, 443–88. Berlin/New York: Walter de Gruyter.

Koopman, Paul L. (1983) 'Management strategies in organizational reduction'. Paper presented to the *North-West European Conference on the Psychology of Work and Organizations*. Nijmegen, The Netherlands.

Kort-Krieger, Ute, and Peter Schmidt (1982) 'Participation and legitimacy conflict at West German universities'. *Organization Studies*, 3/3: 297–320.

Levitt, Ruth (1976) *The Reorganized Health Service*. London: Croom Helm.

Lindblom, Charles (1959) 'The science of muddling through'. *Public Administration Review* xix/2: 79–88.

Lodahl, Janice B. and Gerald Gordon (1972) 'The structure of scientific fields and the functioning of university graduate departments'. *American Sociological Review*, 37: 57–72.

Lukes, Stephen (1974) *Power: a Radical View*. London: Macmillan.

Lustick, Ian (1980) 'Explaining the variable utility of disjointed incrementalism: four proposisions'. *American Political Science Review* 74:342–53.

McMillan, Charles J. (1980) 'Qualitative models of organizational decision-making'. *Journal of General Management*, 5, 4, 22–39.

278 *Bibliography*

Mallory, Geoffrey R., Richard J. Butler, David Cray, David J. Hickson and David C. Wilson (1983) 'Implanted decision making: American owned firms in Britain'. *Journal of Management Studies*, 20/2: 191–211.

Mallory, Geoffrey R. and David Cray (1982) 'Strategic and tactical decision making'. Presented at Annual Meetings of the American Sociological Association, San Francisco.

March, James G. (1981) 'Decision making perspective: decisions in organizations and theories of choice', in *Perspectives on Organization Design and Behavior*. Andrew H. Van de Ven and William F. Joyce (eds), New York: Wiley.

March, James G. and Johan P. Olsen (1976) *Ambiguity and Choice in Organizations*. Bergen, Oslo, and Tromso: Universitetsforlaget.

March, James G. and Johan P. Olsen (1983) 'Organizing political life: what administrative reorganization tells us about government'. *American Political Science Review*, 77/2: 281–96.

March, James G. and Pierre J. Romelaer (1976) 'Position and presence in the drift of decisions' in *Ambiguity and Choice in Organizations*. James G. March and Johan P. Olsen (eds), 251–76. Bergen, Oslo and Tromso: Universitetsforlaget.

March, James G. and Herbert A. Simon (1958) *Organizations*. New York: Wiley.

Mayntz, Renate (1976) 'Conceptual models of organizational decision-making and their application to the policy process', in *European Contributions to Organization Theory*. G. Hofstede and M. S. Kassem (eds), 114–25. Amsterdam: Van Gorcum.

Miles, Robert H. (1980) *Macro organizational Behavior*. California: Goodyear.

Mintzberg, Henry (1978) 'Patterns in strategy formation'. *Management Science*, 24/9: 934–48.

Mintzberg, Henry (1979) *The Structuring of Organizations*. Englewood Cliffs, New Jersey: Prentice-Hall.

Mintzberg, Henry (1983) *Power in and around Organizations*. Englewood Cliffs, New Jersey: Prentice-Hall.

Mintzberg, Henry, D. Raisinghani and A. Theoret (1976) 'The structure of "unstructured" decision processes'. *Administrative Science Quarterly*, 21: 246–75.

Mintzberg, Henry and James A. Waters (1982) 'Tracking strategy in an entrepreneurial firm'. *Academy of Management Journal*, 25, 3, 465–99.

Mohr, Lawrence B. (1982) *Explaining Organizational Behavior*. San Francisco: Jossey-Bass.

Morgan, Gareth (1981) 'The schismatic metaphor and its implications for organizational analysis'. *Organization Studies*, 2/1: 23–44.

Nutt, Paul (1984) 'Types of organizational decision processes'. *Administrative Science Quarterly*, 29/3: 414–50.

Pennings, Johannes M. (1981) 'Strategically interdependent organizations', in *Handbook of Organizational Design, Vol. I*. Paul C. Nystrom and William H. Starbuck (eds), 433–55. Oxford: Oxford University Press.

Perrow, Charles (1970) 'Departmental power and perspectives in industrial firms' in *Power in Organizations*. Mayer N. Zald (ed.), 59–89. Nashville: Vanderbilt University Press.

Pettigrew, Andrew M. (1972) 'Information control as a power resource'. *Sociology*, 6:187–204.

Pettirew, Andrew (1973) *The Politics of Organizational Decision-making*. London: Tavistock.

Pfeffer, Jeffrey (1981) *Power in Organizations*. Marshfield, Mass: Pitman.

Pfeffer, Jeffrey and Gerald R. Salancik (1974) 'Organizational decision making as a political process: the case of a university budget'. *Administrative Science Quarterly*, 19: 135–51.

Pfeffer, Jeffrey and Gerald R. Salancik (1977) 'Organization design: the case for a coalitional model of organizations'. *Organizational Dynamics*, 6: 15–29.

Pfeffer, Jeffrey and Gerald R. Salancik (1978) *The External Control of Organizations: a Resource Dependence Perspective*. New York and London: Harper and Row.

Pugh, D. S. and D. J. Hickson (1976) *Organizational structure in its Context: the Aston Programme I*. Farnborough: Gower Publishing (and formerly D. C. Heath).

Pugh, D. S. and C. R. Hinings (1976) *Organizational structure – Extensions and Replications; the Aston programme II*. Farnborough: Gower Publishing (and formerly D. C. Heath).

Quinn, James B. (1978) 'Strategic change: logical incrementalism'. *Sloan Management Review*, Fall 1978: 7–21.

Quinn, James B. (1980) *Strategies for change: logical incrementalism*. Homewood, Illinois: Irwin.

Rainey, Hal G., Robert W. Backoff and Charles H. Levine (1976) 'Comparing public and private organizations'. *Public Administration Review*, 36: 233–44.

Rhenman, Eric (1973) *Organization Theory for Long-range Planning*. London and New York: Wiley.

Rodrigues, Suzana Braga (1980) *Processes of Successful Managerial Decision-Making in Organizations*. PhD thesis, University of Bradford, England.

Schulman, Paul R. (1975) 'Nonincremental policy making: notes towards an alternative paradigm'. *American Political Science Review*, 69: 1354–70.

Simon, Herbert A. (1945) *Administrative Behavior* (2nd edn). New York: Free Press.

Simon, Herbert A. (1960) *The New Science of Management Decision*. New York: Harper and Row.

Starbuck, William H. (1983) 'Organizations as action generators'. *American Sociological Review*, 48: 91–102.

Stein, Jorge (1981*a*) 'Contextual factors in the selection of strategic decision methods'. *Human Relations*, 34/10: 819–34.

Stein, Jorge (1981*b*) 'Strategic decision methods'. *Human Relations*, 34/11: 917–33.

Strauss, George (1962) 'Tactics of lateral relationship: the purchasing agent'. *Administrative Science Quarterly*, 7, 161–86.

Tannenbaum, Arnold S. (1968) *Control in Organizations*. New York: McGraw-Hill.

Tannenbaum, Arnold S. and Robert A. Cooke (1979) 'Organizational control: a review of studies employing the control graph method' in *Organizations Alike and Unlike*. Cornelis J. Lammers and David J. Hickson (eds), 183–210. London and Boston: Routledge.

Teulings, A. (1982) 'Interlocking interests and collaboration with the enemy: corporate behaviour in the Second World War'. *Organization Studies*, 3/2: 99–119.

Thibaut, J. W. and H. H. Kelley (1959) *The social psychology of groups*. New York: Wiley.

Thompson, James D. (1967) *Organizations in action*. New York: McGraw-Hill.

Thompson, James D. and Arthur Tuden (1964) 'Strategies, structures and processes of organizational decision' in *Readings in Managerial Psychology*. H. J. Leavitt and R. Pondy (eds), 195–216. Chicago: University of Chicago Press.

Walsh, Kieron, Bob Hinings, Royston Greenwood and Stewart Ranson (1981) 'Power and advantage in organizations'. *Organization Studies*, 2/2: 131–52.

Wamsley, G. and M. N. Zald (1973) 'The political economy of public organizations'. *Public Administration Review*, 33: 62–73.

Weick, Karl E. (1976) 'Educational organizations as loosely coupled systems'. *Administrative Science Quarterly*, 21/1: 1–19.

Weiss, Joseph W. (1981) 'The historical and political perspective on organizations of Lucien Karpik' in *Complex Organizations: Critical Perspectives*. Mary Zey-Ferrell and Michael Aiken (eds), 382–96. Illinois: Scott, Foresman.

Wilson, David C. (1980) 'Organizational Strategy'. PhD thesis, University of Bradford, England.

Wilson, David C. (1982) 'Electricity and resistance: a case study of innovation and politics'. *Organization Studies*, 3/2: 119–40.

Wilson, David C., Richard J. Butler, David Cray, David J. Hickson and Geoffrey R. Mallory (1982) 'The limits of trade union power in organizational decision making'. *British Journal of Industrial Relations*, xx/3, 322–41.

Wilson, David C., Richard J. Butler, David Cray, David J. Hickson and Geoffrey R. Mallory (1985) 'Breaking the bounds of organization in strategic decision making'. (In draft.)

Wilson, J. Q. (1966) 'Innovation in organizations: notes toward a theory' in *Organizational Design and Research*. J. D. Thompson (ed.). Pittsburgh: University of Pittsburgh Press.

Witte, Eberhard (1972) 'Field research on complex decision-making processes – the phase theorem'. *International Studies of Management and Organization*, II, 2, 156–82.

Author Index

Subject Index